Not the Marrying Kind
A Feminist Critique of Same-Sex Marriage

Palgrave Macmillan Socio-Legal Studies

Series Editor

David Cowan, Professor of Law and Policy, University of Bristol, UK

Not the Marrying Kind

A Feminist Critique of Same-Sex Marriage

Nicola Barker
Kent Law School, University of Kent, UK

palgrave
macmillan

First published 2012 by
PALGRAVE MACMILLAN

Palgrave Macmillan in the UK is an imprint of Macmillan Publishers Limited,
registered in England, company number 785998, of Houndmills, Basingstoke,
Hampshire RG21 6XS.

Palgrave Macmillan in the US is a division of St Martin's Press LLC,
175 Fifth Avenue, New York, NY 10010.

Palgrave Macmillan is the global academic imprint of the above companies
and has companies and representatives throughout the world.

Palgrave® and Macmillan® are registered trademarks in the United States,
the United Kingdom, Europe and other countries.

ISBN: 978–1–137–34803–6

This book is printed on paper suitable for recycling and made from fully
managed and sustained forest sources. Logging, pulping and manufacturing
processes are expected to conform to the environmental regulations of the
country of origin.

A catalogue record for this book is available from the British Library.

A catalog record for this book is available from the Library of Congress.

10 9 8 7 6 5 4 3 2 1
22 21 20 19 18 17 16 15 14 13

For my mother and my grandmother,
Barbara Barker and Honorah Barker

Contents

Part II

Table of Cases

Table of Legislation

Acknowledgments

Throughout the process of writing this book my colleagues and friends in the Law School at Keele and the Arts and Humanities Research Council Centre for Law, Gender and Sexuality (CLGS) have provided a supportive, collegial and intellectually stimulating space for me to begin to develop my scholarship and I would like to thank them for creating such a vibrant and welcoming environment for PhD students and career-young scholars. I would like to thank Ruth Fletcher and Michael Thomson for their intellectual engagement, support and perseverance in helping me to develop this work over several years in supervising my PhD. I would particularly like to thank Didi Herman for her generosity in taking the time to read an entire draft at a very early stage and providing valuable guidance and direction. Many thanks also to Rosemary Auchmuty, Emily Grabham, Sarah Lamble and Carl Stychin for their searching questions and feedback on the manuscript, and Davina Cooper, Lieve Gies, Reg Graycar, Ewa Majewska, Julie McCandless, Sally Sheldon, Antu Sorienen, Matthew Weait and Yvonne Zylan, who read drafts of individual chapters and provided valuable comments.

I have had the opportunity to present my work at several conferences and I would particularly like to thank the organizers and participants of those and Keele University and CLGS for providing the funding to attend them. In particular, the Graduate School at Keele University provided the forum to present my work for the first time at the Graduate Symposium in June 2003. The participants at the University of British Columbia/CLGS workshop 'Why and How? Theoretical and Methodological Directions in Law, Feminism, Gender and Sexuality' in Vancouver, August 2006, listened supportively to a very early draft of Chapters 5 and 6 and gave me valuable advice on progressing those chapters. Finally, the participants at the Tata Institute of Social Sciences/CLGS workshop 'Agency, Sexuality and Law – Globalising Economies, Localising Cultures' in Goa, December 2007, gave me encouraging feedback on a paper which drew from Chapters 4 and 5. I would also like to thank both the CLGS at Kent and the Feminism and Legal Theory Project at Cornell University for hosting me and giving me the opportunity to present my work in progress.

Some of the discussion about South Africa, in Chapters 3 and 4, and the Butler/Fraser debate, in Chapter 6, has appeared in Barker (2011).

Nicola Barker

Introduction

Reforms may make things better for a while: changes in the law can make straight people a little less hostile, a little more tolerant – but reform cannot change the deep-down attitude of straight people that homosexuality is at best inferior to their own way of life, at worst a sickening perversion. It will take more than reforms to change this attitude, because it is rooted in our society's most basic institution – the Patriarchal family. (Gay Liberation Front (GLF), 1971, p. 321)

Not the marrying kind?

The GLF's manifesto identified the family as the starting point for the oppression of gay people and rejects law reforms in favour of 'a revolutionary change in our whole society' (ibid.). There are clear feminist influences in the manifesto's concern about patriarchy and its determination to challenge institutionalized sexism and build an alliance with the women's liberation movement (p. 328). However, four decades later, gay liberation has become gay rights, same-sex marriage has become a litmus test of how gay-friendly society is, and feminism is too often separated from gay rights claims, especially in relation to marriage. In this book I examine the issue of same-sex marriage from a new perspective, which draws inspiration from these 'old' values of the GLF. Rather than ask whether same-sex couples should be granted access to marriage, I focus my analysis on the institution of marriage itself using second-wave (socialist) feminist and queer theoretical insights to critique the marriage model of relationship recognition. I highlight the various provisions through which same-sex relationships have been legally recognized across several jurisdictions and the ways in which the reliance on the marriage model limits the transformative and transgressive potentials of the law reforms. Instead, I demonstrate why a revolutionary approach is needed,

1

one that rejects the marriage model and takes seriously the critiques of marriage from both feminism and queer theory.

Background

The last two decades have seen increasingly successful claims by or on behalf of same-sex couples seeking to access the institution of marriage or a separate marriage-like institution in several jurisdictions. These successes represent a positive shift from the previous overt homophobia of the state, which in the United Kingdom has been gradually eroded since the 1957 Report of the Committee on Homosexual Offences and Prostitution (Cmnd. 247) – the Wolfenden Report – and the resulting partial decriminalization of gay male sex in the Sexual Offences Act 1967. This was a very tentative first step with an enduring emphasis on privacy rather than celebration; an attitude perhaps best illustrated two decades later by the prohibition on the 'promotion' of homosexuality in schools and the disparagement of lesbian and gay families as 'pretended' under s. 28 of the Local Government Act 1988. The repeal of s. 28 by the Local Government Act 2003 and the introduction of the Civil Partnership Act 2004 form part of a series of recent major legal developments in the law relating to lesbians and gay men. For example: the Sexual Offences (Amendment) Act 2000 brought the age of consent for sex between men in line with that between a man and a woman; the Adoption and Children Act 2002 allows same-sex couples to jointly adopt a child; and discrimination on the grounds of sexual orientation in employment (the Employment Equality (Sexual Orientation) Regulations 2003) and in the provision of goods and services (the Equality Act (Sexual Orientation) Regulations 2007) has been prohibited.

A similar pattern of liberalizing law reform is also identifiable in other jurisdictions, particularly Canada, South Africa and some jurisdictions in Australia, Europe and the United States, with the legal recognition of same-sex relationships through marriage or a marriage-like provision being seen as the final step in this sequence, following decriminalization and anti-discrimination provisions (Waaldijk, 2001, pp. 439–40). Therefore, in addition to providing access to important legal protections and recognition, same-sex marriage is also posited as the final step towards 'full equality' for lesbians and gay men. Legal protections include both financial provisions, such as tax exemptions (though the financial consequences of marriage can be detrimental, particularly to lower-income couples, as discussed in chapters 4 and 5), and also what are generally referred to as 'next-of-kin' rights.[1] In other words, marriage provides an easy way to communicate the nature and status of a same-sex

---

1 There is no single legal definition of 'next of kin' in the UK so it is not technically accurate to refer to a group of next-of-kin benefits in this context (Auchmuty, 2004).

relationship to, for example, hospital workers. This also links in with the parallel, and equally important, reason why same-sex marriage is considered by some to be necessary: it may provide symbolic as well as substantive legal recognition. A state's recognition of same-sex relationships signals to wider society not only that same-sex relationships are no longer to be denigrated but also that they must be positively recognized and respected. Recognition from the state is, then, both an end in itself and a means to an end in that those who seek same-sex marriage not only seek recognition from the state but also from members of birth families, religious institutions and employers (see Chapter 4). In fact the expected value of legal status in prompting recognition from non-state entities, particularly birth families, has been found to be one of the key reasons for lesbians and gay men supporting the marriage-like civil partnerships in the UK (Shipman and Smart, 2007).

The push for same-sex marriage is, however, not a universally welcome move within the gay and lesbian communities. I share the long-held scepticism of many feminists, gays, lesbians and queers about the institution of marriage (see Chapters 5 and 6). As Paula Ettelbrick argues in response to Thomas Stoddard (1989) and other same-sex marriage advocates:

> Steeped in a patriarchal system that looks to ownership, property, and dominance of men over women as its basis, the institution of marriage has long been the focus of radical-feminist revulsion. (Ettelbrick, 1989, p. 119)

It may be that there are compelling arguments for same-sex marriage despite these concerns. Yet, for the most part, those leading the drive towards marriage have not engaged with the feminist critiques of the institution, which have been absent from the mainstream debates on both sides of the Atlantic (Auchmuty, 2007; Young and Boyd, 2006). In addition, queer theorists have expressed concern about marriage in that, among other things, it would require the assimilation of same-sex relationships to a 'traditional' heterosexual marriage norm. These concerns have also been absent from mainstream debates and largely overlooked by those seeking same-sex marriage and this marginalization of feminist and queer voices leaves the conservative, heteronormative discourses about marriage and family unquestioned (Young and Boyd, 2006, p. 214).

This absence of any real engagement with feminist and queer critiques of marriage, particularly from those organizations representing lesbian and gay communities, is, while troubling, perhaps not surprising given the need to confront homophobic opposition in many jurisdictions, as well as the necessity to strategically engage the types of arguments that are likely to be successful according to the dominant political and legal ideologies of the jurisdiction. For example, in the UK, Stonewall (2004a) drew on aspects of New Labour's Third Way ideology to make arguments of social inclusion and responsibility, among others (Stychin, 2006b). In Canada, the litigants in the same-sex marriage cases relied on arguments that it was necessary for equality under s. 15 of the Canadian Charter of Rights and Freedoms 1982 (see further Chapter 3).

Another reason why feminist voices in particular may have been absent from same-sex marriage debates is that the feminist critiques of marriage, originating from second-wave feminism, are seen as *no longer relevant* to contemporary marriage. There is, perhaps, a myth of equality, which along with increasing neoliberal and post-feminist discourses of freedom of choice in this context, lead to an assumption which posits those *individual* women who are still exploited within heterosexual marriage as willing victims who have *chosen* this rather than being structurally disadvantaged by the institution. While there are other reasons why feminist voices are absent (see Auchmuty, 2007), I am interested in this issue of the continuing relevance of second-wave feminist theory for two reasons. First, despite acknowledging problems with the institution, some feminists have made arguments *for* same-sex marriage (see Calhoun, 2000; Hunter, 1995, discussed in Chapter 4). They claim that same-sex marriage would be different from heterosexual marriage and as such would challenge its traditional heteronormative ideologies: same-sex marriage might 'rock marriage towards its egalitarian shore' (Graff, 1996, p. 137). Second, I am more generally interested in the move by some contemporary feminists away from the principles of the second wave and want to question whether this is appropriate in the context of same-sex marriage.

However, I am not seeking to merely apply second-wave feminist critiques to contemporary same-sex marriage debates but rather to examine how these feminist critiques might be further developed in order to more fully analyse same-sex marriage. In particular, I foreground the feminist analysis that has been largely absent in the mainstream debates, providing a direct response to arguments that such critiques are no longer relevant or not applicable to same-sex marriage. Although I argue that the feminist critiques, particularly in relation to the privatization of care and dependency, are in themselves relevant to both contemporary heterosexual marriage and same-sex marriage, I also demonstrate some ways in which queer theory might inform these feminist critiques in order to develop them further.

I additionally seek to make a contribution to the broader literature on marriage. Same-sex marriage debates, in the contexts of both policy and academic arguments, generally focus on the 'pros and cons' of recognizing same-sex relationships without analysing marriage as an institution or as a normative framework (see, for example, Sullivan, 1997). There is an assumption that the institution of marriage has a clear and universal definition (that can be either supported or critiqued in relation to same-sex relationships) but I argue that this is not the case. The formulation of marriage expressed by Lord Penzance in the English case *Hyde v Hyde and Woodmansee* [1866] L Rev 1 P&D 130 has been criticized on a number of grounds (as discussed in Chapter 1) and yet remains consistently cited internationally, in both case law and academic writing, as *the* definition of marriage. I move away from the *Hyde* formulation, arguing that the key features of marriage should be identified instead by examining the structure, legal consequences and ideologies of marriage. However, I also argue that there is no fixed, universal essence of marriage. In order to both acknowledge this and recognize that the reach of the marriage framework extends beyond actual marriages (that is, non-marital, cohabiting relationships also fall within the feminist critiques of marriage), I argue that we should refer to the *marriage model* as the focus of critique rather than only the institution of marriage itself.

Therefore, this book departs from previous analyses of same-sex marriage in two ways: first, through identifying the marriage model and demonstrating how the marriage model informs the legal recognition of same-sex relationships; and then by modifying existing feminist critiques of marriage in light of this new formulation of the marriage model and to more specifically relate these feminist critiques to *same-sex* marriage. More broadly, I identify the continuing relevance of second-wave feminist critiques to the contemporary marriage model and specifically whether and how these critiques can be extended to same-sex relationships. This, therefore, not only contributes to discourses about marriage and the legal recognition of same-sex relationships but also demonstrates the continuing usefulness and applicability of second-wave feminist theory (in conjunction with queer theory) to contemporary social issues.

This book is not restricted to one jurisdiction but rather draws on materials from several jurisdictions that have had significant legal and political debates in relation to same-sex marriage. I analyse the theoretical arguments made for same-sex marriage and revisit the feminist and queer critiques of marriage in the context of the different legal provisions that have been created in these jurisdictions. My approach raises two methodological issues that require further discussion. First, because I refer to both primary and secondary materials from a number of jurisdictions, I begin by discussing the reasons for and justifying this approach. Second, both feminism and queer theory are terms that are used in a number of ways by different theorists, and sometimes in ways that potentially make them incompatible. Therefore, I outline my use of these terms and the reasons why I draw on both approaches below.

Cross-jurisdictional comparisons

A number of diverse social, economic and political factors have influenced the legal developments relating to same-sex marriage in different jurisdictions, ranging from a 'natural' evolution in the Netherlands and some other countries, where same-sex marriage became the *next step* in a sequence of liberal law reforms giving positive recognition to same-sex couples (Waaldijk, 2001, pp. 437–9) to the United States where the backlash began even before same-sex marriage was legally recognized (see, for example, Jesse Helms' speech in favour of the Defense of Marriage Act 1996: 1997, pp. 21–3; see also Wolfson, 2001, p. 170). However, it is not my intention to engage in a comparative analysis of the legal and political contexts of jurisdictions with various forms of relationship recognition (for this, see Merin, 2002; Sumner, 2002; Waaldijk, 2005; Bamforth, 2007; Smith, 2007). Instead, my intention is to identify the common themes in the arguments that have been used across jurisdictions.

While there can be problems with attempting straightforward cross-cultural comparisons in relation to gay and lesbian legal rights and with transposing strategies and arguments from one jurisdiction to another (see Graycar and Millbank, 2000, p. 274; Millbank and Morgan, 2001, p. 295; Stychin, 2001, p. 347), a broad approach is useful in this context because there is a clear cross-jurisdictional influence in the development of same-sex marriage claims. This is evidenced in two ways. First, similar arguments have been made both for and against same-sex marriage in different jurisdictions, albeit sometimes with variation to account for different constitutional or human rights provisions. For example, Miriam Smith (2007, p. 6) argues that a similar 'rights frame' is used to argue for same-sex marriage in both Canada and the US despite legal, political and policy differences between the countries; Nicholas Bamforth (2007, pp. 47–8) notes that arguments made for same-sex relationship recognition in Canada, South Africa, the UK and the US are analogous; and Nancy Maxwell argues that despite the very different legal and political cultures and routes taken towards same-sex relationship recognition in the Netherlands and the US, 'the issues argued and decided are almost identical' (2001, p. 200). Both Smith and Bamforth argue that political and cultural differences between countries influence the *reaction* to arguments (both legally and socially) for same-sex marriage rather than the actual legal arguments that are made. This argument is supported by my findings in Chapter 3, where I analyse the arguments that have been made for same-sex marriage, primarily in the context of litigation, and argue that there are a number of common themes across the jurisdictions (though there were also a number of jurisdiction-specific claims that were made, particularly those resting on constitutional provisions in the various jurisdictions). However, the commonalities between jurisdictions in terms of the arguments made may belie the extent to which these arguments have already been transplanted from one legal and cultural context to another. In particular, there are several examples of arguments that have clearly mirrored those made in the US context and simply been applied in a different jurisdiction.[2] Therefore, while it remains necessary to examine this issue in a cross-jurisdictional context, I do so cautiously.

Second, same-sex couples have travelled to a different jurisdiction to marry and then returned home seeking recognition of that marriage (see, for example: *Wilkinson v Kitzinger* [2006] EWHC 2022 (Fam); *Zappone and Gilligan v Revenue Commissioners* [2008] 2 IR 417; *Ben-Ari v Director of the Population Administration in the Ministry of the Interior* (2005) HCJ 3045/05 (see Association for Civil Rights in Israel, 2006; Gross, 2006); and *Hennefeld v Township of Montclair* [2005] 22 NJ Tax 166). As such, the developments in one jurisdiction have had an impact on others, whether or not the marriage (or marriage-like provision) was subsequently recognized in the home jurisdiction.[3]

Theoretical frameworks

My research questions lead to a theoretical framework that draws primarily from feminist literatures that are grounded in the second wave, especially those within the radical and socialist feminist traditions. I explore these traditions in more depth in Chapter 5, but I focus on these perspectives because they have well-established and, in my view, strong critiques of marriage, yet these critiques are (as noted above) largely absent from contemporary debates about same-sex marriage. However, in order to address some of the arguments for same-sex marriage, particularly those that were based on the (perceived) need for positive state recognition of same-sex relationships in the context of 'previous' overt state homophobia, I found some of the insights of queer theory a useful addition. These insights provided another dimension to my feminist critique but drawing on these theories together also raises potential problems because of high-profile disagreements between them. Sheila Jeffreys, who argues that queer theory is 'deeply hostile to feminism' (1994, p. 467), is perhaps the most vociferous feminist critic of queer theory.[4] As such, I will

---

2 See, for example, some of the arguments made by Wilkinson and Kitzinger (2006) in relation to their case, particularly regarding separate and unequal, where they explicitly reference US and South African contexts; and arguments made by the Constitutional Marriage Amendment Campaign (2006) in South Africa, which were influenced and supported by American right-wing Christian organizations, particularly the Southern Africa chapter of Focus on the Family (see Dobson, 2005).

3 Relating to the recognition of same-sex relationships within the EU countries, it has also been suggested that cross-jurisdictional recognition may be necessary for the purposes of the free movement of persons (Guild, 2001), particularly following Directive 2004/58/EC. As Stychin argues, by directing member states to treat registered partners as spouses for the purposes of free movement, the directive attempts to 'impose transnational coherence upon the culturally diverse pattern of regimes of recognition emerging across the E.U.' (Stychin, 2005b, pp. 571–2).

4 Another illustration of the divergence between (second-wave) feminist theory and queer theory is the recent work of Janet Halley, a queer theorist who argues that we should 'take a break from feminism' (2006). See also the discussion in Cossman *et al.* (2003).

briefly outline her objections to queer theory as an example, before explaining why I nevertheless draw on both frameworks in my analysis of marriage.

Jeffreys' feminist critique of queer theory is based on three key points. First, she argues that 'queer' is a supposedly inclusive generic term but it does not include lesbian points of view unless they fit a gay male agenda.[5] Second, the goal of transgressing gender actually serves to re-inscribe rather than eliminate it; for example, the practice of drag depends on 'the existence of a subordinate class of women' (2003, p. 106). This is based on a radical feminist position that 'gender' should be understood as 'dominant and subordinate forms of behaviour' (Jeffreys, 2003, p. 44). Following Christine Delphy, Jeffreys argues that there can only be two genders: the behaviours of male dominance and female subordination.[6] It is, therefore, necessary to eliminate dominant and submissive behaviours in order to have equality between men and women (2003, p. 44). This relates to Jeffreys' third point, that queer theory provides theoretical justification for sexual practices (including camp, drag, public sex, pornography and sadomasochism) that are male and in many cases depend on domination and submission (2003, p. 55).

In this section I will explain why I nevertheless see queer theory as providing a helpful and necessary contribution to a feminist critique of marriage. My intention here is not to attempt to reconcile the differences between these theories. Instead, I will accept that there may be *some* ways in which these theories are inherently incompatible and focus on why it is nevertheless important to draw upon both in this context. There is, however, much more common ground than is acknowledged through the caricatures of lesbian feminism as anti-sex and queer theory as an 'anything goes' libertarianism. For example, Suzanna Walters (1996, p. 860) shares some of Sheila Jeffreys' concerns but argues that an alliance between feminism and queer theory 'has important political and intellectual potential'. This alliance, Walters emphasizes, must move away from 'the tendency to assume gay male sexuality and iconography as the pinnacle of radical transgression and lesbianism and lesbian feminism as a tired, PC remnant of days long gone' (1996, p. 860). As I argue next, queer theory is not wholly incompatible with some of the aims of feminism and a number of feminists have drawn on concepts that could also be termed queer, particularly in relation to same-sex marriage (see, for example, Robson, 2002; Boyd and Young, 2003). I see four main

---

5 There are repeated instances in Jeffreys' analysis where she appears to use gay male as a synonym for queer men, which is a misinterpretation of queer: there are a significant number of gay men who could not be referred to as queer and who are, in fact, deeply critical of queer theory and practices (see, for example, the gay male advocates of same-sex marriage discussed in Chapter 4). However, for the sake of argument, I am interpreting the term 'gay male' in this context as intending to refer to the interests of queers who are men.

6 This would not be the way that many other feminists would use the term gender and is in contrast to the way I use gender in this research (see Chapter 5). My intention here is only to present an overview of Jeffreys' views in relation to queer. Jeffreys is also critical of trans but this is outside the scope of this book.

ways in which queer theory contributes to my feminist critique of same-sex marriage.

First, like radical and socialist feminisms, queer theory provides a critical response to a liberal gay agenda. In the US context, Steven Seidman relates the evolution from a theory and politics of liberation in the 1970s, concerned with freeing people from the constraints of 'mutually exclusive homo/hetero and feminine/masculine roles' (1993, p. 110), to an 'ethnic/essentialist' model and socio-political agenda in the late 1970s and 1980s, which constructed gays and lesbians as an oppressed minority in civil rights discourse (see also Stychin, 2005a). For Seidman, queer is a reaction against this development by those who were marginalized by the white, middle-class dominant paradigm, such as sex radicals and lesbians and gay men of colour: the post-modern queer is 'the true radical heir to a fading liberationist ideal' (1993, p. 110). This evolution can also be seen in the context of UK activism. For example, Chris Woods, one of the founders of the direct action group Outrage!, describes the 'generational struggle' around queer:

> Queer politics was a new politics. It was post lesbian and gay, but was very different, very exciting.... To me, sexuality is in a state of flux, it's a changing thing, a metamorphosing thing. Gay, which had been a radical, revolutionary concept in the early seventies, had become this conservative, strained value system in the nineties, which commercial organizations had a vested interest in maintaining. (Lucas, 1998, p. 56)

I am not, however, arguing that queer theory is merely the rebirth of gay liberation: there are significant differences between these movements (see Lent, 2003). Instead, I am suggesting that queer theory and radical feminism share an opposition, albeit for different reasons, to the gay rights agenda that is promoting same-sex marriage. This also includes a shared opposition to gay as a consumer identity (see Stychin, 2005a). This setting up of queer theory in opposition to the 'ethnic/essentialist model' of the gay mainstream is not unproblematic. For example, Nikki Sullivan argues that this 'overly simplistic' distinction and the dichotomies that it creates of queer and heterosexual, and queer and gay/lesbian mean that:

> all heterosexuals, it is often implied, are situated in a dominant normative position, and all gays and lesbians simply aspire to be granted access to this position, whereas all queers are marginalized and consciously and intentionally resist assimilation of any kind. (Sullivan, 2003, pp. 48–9)

In terms of the same-sex marriage debate, however, there *is* a clearly identifiable conflict between a lesbian and gay mainstream seeking 'inclusion' and 'recognition' through marriage (see further Chapter 4) and a more radical, though less visible, queer opposition to marriage, discussed in Chapter 6.

Second, despite the differences in the ways that sexuality and gender are theorized, queer theory shares with radical feminism the view that sexuality is a 'constructed reality, a social and not a natural reality' (Halperin, 1995, p. 45). Furthermore, the suggestion of queer theorists, following Gayle Rubin (1984), that gender and sexuality are separate forms of oppression is one of the reasons why it is useful for feminists to draw upon queer theory in the context of same-sex marriage debates. Rubin argues that:

> Feminism is the theory of gender oppression. To assume automatically that this makes it the theory of sexual oppression is to fail to distinguish between gender, on the one hand, and erotic desire, on the other. (1984, p. 32)

While, like many lesbian feminists, I would not accept the premise of this separation of sexuality and gender, as I outline in Chapter 4 one argument that is made for same-sex marriage acknowledges the feminist critiques of the institution but relies on differences in the oppression of heterosexual women and lesbians to argue that same-sex marriage is nevertheless necessary. Feminist theory can respond to that argument, as I demonstrate in Chapter 5, but a much more effective response can be made from queer theory. This is because queer theorists who follow Rubin may accept the premise of the claim that the modes of oppression are different but *still* deny that same-sex marriage is the solution to overcoming this oppression for reasons that I explore in Chapter 6.

Third, queer theory provides a means to protest exclusion without claiming sameness and demanding inclusion. Instead, queer theory seeks to 'decentre' law and have a 'more directly cultural impact' (Morgan, 1995, p. 39). As such, like both radical and postmodern feminisms, queer theory is rejecting the liberal assumption that law can provide 'the answer' to lesbian and gay oppression:

> Queer theory coalesced out of the growing sense among some feminists and sexual minorities that their access to equal rights and treatment would depend not on working out the glitches in an otherwise workable system but on rethinking from the ground up categories of persons and the distributions of power among them. (Turner, 2000, p. 15)

For queer theorists, the homophobia of law is as apparent (though perhaps in different ways) in 'law's "gay friendly" voice', such as anti-discrimination law, as it was in the 'gay unfriendly' voice of criminalization (Morgan, 1995, p. 39). Therefore, Morgan concludes that queer theory may be useful for the following reasons. First, it reminds us that rather than assuming that natural coalitions lie with those who share a sexual orientation, we must seek out 'conscious coalitions' and address issues of multiple identities (1995, p. 43). Second, we must be 'very careful about the stories we tell about gay and lesbian lives in legal fora', avoiding the language of sameness and encouraging 'legal institutions to view diversity favourably in reality rather than just formally in rhetoric' (ibid.). Third, although compromise is inevitable when dealing with legal institutions, we should beware of co-option in the name of 'political necessity' (1995, pp. 43–4). Finally, queer theory reminds us that 'law is only one of the discourses...which construct views about homosex' so it is important to remember that formal legal reform alone will not contest this power (1995, p. 44). None of these points are fundamentally incompatible with second-wave radical or socialist feminisms and they are all points that are very relevant in the context of some of the arguments that are being made in the same-sex marriage debates.

Finally, one of the ways in which (second-wave) feminist legal method explores the silencing and marginalization of women by the law is 'asking the woman question' (Bartlett, 1990, p. 371; see also Conaghan, 2000). In response to critiques that the woman question is exclusionary in its assumption of the universal category woman, who is almost always white, heterosexual and middle-class (see further Rich, 1981; Carby, 1992), Bartlett suggests asking 'the question of the excluded':

> This inquiry would require a general and far-reaching set of questions that go beyond issues of gender bias to seek out other bases of exclusion: what assumptions are made by law (or practice or analysis) about those whom it affects? Whose point of view do these assumptions reflect? Whose interests are invisible or peripheral? How might excluded viewpoints be identified and taken into account? (Bartlett, 1990, p. 376)

Taking this approach means that central to my analysis is the question of what marriage is and which relationships are included and excluded from its definition; what assumptions are made by the law in relation to marriage; who stands to gain/lose from same-sex marriage; and whose interests are invisible or peripheral to the question of same-sex marriage. The final question of how it would be possible for these interests to be taken into account through changes in marriage law is outside the scope of this project.

Some of these questions are easily addressed through the application of second-wave feminist analysis, but in order to comprehensively answer questions of recognition and exclusion it is impossible to ignore the contributions of queer theorists. While one of the stronger arguments for same-sex marriage is that it is necessary to have public, state recognition of the legitimacy of same-sex relationships, queer theoretical frameworks are particularly helpful in highlighting the relationships and forms of sexuality that would continue to be excluded and/or stigmatized after same-sex marriage is available. In conjunction with a postmodern feminist critique of law, which questions the idea of law reform as liberation, queer perspectives add an important dimension to second-wave feminist critiques of marriage in the context of same-sex relationships. Together, second-wave feminist and queer theories can provide a stronger critique of *same-sex* marriage than second-wave feminist theory alone.

Chapter outline

In the first part of this book (Chapters 1–3), I critically examine the legal provisions that currently exist in terms of (same-sex) relationship recognition. I argue that the same-sex marriage debates tend to focus on *access* to the institution at the expense of examining what it actually is that some same-sex couples are seeking access to and what it means to *be* married, legally, socially or ideologically. This leaves unexplored a vital aspect of the meaning of same-sex marriage. This unexplored terrain permits an uncritical reliance on formal equality in support of same-sex marriage and wholesale acceptance of the institution, even though there may be recognized problems with a particular provision. For example, referring to the absence of adultery in the UK's Civil Partnership Act 2004 (see Chapter 2), Ian Sumner argues:

> Although the current author is not in favour of adultery as a ground for the termination of a marriage, it is argued that if this *is still* a ground for the dissolution of marriage, then this should also be a ground for the dissolution of a civil partnership. (2004, p. 38)

Similarly, arguments against same-sex marriage may fail to acknowledge the possibilities it could hold for subverting, or even transforming, the institution. Therefore, as Janet Halley argues, we must approach the question of same-sex marriage with 'an honest, beady-eyed understanding of *what marriage is*' (2001, p. 111). As such, the first question I ask is: 'What is marriage?' This close examination of the institution in Chapter 1 then forms the basis of my critical analysis of same-sex marriage in subsequent chapters.

There are a number of statutory requirements for enacting a valid marriage (as well as dissolving one) and a considerable number of legal consequences that flow from this status. In combination with the judicial ideological narratives of marriage, these form what I will term the marriage model. I refer to marriage as a model to both acknowledge it as an 'ideal' and to reflect the fact that the reach of the ideal extends beyond marital relationships.

In some jurisdictions legal recognition is also given to relationships through institutions that are separate from marriage. This raises the question of whether these separate forms of same-sex relationship recognition, such as civil partnership, map on to the marriage model. While some marriage advocates criticize these provisions as inferior to marriage, there is growing support amongst activists as well as academics for the creation of 'alternatives' to marriage (see, for example, Beyond Marriage, 2006). In chapter 2, I examine these separate legal provisions in the context of the structure, legal consequences and ideologies of the marriage model. I argue that the separate provisions are informed by this model to the extent that many of them can be easily encompassed within it.

The final question in relation to the legal provisions is what types of legal arguments are being made in order to gain marriage. In Chapter 3, therefore, I analyse the routes to same-sex marriage that have been taken in several of those jurisdictions that now recognize it and identify several common themes that recur in (legal) arguments for same-sex marriage.

In the second part of the book, my focus turns to the theoretical arguments that have been made for and against same-sex marriage. In Chapter 4, I deconstruct, classify and critique the arguments for same-sex marriage in order to identify the strongest arguments from a feminist perspective. This is important because, while there are some arguments that are clearly incompatible with feminism, other arguments do have some merits that should be acknowledged. In the mainstream arena, arguments for same-sex marriage are most frequently made on the basis of formal equality, that same-sex relationships are functionally and structurally similar to heterosexual relationships and therefore should have access to the same legal provisions (protections) and recognition of the relationship from the state and other third parties. Arguments are also made from conservative perspectives, which stress the role of (same-sex) marriage in strengthening and supporting 'the family' and promoting 'family values' amongst gay men and lesbians. However, all of these arguments stress the ways in which same-sex relationships are (or, in the case of conservative perspectives, should be) the same as heterosexual relationships.

Some of these arguments might carry more weight than others from a feminist perspective: it is much more difficult to argue against the legal and symbolic importance of *recognition* of same-sex relationships in a context of heterosexism and homophobia, often perpetuated by state policies, than it is to argue against access to tax breaks for the wealthy. However, relying on arguments that same-sex relationships are just the same as heterosexual relationships, and as such should have access to the institution on the same terms, does not pose a particularly strong challenge to the feminist critique of marriage.

In contrast, other writers move away from sameness arguments, exploring the ways in which same-sex marriages might be different to heterosexual marriages, might have a transformative effect on the institution as a whole, or might transgress the boundaries of marriage in various ways. Finally, Cheshire Calhoun (2000) argues that same-sex marriage is important *despite* the feminist critiques of the institution because the issue of family is one point at which lesbian (and gay) subordination differs from that of heterosexual women. She argues that while heterosexual women are oppressed within marriage and the family, lesbian and gay subordination arises principally through exclusion from these institutions. As such, access to marriage should, she argues, be central to lesbian theory and politics.

In Chapters 5 and 6, I respond to these arguments through expanding upon and revising the critiques of marriage. In Chapter 5, I examine the history and context of feminist theorizing of marriage. I begin by reviewing the second-wave feminist literature. The key criticisms made by second-wave feminists related to not only the gendered division of labour and other unequal power relations within individual marriages but also the privatization of reproduction and caretaking within the family. I argue that these concerns are no less relevant to contemporary marriage, despite discourses that would suggest a more egalitarian household division of labour. Not only do government statistics and empirical research belie such egalitarianism in contemporary marriages, but also the issue of privatization is, as Boyd and Young (2003) and others argue, *increasingly* relevant in the contemporary neoliberal (or neoconservative) political contexts. As such, I will argue that claims that same-sex couples should have access to the legal provisions and framework of marriage and that same-sex marriage would be more egalitarian and possibly transformative of the institution as a whole do not overcome these feminist critiques.

However, two questions remain. First, could same-sex marriage, as conservative opponents fear, destabilize the (hetero) norms of the institution? In other words, could marriage be 'queered' through the transgression of norms such as the primacy of the monogamous sexual family? In the context of the UK Civil Partnership Act 2004, some aspects of the legislation may allow for these possibilities. Second, would same-sex marriage provide the legal and symbolic *recognition* of same-sex relationships *as* family that Calhoun argues is necessary to challenge their stigmatization as 'outlaws' to the family?

These questions are addressed in Chapter 6, where I take up Calhoun's challenge to treat lesbian and gay subordination as a separate (though related) axis to gender oppression. Drawing on queer theoretical perspectives, I conclude that this highlights an additional, related set of problems with the institution of marriage, which for the most part complement rather than undermine the feminist critiques of the institution. While same-sex marriage *would* be hugely significant in providing symbolic recognition that lesbians and gay men are fit to participate in the institution of marriage and family, a queer and feminist lens also highlights the privileging of the monogamous, sexual relationship over other forms of family. It makes lesbians and gays complicit in the labelling of casual sexual encounters as not responsible and it forecloses more imaginative kinship possibilities that move away from the privatized, nuclear family model. Most significantly, in terms of the feminist critiques of marriage, I argue that lesbians and gay men should be regarded as one of Nancy Fraser's 'bivalent collectivities' (1997a, p. 19). This means that injustices are not just cultural (requiring recognition) but *also* economic and therefore requiring redistribution.

Recognition and redistribution remedies can, according to Fraser, be either affirmative or transformative. In terms of redistribution, there is no question that same-sex marriage would be an affirmative remedy: it would merely give same-sex couples access to existing social structures rather than challenge them. The question is whether same-sex marriage could be a transformative remedy in terms of recognition, changing the meaning of marriage in some way. I argue that even if the recognition could be transformative, when this remedy is coupled with an affirmative redistribution remedy it is difficult to envisage this as a radically transformative strategy.

Part I

1
The Marriage Model

It is clear, then, that marriage is in its essence a simple contract which any person of either sex of normal intelligence should readily be able to comprehend. (per Karminski J, *In the Estate of Park, Dec'd* [1954] P 89 at 100)

Introduction

Marriage is frequently claimed, as above, to be a simple and universally under-stood institution. However, I suggest that it lacks a clear definition from either statute or common law in the UK and, despite Mr Justice Karminski's clarity on the issue, the 'essence' of marriage is perhaps not as readily comprehensible as he suggests. While Lord Penzance's formulation of marriage as 'the voluntary union for life of one man and one woman to the exclusion of all others' (*Hyde v Hyde and Woodmansee* [1866] L Rev 1 P&D 130 at 133) is generally cited in both case law and academic commentary as a common law definition (see, for example, Probert, 2007; see also Sharpe, 1997, and Bainham, 2002, describing it as the 'classic' definition; and Murphy, 2004 referring to it as the 'traditional' definition), it has been undermined by evolutions in the law of marriage (see also Murphy, 2002, p. 188). In fact, Sebastian Poulter argues that it was never wholly accurate, particularly in relation to the 'for life' requirement, since divorce was available before 1866 (1979, pp. 418–19). He also notes that the 'actual rule' in *Hyde* (that potentially polygamous marriages contracted abroad would not be recognized by English law) has disappeared following legislative reform (1976, p. 508). Despite this, the atti-tudes underlying Lord Penzance's formula survive 'through their very famil-iarity and constant repetition' (1976, p. 508). Rebecca Probert also refers to the *Hyde* formula as 'positively misleading as a definition of marriage' (2007) and claims that Lord Penzance's view was more a *defence* of marriage than a definition. She argues that, in the context of a perceived threat to Christian marriage by the potentially (though not actually) polygamous Mormon marriage of Mr and Mrs Hyde, 'the desirability of the *idea* of marriage set out in *Hyde* was more important than its accuracy' (2007, p. 322, emphasis added).

Examining each part of the 'definition' in the context of current marriage law bears this out.[1] A marriage entered into *in*voluntarily is voidable rather than automatically void and as such could be upheld as legally valid (Matrimonial Causes Act 1973 (MCA) s. 12(c)). The availability of divorce means that marriage is not necessarily for life and the parties arguably need not intend it to be for life when they enter into a marriage. Though the Court of Appeal did suggest in *Nachimson v Nachimson* [1930] P 217 that the parties must intend a marriage to be for life, this 'gloss' put on the *Hyde* definition is described as 'unsatisfactory' by Lowe and Douglas (2007, p. 41) and it has subsequently been held that a marriage not intended to be for life was valid, though this case was confined to its facts (*Vervaeke v Smith* [1982] 2 All ER 144). Wade (1982) suggests that the courts may respond to 'limited purpose' marriages (that is, those that comply with the formal requirements but which are intended only for a limited purpose, such as immigration or tax avoidance) by resurrecting the historical concept of 'mental reservations' but, as I demonstrate below, the approach the courts have taken recently points to developments in the enforcement of romantic marriage ideologies of love and companionship rather than the absence of actual consent that mental reservations would imply.

While the criminal offence of bigamy enforces the '*one* man and *one* woman' (or, in the case of jurisdictions that now allow same-sex marriage, 'two people') requirements of marriage, there are some, albeit limited, circumstances under which polygamous marriages can be recognized in the UK (see, for example, *Radwan v Radwan* (No 2) [1972] 3 WLR 939; MCA s. 11(d)). Furthermore, while non-monogamy is grounds for divorce (MCA s. 1(2)(a)), this would not make the marriage *void* but rather potentially bring it to an end: therefore a valid marriage exists despite the fact that it is not 'to the exclusion of all others'. Additionally, adultery alone is not sufficient in itself to provide grounds for divorce, rather s. 1(2)(a) provides that the petitioner must also find it intolerable to live with the defendant. Most importantly in the context of this book, in some jurisdictions that had adopted the *Hyde* formula (Canada, Massachusetts), as well as in others where the common law

---

1 In the Canadian context, see Calder (2009), arguing that the only aspect of the *Hyde* definition remaining is that marriage is a sexually monogamous relationship. Nicholson (2005) also argues, in the Australian context, that the *Hyde* definition was strictly speaking inaccurate even at the time it was created.

definition of civil marriage was very similar (South Africa),[2] marriage is now available to two people of the same sex.

This brief examination of the legal institution of marriage casts doubt on any assumption, such as that of Mr Justice Karminski, that it is an essential, universal and natural institution. I suggest that looking at the *Hyde* formulation as an *ideal* rather than as a definition is, therefore, a useful way to think about marriage and invites consideration of what the essence of marriage actually is in contemporary UK law. Yet many of those advocating for same-sex marriage do not engage with these questions.

In this chapter, I explore the *structure, legal consequences* and *ideologies* of marriage to identify those characteristics that are at the core of the institution. I do this by examining statutory frameworks and judicial comments on marriage, primarily in the UK but also drawing on those of other common law jurisdictions. I refer to 'the marriage model' both to recognize that marriage is much more of an ideology than a fixed definition and to highlight the ways in which this ideology may be extended to forms of relationship that are not called marriage, such as the UK's civil partnerships. In other words, the marriage model provides a framework to analyse the extent to which the legal recognition of same-sex relationships reflects the structure, ideology and legal consequences (in terms of the rights, obligations, benefits and burdens) of marriage but the 'essence' of marriage, in the sense of there being a consistent shared understanding of what marriage is, is much less certain.

Marriage and the marriage model

The question of what *is* the essence of marriage has arisen in a number of contexts, including: whether a 21-year-old woman with hydrocephalus and spina bifida who 'functions at the level of a 13 year old' had the capacity to marry a 37-year-old man with a history of sexual violence (*Sheffield County Council v E and Another* [2005] Fam 326 at 328); whether a Muslim couple who had gone through a civil marriage ceremony but did not 'become husband and wife in any real sense' in the absence of a religious ceremony had contracted a valid marriage (*SH v KH* [2005] SLT 1025 at para. 56); whether a long-term cohabiting same-sex partner was a spouse or family member for the purposes of tenancy succession under the Rent Act 1977 (*Fitzpatrick v Sterling Housing Association* [2001] 1 AC 27; *Ghaidan v Godin-Mendoza* [2004]

---

2 Here, the common law definition of marriage was: 'a union of one man with one woman, to the exclusion, while it lasts, of all others' (per Innes CJ in *Mashia Ebrahim v Mahomed Essop* 1905 TS 59 at 61; in *Minister of Home Affairs and Director-General of Home Affairs v Fourie and Bonthuys* (CCT 60/04) [2005] ZACC 19 at 3). Commenting on the 'for life' requirement in *Hyde*, the Constitutional Court of South Africa in *Fourie* said: 'Given the high degree of divorce this would seem to be a misnomer' (per Sachs J at 3).

2 AC 557); and whether a same-sex marriage contracted in Canada could be recognized as a marriage rather than a civil partnership in the UK (*Wilkinson v Kitzinger and Others* [2006] EWHC 2022 (Fam)). In each of these cases, the courts drew on not only the strict legal formalities and requirements contained in the MCA and elsewhere but also, like Mr Justice Karminski, on what they assume are obvious, even universal, (social) understandings and norms of marriage. Partly because of the incorporation of such knowledge into legal precedent, it is impossible to determine where the line is between legal and social understandings of marriage; but that is not my aim here. Instead, I will argue that these are ideologies of marriage which, along with its legal structure and consequences, form the marriage model informing judicial as well as lay people's expectations about how marriages will be lived out and what it means to be living as spouses.

Most significant in terms of upholding a particular understanding of the institution is the first part of the marriage model that I will examine: its (legal) *structure*. This refers to its entry and exit requirements or, in other words, who may marry and dissolve a marriage, under what circumstances and according to what formalities. This is the part of the marriage model that should carry the most weight because these rules are often regarded as integral to, even definitional of, the institution: the requirements for entry into marriage and structural assumptions about the marital unit have been relatively constant, both within UK law and between jurisdictions; and, when the structure is potentially altered (as in the case of same-sex marriage), particularly when this also involves its ideologies being challenged in some way (such as discussions of 'no fault' divorce), this is seen by some as a threat to the core of the institution itself (for examples of this in relation to same-sex marriage, see Sullivan 1997; Baird and Rosenbaum, 1997; 2004).

The second part of the marriage model that I will discuss are the legal *consequences* of marriage. These are, I suggest, the least 'telling' aspect of the marriage model, while nevertheless forming a part of it. The legal consequences are significant because they are set by the state rather than the parties themselves:

> Its [marriage's] distinctive character lies in the fact that English law will not allow husband and wife by contract (whether pre- or post-nuptial) to exercise the right, which it accords virtually all other partners, to make their own agreement as to the terms. (Cretney, 2003, p. 9)

The consequences that the state chooses to attach to marriage may provide an indication of the type of relationship it is intended to be. However, I put less weight on this aspect than on its structure and ideology because it has less public impact. Unlike the structure of the institution, the detail of the resulting legal consequences may be changed relatively easily without attracting much critical attention[3] and varies significantly between jurisdictions (see Waaldijk, 2005 for illustrations of the differences between the legal consequences of marriage in nine European countries). I would suggest that, while people are generally aware of both the structure and ideologies of marriage, there is little awareness of its legal consequences. This is borne out by empirical research, which suggests that the legal consequences of marriage play a limited role in the factors that contribute to a decision to marry. Instead, people marry for a variety of reasons, such as demonstration of love, commitment and a sense of tradition or 'old-fashioned' values, that are much more closely linked to the ideologies of marriage as an institution than a recognition of its legal consequences (see Eekelaar and Maclean, 2004, pp. 517–23; Hibbs, 2001).

Finally, I return to the cases mentioned above to examine the *ideologies* invoked by the courts in deciding what marriage is. Ideology plays a significant role in family law and in this context often refers to a particular set of (conservative) ideologies. For example, Eva Havas (1995) discusses the role of family ideology in maintaining an individualized social system. There is, however, disagreement between theorists on the meaning of 'ideology' as a term and a concept, as well as with regard to its role in relation to law (see Eagleton, 1991; Hunt, 1985). For example, Eagleton outlines six possible definitions from a 'general material process of production of ideas, beliefs and values in social life' (1991, p. 28) to deceptive or false beliefs that arise from the material structure of society as a whole (1991, p. 31). Other definitions of ideology move away from its Marxist base towards language and discourse (Purvis and Hunt, 1993). I am using the term ideology to refer to the beliefs and discourses that underpin judicial understandings of marriage as natural and universal. Ideology here is the manifestation of an 'ideal' image of marriage. This is consistent with several theorists who argue that family law promotes an ideal family form: for example, Shelley Gavigan refers to familial ideology (discussed further in Chapter 5); and, as already noted, Alison Diduck (2003) distinguishes between families we live *by* and families we live *with* (see also, in the US context, discussions of the 'channelling function of family law': Schneider, 1992; McClain, 2007; for an argument that law more generally is used for 'purposive social engineering' see Smart, 1997, p. 312). The ideologies of marriage would be those pronouncements that tell us about the marriages we live by, our collective image of what marriage ought to be.

---

3 Though this is not to say that is always the case: for example, large awards made to wives on divorce as a result of the 'yardstick of equality' introduced in *White v White* [2001] 1 AC 596 (at 605) attracted a significant amount of media coverage (*Miller v Miller; McFarlane v McFarlane* [2006] 2 AC 618), although the commentaries did not suggest that this change would alter the institution of marriage itself in any way.

This may bear little relation to the actual marriages that we live with but, through its incorporation into what have generally been accepted as judicial definitions, such as in the case of *Hyde*, what marriage 'ought to be' becomes what marriage is. In this way, ideologies of marriage form part of its (perceived) essence.

The structure, legal consequences and ideologies of marriage are interlinked and overlapping – in particular, the structure and consequences reflect as well as inform the ideologies of the institution – but, for the purposes of identifying the key features of marriage, I will discuss them separately here.

Structure

By structure, I refer to the parameters of marriage. In other words, as stated above, I refer to its entry and exit requirements: who may marry and dissolve a marriage and under what circumstances. In the UK, the structure of marriage is governed primarily by the MCA, which provides the circumstances under which a marriage will be void, voidable or may be dissolved. Parties must 'opt-in' to marriage through registering with the state in adherence with the formalities required by the Marriage Act 1949 (as amended). I argue that the provisions relating to the validity and formalities of marriage can be grouped into four overlapping categories: sexuality; monogamy; commitment; and protection.

The clearest indications that *sexuality* forms an integral part of the structure of marriage are the provisions relating to consummation, venereal disease and prohibited degrees of relationship. A marriage is voidable if it is not consummated due to one party's incapacity or wilful refusal (s. 12(a) and (b)), or if one party was suffering from a communicable venereal disease at the time of the marriage. Consummation is defined as 'sexual intercourse in the proper meaning of the term'. That is, *'ordinary and complete* intercourse; it does not mean *partial and imperfect* intercourse' (per Dr Lushington in *D-e v A-g (falsely calling herself D-e)* [1845] 1 Rob Ecc 280 at 1045 (emphasis added); see Collier, 1995, p. 152). The definition of consummation, as upheld in *Corbett v Corbett* [1971] P 83, as well as the fact that a marriage is automatically void unless the parties are 'respectively male and female' (MCA s. 11(c)) indicate that marriage in the UK is not only a sexual institution but also that it remains a *hetero*sexual one, at least as far as sexual performance is concerned.

It is possible for a marriage that has not been consummated to exist as a valid marriage. This is because non-consummation as such does not provide the ground for nullity, but rather the incapacity or wilful refusal to consummate does (see also Brunner, 2001). In fact if, *inter alia*, the petitioner was aware that the marriage would not be consummated at the time it was contracted, or had led the respondent to reasonably believe that she/he would not seek a decree, MCA s. 13 provides that a decree of nullity will not be granted. Furthermore, like any voidable provision, it will not be voided until one party petitions the court to do so. There is, however, a clear expectation within the MCA that marriages will be consummated. As such, (hetero)-sexuality is a part of its structure. It also appears that there may be a duty to maintain a sexual relationship, arising historically from the doctrine of consortium (Gaffney-Rhys, 2006; see legal consequences, below). Gaffney-Rhys examines two cases where the husband petitioned for divorce on the basis of infrequent sexual intercourse (*P (D) v P (J)* [1965] 2 All ER 456; *Mason v Mason* (1980) 11 Fam Law 143) and finds that: 'These cases suggest that spouses are expected to engage in sexual intercourse during their marriage, but they do not indicate that a particular degree of regularity is required.'[4]

The exclusion of close relatives from marrying each other also indicates that marriage is expected to be a sexual relationship. If incest were not a presumed consequence of marriage between relatives, there would be little reason to prevent consenting adults from entering into marriage as a reciprocal legal arrangement, though other aspects of the structure of the institution would pose practical problems.[5] Furthermore, the Law Commission explained the prohibited degrees provision in the Marriage Act 1949 by referring to sexual relations between family members as 'unnatural and wrong' (Gaffney-Rhys, 2006).

Second, and related to sexuality, is monogamy. In the Canadian context, Gillian Calder (2009, pp. 26–7) argues that the only part of the *Hyde* definition that remains essential in contemporary marriage is that it must be sexually monogamous. Monogamy is a central part of marriage in that bigamy/polygamy remains one of the few grounds upon which a marriage contracted in the UK will be automatically void (MCA s. 11(b)). This does not mean that 'open' marriages (a marriage that is between two people but non-monogamous in the sense that they also have non-marital sexual relationships with other people) will be void, or even provide grounds for divorce. The only ground for divorce in the UK is that the marriage has irretrievably broken down (MCA s. 1(1)). This can be established by one of five facts, including 'that the respondent has committed adultery *and* the petitioner finds it intolerable to live with the respondent' (MCA s. 1(2)(a), emphasis added). Significantly, the intolerability clause was included so that adultery would not provide grounds

---

4 Interestingly, though evidently related to conserving resources, there *is* a prescribed 'degree of regularity' for men who access Viagra through the National Health Service: doctors may only prescribe four pills per patient per month (Thomson, 2006, p. 270).

5 In fact, during the passage of the Civil Partnership Act 2004, some Members of Parliament argued that close relatives should be included within the Act, which was legally identical to marriage in most respects. However, even in the absence of a sexual element, some of its provisions such as its restriction to two people would pose other problems for family members who married each other (see Barker, 2004; 2006).

for divorce where it had not had an impact on the relationship (Booth and Jenkinson, 2007, p. 530). Therefore, it is for one party to petition for divorce on the basis that the other's adultery makes it intolerable for them to live together but, if they had earlier agreed to a non-monogamous relationship, this ground might be more difficult to demonstrate to the court. Furthermore, a non-monogamous relationship is not a bar to marriage in that a valid marriage will exist until one party petitions for divorce; at that point divorce is a means to bring a valid marriage to an end. However, marriage is structurally monogamous in the sense that one can only enter into a legally recognized marriage with one person at a time: bigamy is a criminal offence (Offences Against the Person Act 1861 s. 57) and a marriage will be void if one of the parties is already lawfully married (MCA s. 11(b)). Polygamous marriages are, however, recognized unless one of the parties was domiciled in England and Wales at the time of the marriage (s. 11(d)).

Third, the structure and formalities of marriage contain several indications that marriage requires some level of *commitment* from the parties. As the divorce rate rises, it is tempting to suggest that a long-term (and certainly a life-long) commitment is no longer required: in fact one participant in Eekelaar and Maclean's research suggested that it was children rather than marriage that created commitment in a relationship (2004, p. 522). The intention to make a long-term commitment is not necessarily required to enact a valid marriage. For example, in some cases, such as 'sham' marriages for immigration purposes (where the parties have not intended the marriage to be for life), the marriage has been upheld as valid, though others in similar circumstances have been declared void (see *Vervaeke v Smith*; cf. *Nachimson v Nachimson*).

The availability and prevalence of divorce means that marriage is in many cases not actually for life. However, through the formalities required to enter and dissolve a marriage there remains an element of commitment in its structure. Divorce proceedings may not be brought during the first year of marriage (MCA s. 3(1)) and the parties must demonstrate that the relationship has *irretrievably* broken down (MCA s. 1(1)). Other than adultery (discussed above), a party may petition for divorce on the grounds that 'the respondent has behaved in such a way that the petitioner cannot reasonably be expected to live with the respondent' (MCA s. 1(2)(b)). This requires more than the parties being merely incompatible, no longer having anything in common or being unable to communicate (*Buffery v Buffery* [1988] 2 FLR 365; see also Lowe and Douglas, 2007, p. 268). That one party is bored with the marriage is also insufficient (*Kisala v Kisala* (1973) 117 Sol Jo 664; Lowe and Douglas, 2007, p. 268). The test for 'behaviour' is, though, a 'quasi-subjective' test devised in *Ash v Ash* [1972] Fam 135 (per Bagnall J at 140), which asks whether *this* petitioner with their particular attributes can *reasonably* be expected to live with *this* respondent (Bailey-Harris, 2002, p. 883). If the parties wish to demonstrate the irretrievable breakdown of the marriage through a period of separation (rather than a fault-based ground), the relevant time periods are two years (with the consent of the other party or in the case of desertion) or five years (without consent) (MCA s. 1(2)(c), (d), (e)). This suggests that a decision to end a marriage is not to be taken lightly.

Finally, the *protection* category refers primarily to those provisions that prevent minors and those within the prohibited degrees of relationship from contracting a valid marriage in any circumstances: MCA s. 11(a)(i) and (ii) provide that such marriages will always be void. However, I also include those provisions that may have an element of protection even where that may be based partly on prejudice, discrimination or biological constructions of parenthood: a marriage is voidable if it was not voluntary (MCA s. 12(c)), if either party was suffering from a mental disorder to the extent that they were 'unfit' to marry (MCA s. 12(d)), or if at the time of the marriage the respondent was pregnant by someone other than the petitioner (MCA s. 12(f)). The formalities required to marry not only indicate the level of commitment expected (above) but also suggest an element of protection, particularly in relation to third parties. In order for a valid marriage to be formed, the parties must publicize their intention to marry. For a civil marriage, they must give written notice of the proposed marriage to the district superintendent registrar, who must then display notice of the marriage for 15 successive days (Marriage Act 1949 s. 27). A civil marriage must take place in an 'approved premises' (Marriage Act 1994), which is open to the public, and in the presence of the superintendent registrar and a registrar of marriages (Lowe and Douglas, 2007, p. 61). These formalities also indicate that marriage is a *public* commitment. However, if the formalities are not followed, the marriage may nevertheless be upheld where the parties genuinely believed they had contracted a valid marriage (see, for example, *Chief Adjudication Officer v Bath* [2000] 1 FLR 8). Again, this is a measure of protection for parties who are acting under the genuine belief that they are married:

> because of the importance that English law attaches to marriage and the consequent legal disadvantages inherent in a finding that a party is not married, the law has long treated any challenge to the integrity of an individual marriage with suspicion. (Bradney, 2000, p. 352)

These aspects of the structure of marriage suggest that, at its core, it is a committed sexual relationship between two people who register their relationship with the state. Sexuality, commitment and monogamy characterize marriage. The protection provisions are necessary to prevent both abuse of minors and incest, and to protect third parties by giving public notice of the marriage.

Legal consequences

Marriage is a distinct form of relationship, in part because the legal consequences of entering into marriage are controlled by a third party: the state. These legal consequences of marriage are, nevertheless, difficult to quantify or codify. In the US, the General Accounting Office counted 1138 federal consequences of marriage, with many more provided by each state (Human Rights Campaign, 2007b). No such tally has been attempted in the UK but the length of the Civil Partnership Act (at 429 pages, 30 schedules and 264 sections), which incorporates civil partners into most of the spousal provisions of marriage through amending each individual provision, gives some indication of the amount of law in this area. As a result, 'it is virtually impossible to give an account of the legal consequences of marriage which is coherent, much less comprehensive' (Cretney et al., 2003, p. 69). It is not, then, my intention to describe all of the legal consequences of marriage. Instead, I will focus on a few key provisions that provide some insight into what the essence of marriage and the shape of the marriage model might be.

In the absence of a comprehensive and coherent account of the legal consequences of marriage some leading family law writers in the UK highlight the 'historical' common law features of marriage as a starting point (see for example: Cretney et al., 2003, pp. 69–75; Lowe and Douglas, 2007, pp. 106–11). These are: the doctrine of unity; consortium; and the duty to maintain. Though these are a way of contextualizing contemporary provisions, they also form the basis of some existing legal consequences of marriage. I argue that the doctrine of unity has some (though limited) contemporary reflection in the legal consequences of marriage, while modern-day versions of consortium and a duty of maintenance remain integral to the marriage model in the form of expectations of intimacy, confidence, companionship and (inter)dependence that *are* protected by its current legal consequences.

The doctrine of unity is explained in the famous statement of Blackstone's Commentaries:

> By marriage, the husband and wife are one person in law; that is, the very being or legal existence of the woman is suspended during the marriage, or at least is incorporated and consolidated into that of the husband; under whose wing, protection, and *cover*, she performs everything.... Upon this principle of a union of person in husband and wife, depend almost all the legal rights, duties, and disabilities, that either of them acquire by the marriage. (in Lowe and Douglas, 2007, p. 107, original emphasis)

Though it is generally accepted now that this principle was 'a mediaeval axiom which was never wholly accurate' (Oliver J, *Midland Bank Trust Co.*

Ltd and Another v Green and Another (No 3) [1979] Ch 496 at 527), it did, as Blackstone suggests, provide the basis for many, 'almost all', of the legal consequences of marriage. For example: women's lack of property rights; that spouses could not sue each other in tort; that husbands were liable for any torts committed by their wife; that spouses could not be convicted of stealing each others' property; the presumption that if a married woman committed certain criminal offences in the presence of her husband she was acting under his coercion; and that spouses could not give evidence against each other.

As Oliver J explains in *Midland Bank Trust v Green*, the rationale of the doctrine appears to have shifted over time. Whereas its roots were in the 'biblical notion of unity in one flesh', it was also later deemed to rest on the assumption that a wife acts under her husband's instruction and public policy considerations of the extent to which the law should interfere in marital relations (per Oliver J, at 512–13). Whether it was in fact based upon the Bible, the assumption and enforcement of male dominance, or public policy, it is clear that, as Lowe and Douglas argue, it 'became the legal justification for subordinating the wife's will and acts to those of her husband, and the embodiment of patriarchy' (2007, p. 107). The notion that a wife should be subordinated to her husband has been rejected in favour of a presumption of egalitarianism within marriages (cf. Chapter 5). However, some of the remnants of the doctrine of unity remain in that some legal consequences that arose from it continue to be applicable today. For example: spouses cannot be convicted of conspiracy together (Criminal Law Act 1977 s. 2(2)(a); see also Rees, 1993, p. 890), though they *are* liable for the tort of conspiracy (*Midland Bank Trust v Green*; a person cannot be liable for defamation in respect of statements made to their spouse (*Wennhak v Morgan and Wife* (1888) LR 20 QBD 635; Cretney et al., 2003, p. 91); spouses are treated as a unit for some tax purposes, such as exemption from inheritance and capital gains taxes (Barter and Hodgwood, 2005, p. 568); 'marital confidences' are protected (*Argyll v Argyll* [1967] Ch 302; Coad, 2001, p. 227); and spouses have an unlimited insurable interest in each other without having to prove financial loss (Life Assurance Act 1774; *Griffiths v Fleming* [1909] 1 KB 805; Cretney et al., 2003, p. 71).

Although Oliver J describes the doctrine of unity as a legal fiction that is 'as real as the skeleton of the brontosaurus in a museum of natural history' (*Midland Bank Trust v Green*), the legal consequences of marriage that are based on this legal fiction, while they may be dinosaurs, are not yet skeletons. Cretney et al. suggest that though unity was never consistently applied and little of it remains, it is difficult to know how significant that little is (2003, pp. 70–1). On the basis of these remaining vestiges of unity in the form of the legal consequences of marriage, combined with the judicial pronouncements of marriage ideologies discussed below, I would argue that the contemporary version of 'unity' is actually an assumption of intimacy, confidence and interdependence. This, then, retains some significance in the context of contemporary marriage.

Consortium and duty to maintain also have clear links to some contemporary legal consequences of marriage. Consortium was:

> An abstract notion which appears to mean living together as husband and wife with all the incidents (insofar as these can be defined) that flow from that relationship. At one time it would have been said that the husband had the right to his wife's consortium whilst the latter had not so much a reciprocal right to her husband's consortium as a correlative duty to give him her society and her services...The wife's basic duty was to submit to her husband, in return for which the husband would protect and support her. (Lowe and Douglas, 2007, pp. 108–9)

In other words, consortium is about 'society, comfort and protection' (per Lord Goddard, *Best v Fox & Co. Ltd* [1952] AC 716 at 729–30). In order to enforce his right to consortium, a husband could physically restrain his wife or confine her to the house, and claim for damages against anyone who interfered with his right (Lowe and Douglas, 2007, pp. 109–10). The duty to maintain was linked to this and referred to the husband's obligation to support his wife. This duty was, according to Cretney et al., 'conceptually important' but the wife had limited ability to enforce it, it was for the husband to determine their standard of living, it only gave the wife a right to 'bed and board' (*Lilley v Lilley* [1960] P 169 at 178, per Hodson LJ; Cretney et al., 2003, p. 73), and it was not possible for the wife to enforce it if they were living apart for any reason other than the husband's misconduct.

In *Sheffield County Council v E*, Mr Justice Munby emphasized that wives are no longer subservient as assumed by these concepts (at para. 130). At the same time, however, he demonstrated their continuing applicability, albeit in a contemporary, 'egalitarian' and reciprocal form:

> Today both spouses are the joint, co-equal heads of the family. *Each has an obligation to comfort and support the other.* It is not for the husband alone to provide the matrimonial home or to decide where the family is to live. Husband and wife both contribute. And where they are to live is, like other domestic matters of common concern, something to be settled by agreement, not determined unilaterally by the husband. In so far as the concept of consortium...still has any useful role to play, the rights of husband and wife must surely now be regarded as exactly reciprocal. (para. 131, emphasis added)

Consortium and the duty to maintain, reconstituted in a less specific and more gender-neutral way for the contemporary marriage, thus remain embedded in some of its legal consequences. There are some very clear examples of the contemporary duty to maintain. For example under the MCA s. 27 and the Domestic Proceedings and Magistrates' Courts Act 1978, spouses are each able to claim maintenance from the other. Spouses are also assumed to pool their income for the purposes of state benefits: under the Social Security Contributions and Benefits Act 1992 s. 136 spouses must claim jointly rather than individually and their income will be combined for the purposes of determining eligibility and amount of support received. This would suggest that an assumption of financial interdependence forms part of the essence of marriage.

Mr Justice Munby defines consortium as 'the sharing of a common home and a common domestic life, and the right to enjoy each other's society, comfort and assistance' (*Sheffield County Council v E* at para. 131). The extent to which these remain legally enforceable consequences of marriage is questionable. However, because Munby J discusses cohabitation, society, comfort and assistance in the context of his discussion of the rights and responsibilities of marriage, this suggests that he does consider these to be part of those rights and responsibilities, or its legal consequences (Gaffney-Rhys, 2006). Ruth Gaffney-Rhys explores each of these. She claims that the duty to cohabit, though its enforcement and remedy was abolished in 1970, remains. To support this argument, she notes the following facts: that separation is one of the ways of demonstrating that a marriage has broken down irretrievably (MCA s. 1(2)); that a decree of judicial separation can be granted on the basis of separation or desertion; and that the MCA s. 18(1) provides that once such a decree is granted, it is *no longer* 'obligatory for the petitioner to cohabit with the respondent'. Cohabitation is, then, at the very least assumed in the legal consequences of marriage and could reasonably be argued to be a default requirement (that is, one that exists unless both parties agree otherwise). Nevertheless, a marriage remains valid until one party chooses to petition for divorce so it is possible for a valid marriage to exist in the absence of cohabitation, comfort, society and assistance. As Gaffney-Rhys goes on to note, it is also possible on the basis of *Hamer v UK* (1979) 24 DR 5 for the parties to 'exclude [the cohabitation] duty by entering into an agreement to live apart whilst married' and to exclude the duty to share a common life by agreement. Such agreements would make it more difficult for one spouse to argue that it constituted 'behaviour' under the MCA s. 1(2)(b) but agreements such as these are not binding on the grounds of public policy (Gaffney-Rhys, 2006). This gives additional weight to the suggestion that they are central attributes of marriage.

Whether a requirement of society, comfort and assistance exists in contemporary marriage is, according to Gaffney-Rhys, unclear. However, I would argue that such requirements *do* exist. Gaffney-Rhys' conclusion is based on her examination of two divorce cases concerning the absence of these within the marriages. *Bannister v Bannister* (1980) 10 Fam Law 240 was an undefended divorce petition on the grounds that the husband's behaviour was such that the wife could not reasonably be expected to live with him. The facts were undisputed:

> He does not speak to her except when it is unavoidable; he has not taken her out for two years and it is obvious that he has been living an entirely independent life, ignoring his wife completely, staying away for nights giving her no idea where he is going, and so on. (per Ormrod LJ)

The Court of Appeal held that it was clear that this marriage had irretrievably broken down and granted the divorce. In this case, a failure to provide society, comfort and assistance within the marriage was held to be intolerable behaviour and thus grounds for divorce. However, Gaffney-Rhys' analysis of an earlier case appears to contradict Mr Justice Munby's view of these as obligations of marriage. In *Pheasant v Pheasant* [1972] Fam 202 a husband petitioned for divorce, again on the 'behaviour' ground: '[his wife] has not been able to give him the spontaneous demonstrative affection which he says that his nature demands and for which he craves' (per Ormrod J at 205). In this case, also heard by (then) Mr Justice Ormrod in the Family Division, the husband's petition was unsuccessful because the wife's behaviour could not 'be regarded as a breach on her part of any of the obligations of the married state' (at 209). Gaffney-Rhys interprets this to mean that Mr Justice Ormrod is denying the existence of an obligation for affection within marriage. However, I would argue instead that Mr Justice Ormrod's decision is based on a finding of *fact* that the wife had not actually behaved in the manner of the husband's allegations. Mr Justice Ormrod finds that the breakdown of the marriage was not caused by the respondent's behaviour but, instead, 'by a change in the personality of the petitioner and the development in him of some psycho-neurotic condition which has made him totally egocentric and obsessed with grievances' (at 209). He goes on:

> I do not intend in the petitioner's own interests to summarize the evidence in this case. I have no wish to add to his humiliations by exposing them to a wider audience and no useful purpose will be served in doing so. Suffice it to say that where their evidence differs I prefer the evidence of the respondent. *I am satisfied that she has shown him all the affection which she can* and that she is sincere in saying that she would welcome him back. (at 209, emphasis added)

This petition was, therefore, denied on the basis that Ormrod J was unconvinced that the marriage *had* irretrievably broken down (and that he was unconvinced that any marital problems were the respondent's fault as opposed to the petitioner's neuroses) rather than because affection was not a requirement of marriage. Furthermore, even if examination of divorce cases is inconclusive as to whether there is a strict legal obligation to provide society, comfort and assistance, Mr Justice Munby's views are nevertheless present in other judicial pronouncements on marriage. For example, in the context of identifying 'sham' marriages contracted for purposes such as by-passing immigration restrictions, the courts have required these obligations to be met in some degree for a valid marriage to exist (see for example *SH v KH,* discussed below; cf. *Vervaeke v Smith* confined to its facts by Lord Diplock at 158–9). As such, I would argue that, whether or not this legal consequence of marriage is enforceable as between the parties, its demonstration certainly has been required by the courts in some contexts. This indicates that some form of 'society, comfort and assistance', or companionship, is part of the essence of marriage, in addition to financial interdependence.

As argued above, the precise legal consequences of marriage will vary (sometimes widely) across jurisdictions and form a relatively minor aspect of the marriage model. However, they can be characterized by the fact that they are set by the state and not the parties themselves. I suggest that in both assuming and protecting a degree of financial and emotional interdependence between spouses, and in the ways in which spousal relationships are privileged and protected over and above other relationships, the legal consequences of marriage indicate that *some level* of intimacy, companionship and interdependence are essential ingredients for a valid marriage.

Ideology

Perhaps unsurprisingly, despite the tendency (noted above) to move away from the *Hyde* formula in specific circumstances, the courts have generally cited and upheld it as the ideal to aspire to. So, for example, Mr Justice Munby's view of marriage was that:

> Marriage, whether civil or religious, is a contract, formally entered into. It confers on the parties the status of husband and wife, *the essence of the contract being an agreement between a man and a woman to live together, and to love one another as husband and wife, to the exclusion of all others.* It creates a relationship of mutual and reciprocal obligations, typically involving the sharing of a common home and a common domestic life and the right to enjoy

each other's society, comfort and assistance. *(Sheffield County Council v E* at 361, emphasis added)

As outlined above, society, comfort and assistance are clearly identifiable in the legal consequences of marriage but they also form an integral part of its ideology to the extent that where they are absent an otherwise valid marriage may be rejected by the courts. For example, citing with approval Mr Justice Munby's definition, the Scottish Court of Session held in *SH v KH* that, while marriage in a 'real sense' need not include *all* of the characteristics that Mr Justice Munby identifies (above), 'the stage may come at which the *nature and extent of the derogation from the norm* leaves a relationship that simply cannot be described as marriage' (Lord Penrose at para. 55, emphasis added). In that case it was not enough that a man and a woman had gone through the legal formalities required to contract a marriage. The parties had married in a civil ceremony to enable KH to remain in the UK but, as they were religious Muslims, they did not consider themselves to be married until a religious ceremony had taken place. KH began a relationship with another woman and subsequently cancelled the religious ceremony; the parties never had a sexual relationship, cohabited or considered themselves to be married. It was held that there must be 'some form of shared life' (per Lord Marnoch at para. 63) for a valid marriage to exist and a decree of nullity was granted.

In the cases of *Fitzpatrick v Sterling Housing Association* and *Ghaidan v Godin-Mendoza* the issue was what constituted a spousal relationship. *Fitzpatrick* was concerned with whether or not a same-sex couple were *living as* husband and wife (or alternatively as family members) for the purposes of tenancy succession. In this case Lord Nicholls described the spousal relationship as being characterized by 'intimate mutual love and affection and long-term commitment' (at 44). Though there was no dispute that these characteristics existed in the same-sex relationship, the House of Lords held that the words 'living as husband and wife' in the Rent Act 1977 could not be interpreted to include same-sex couples. This question was, however, revisited in *Mendoza* after the Human Rights Act 1998 came into force. In that case, the court used its power under s. 3 to read additional words into the Rent Act, holding that a same-sex couple were *living as if they were* husband and wife. In *Mendoza*, Lord Nicholls described spouses as those who 'share each other's life and make a home together' (at 568), while Baroness Hale referred to 'intimacy, stability, and social and financial interdependence' (at 606).

From these judicial pronouncements, then, the ideology of marriage in the UK is a relationship that provides some level of intimacy, companionship, commitment and interdependence between two people who live together. While not all of these must be present in terms of the legal status of the relationship, the parties must have (or have had) some sort of shared life. This is consistent with definitions that were emerging in the context of same-sex marriage cases in other jurisdictions, which had also adopted the *Hyde* definition of marriage. For example, the Massachusetts Supreme Court held that:

> Civil marriage is at once a deeply personal commitment to another human being and a highly public celebration of the ideals of *mutuality, companionship, intimacy, fidelity, and family. ...* [T]he aim of marriage [is] to *promote stable, exclusive relationships.* It advances the two legitimate State interests the department has identified: providing a stable setting for child rearing and conserving State resources. (per Marshall CJ, *Goodridge v Department of Public Health* 440 Mass (2003) 309 at 322, 333–4)

The Ontario Court of Appeal held that marriage is the institution through which 'society publicly recognizes expressions of love and commitment between individuals, granting them respect and legitimacy as a couple' (*per curiam, Halpern v Toronto* (2003) 2003 CarswellOnt 2159 at para. 5).

However, in some cases where the courts have considered same-sex marriage, a different view of the purpose and essence of marriage has emerged: it is not unusual in cases where the issue is same-sex marriage or spousal recognition for those opposed to it to argue that the essence of marriage is heterosexuality and/or procreation. In fact, Lord Millet has gone so far as to suggest:

> Marriage is the lawful union of a man and a woman. It is a legal relationship between persons of the opposite sex. A man's spouse must be a woman; a woman's spouse must be a man. This is the very essence of the relationship, which *need not be loving, sexual, stable, faithful, long-lasting, or contented.* (*Mendoza* (dissenting) at 588, emphasis added)

This view is somewhat anomalous in the context of a trend among his judicial colleagues towards emphasizing the very characteristics he dismisses. Nevertheless, in *Wilkinson v Kitzinger* Sir Mark Potter took a similar line and was adamant that procreation (including child-rearing by both biological parents) was the key feature of marriage:

> It is apparent that the majority of people, or at least of governments, not only in England but Europe-wide, regard marriage as an age-old institution, valued and valuable, respectable and respected, as a means not only of encouraging monogamy but also the procreation of children and their development and nurture in a family unit (or 'nuclear family') in which both maternal and paternal influences are available in respect of their nurture

and upbringing. ... *marriage, is by longstanding definition and accep-*
tance, a formal relationship between a man and a woman, primarily
(though not exclusively) with the aim of producing and rearing chil-
dren. ... to accord a same-sex relationship the title and status of
marriage would be ... to fail to recognize physical reality. (paras
118–20, emphasis added)

The procreation function of marriage is generally only emphasized in cases
involving claims for same-sex marriage. This argument usually takes a familiar
form along the lines of Potter's argument: same-sex couples cannot 'naturally'
procreate as between themselves; therefore (as this is attributed as the primary
aim of marriage) prohibitions on same-sex marriage are justified.[6] In *Morrison*
v Sadler [2005] 821 NE 2d 15 this line of argument took an interesting turn
when the Indiana Court of Appeal appeared to be suggesting that same-sex
couples should not have access to marriage because, since they were already
more responsible procreators than heterosexual couples, same-sex marriage
would not further the state interest in encouraging responsible procreation.
The exclusion of same-sex couples from marriage was, therefore, justified on
the basis of the state's interest in encouraging responsible procreation and a
stable environment for raising children, not because same-sex couples were
not (or should not be) parents, but because they were *already* responsible parents so marriage was not necessary (see also Calder, 2009, pp. 77–8):

Becoming a parent by using 'artificial' reproduction methods is
frequently costly and time-consuming. Adopting children is much
the same. Those persons wanting to have children by assisted
reproduction or adoption are, by necessity, heavily invested,
financially and emotionally, in those processes. Those processes
also require a great deal of foresight and planning. 'Natural' procreation, on the other hand, may occur only between opposite-sex
couples and with no foresight or planning. (per Barnes J, *Morrison*
v Sadler at 19)

While other judgments refer to the role of marriage in discouraging promiscuity and as a site for stable parenthood (see, for example, *Wilkinson*,
above, and Justice Cordy's dissent in *Goodridge*), the *singular* focus of the
Indiana court on accidental pregnancy as a potential consequence of heterosexual penetrative sex is peculiar and anomalous. Nevertheless, it is another

---

6 This argument has been made in some first instance judgments that were later overturned
   on appeal (see *EGALE Canada Inc. v Canada (Attorney General)* 2001 CarswellBC 2071;
   Goodridge v Department of Public Health at 951) and dissenting judgments in same-sex marriage cases that succeeded (see, for example, Cordy J in *Goodridge*; and Zarella J in *Kerrigan*
   v Commissioner of Public Health 289 Conn 135).

example of a court centring procreation as the key feature or even *raison d'être* of marriage.

It is not overly cynical to suggest that procreation has been singled out as the essence of marriage (and usually defined in a biological, genetic way) in these cases precisely because it is 'the one unbridgeable difference between same-sex and opposite-sex couples' (per Marshall CJ in *Goodridge* at 333). The Ontario Superior Court of Justice also noted, in rejecting the submission that procreation was the essence of marriage, that:

> the evidence actually demonstrates that it was only recently – when same-sex couples began to advance claims for the equal recognition of their conjugal relationships – that some courts began to infer that procreation was an essential component to marriage. There is simply no evidence that convinces me that those earlier courts, when developing the common law rules regarding the validity of marriage and capacity, viewed procreation as the purpose of marriage. (per LaForme J in *Halpern* [2002] CarswellOnt 2309 at para. 238)

The comments made by Chief Justice Marshall and Justice LaForme certainly ring true in relation to UK law. As the above discussion of UK cases demonstrates, immediately prior to *Wilkinson* there was no indication that procreation was central to marriage in the UK. In fact, as far back as 1948, the House of Lords, in a case relating to consummation, held:

> Again, the insistence on the procreation of children as one of the principal ends, if not the principal end, of marriage requires examination. ... In any view of Christian marriage the essence of the matter, as it seems to me, is that the children, if there be any, should be born into a family, as that word is understood in Christendom generally ... *But this is not the same thing as saying ... that procreation of children is the principal end of marriage.* Counsel were unable to cite any authority where the procreation of children was held to be the test in a nullity suit. (per Viscount Jowitt LC in *Baxter v Baxter* [1948] AC 274 at 286, emphasis added)

Sir Mark Potter did not consider the precedent of *Baxter* in his judgment and his view that procreation and child-rearing are the essence of marriage is anomalous and, I would argue, wrong in the context of contemporaneous UK judgments and *obiter dicta* on marriage and the House of Lords' judgment in *Baxter*. As the Massachusetts Supreme Court held:

> while it is certainly true that many, perhaps most, married couples have children together (assisted or unassisted), it is the exclusive

and permanent commitment of the marriage partners to one another, not the begetting of children, that is the *sine qua non* of civil marriage. (per Marshall CJ in *Goodridge* at 332; see also *In Re Marriage Cases* 43 Cal 4th 757 at 825, per George CJ)

The ideology of marriage, as expressed by the judiciary, emphasizes not procreation but a shared life, commitment, intimacy and interdependency between adults.

Conclusion

Despite the implicit assumption made in almost all of the judgments cited in this chapter (and articulated by Karminski J) that the essence of marriage is universally understood, an examination of the structure, legal consequences and ideologies of marriage in UK law reveals contradictions, inconsistencies and a surprising level of departure from the *Hyde* 'definition'. This is, perhaps, as much a feature of 'the normal chaos of family law' (Dewar, 1998), the lack of coherence of the law related to families, as it is of marriage itself. However, I would suggest that it builds on Rebecca Probert's (2007) argument that *Hyde* is much more of an ideal than a definition. This is not to suggest that there is a *coherent* agenda to promote one particular ideology of marriage. The case law that I have examined demonstrates that the 'essential' characteristics of marriage differed, sometimes significantly, and often depended on the desired outcome of a particular case. This desired outcome may not necessarily be related to a particular ideology of what marriage should be. For example in *Vervaeke* v *Smith*, a 'sham' marriage was upheld to prevent the claimant from profiting from its nullification, even though there was no doubt about the absence of a shared life. In other cases, such as *Wilkinson*, the desired outcome was inextricably linked with a particular set of ideologies: maintaining the status of (heterosexual) marriage at the top of a hierarchy of relationships and supporting heterosexism and homophobia through discourses of procreation and traditional family values. While not all judges share a coherent agenda in relation to promoting a particular ideology of marriage, I am suggesting that there are nevertheless broad understandings of what marriage is (or, perhaps, what it should be) that underpin judicial decision-making in this area.

These understandings are not part of a consistent, coherent 'definition' but instead are deployed at specific moments to (in Probert's terms) defend a particular ideal of marriage. As such, Probert argues that a more accurate definition of marriage was advanced by Thorpe LJ in his *Bellinger* dissent:

> [Marriage is] a contract for which the parties elect but which is regulated by the state, both in its formation and in its termination

> by divorce, because it affects status upon which depend a variety of entitlements, benefits and obligations. (*Bellinger* v *Bellinger* [2001] EWCA Civ 1140 at para. 128; Probert, 2007, p. 9)

This reflects the legal status of marriage in relation to the state and, as Probert notes, distinguishes marriage from cohabiting relationships in a way that *Hyde* and other definitions do not. This definition describes the parameters of marriage (that it is an 'opt-in' legal relationship whose formation, termination, and legal consequences are regulated by the state) but it does not tell us anything about what is contained *within* these parameters.

Framing a definition of marriage in this way is both more accurate in terms of the legal status of the institution and, most importantly for my purposes, clearly demarcates its legal *parameters* from the ideologies that supposedly form the basis of our common understanding of what marriage should be. These ideologies, however, are nevertheless a significant part of judicial understandings of marriage and as such do form part of marriage law. Furthermore, they actually extend beyond formal marriage and are used in relation to other non-marital relationships such as cohabitation for the purposes of legal recognition. I refer to the marriage model as both the legal framework of marriage and as a means to reflect both this ideological component and its extension to non-marital relationships.

The themes that recur throughout this chapter are those of a committed, sexual, monogamous and interdependent relationship. Similarly, the Law Society in the UK has also suggested that in determining whether a relationship is 'analogous to marriage' the courts should take into account the following factors: whether it is a sexual relationship; whether there are joint finances; whether the parties share a home; whether there is financial support; whether they have a child; and whether they are known as a couple (2002, p. 13). The Law Society also suggested that the court should look at any other factors it deemed relevant and that the absence of any stated factor should not prevent the parties from being marriage-like. However, the list of factors that it chose to highlight does (with the exception of the absence of a direct mention of monogamy) support the key characteristics of the marriage model that I have outlined in this chapter (in the US context see also Halley, 2001, p. 103, referring to 'marriage-like' as being: 'monogamous, sexual, domestic, economically interdependent, and long-term'). Therefore I would suggest that these, along with it being 'opt-in' and having legal consequences that are determined by the state, form the marriage model according to the current legal framework in the UK. Other factors, such as emotional intimacy, companionship and support, were also recurring in the judgments as *ideally* present but, while a relationship that evidences none of these could be held invalid, they are not *all* strictly required in *all* circumstances. They are, however, assumed to exist in the structure and legal consequences of the institution.

In the next chapter, I evaluate the various ways in which same-sex relationships have been legally recognized in different jurisdictions through provisions that are separate to marriage. This is central to a full understanding of the parameters and potential implications of these provisions, as well as consideration of whether they pose a viable alternative to marriage, or a 'stepping stone' to it.[7] In Chapter 3, I outline the process through which the marriage model has been applied to same-sex relationships through same-sex marriage provisions. I return to the question of whether, or how far, same-sex marriage may provide opportunities for challenging the marriage model in Part II.

---

7 For an argument that civil unions in the US context are a stepping-stone to same-sex marriage, see Stefanec, 2004, p. 146. See also Eskridge, 2001; Ettelbrick, 2001.

2
Different Institutions for Same-Sex Relationships: A Departure from the Marriage Model?

Introduction

Over the last two decades, legal action and political activism from same-sex couples and lesbian and gay advocacy organizations seeking relationship recognition has resulted in the introduction of either same-sex marriage or a separate but, to varying degrees, marriage-like provision in some jurisdictions. Separate provisions are generally presented by lesbian and gay organizations as a compromise and a pragmatic way to secure some relationship recognition for same-sex couples in the absence of marriage (Merin, 2002, p. 63). For example, explaining its decision to lobby for civil partnership rather than marriage, Stonewall states: 'Stonewall's main focus was on the outcome in terms of rights and responsibilities, rather than the label. Civil partnership achieves parity with marriage in every respect.' (Stonewall, 2007)

However, not everyone views separate provisions as a compromise. For some, recognizing same-sex relationships through a separate provision (which is, for them, inherently lower-status because it is not marriage) is discriminatory. For example, Evan Wolfson argues that 'separate but equal is inherently unequal' (Wolfson, 1998), and some compare separate provisions to apartheid (Tatchell, 2005): for them, anything 'less' than marriage necessarily conveys second-class citizenship. There is a significant body of literature on the issue of whether 'separate but equal' is justifiable in the context of same-sex relationships, particularly from the US (see, for example: Cox, 2000–2001; Cruz, 2002; Johnson, 2002; Buckel, 2005; see also De Vos, 2007a).[1] The Connecticut Supreme Court has recently described the creation of a separate civil union provision for same-sex couples as a 'cognizable harm' (*Kerrigan v Commissioner of Public Health* 289 Conn 135 at 141; see also *In Re Marriage*

---

1 However, there is an emerging literature criticizing the use of a race analogy in this context: see, for example: Schatschneider, 2004–2005; Kandaswamy, 2007.

Cases 43 Cal 4th 757; *Minister of Home Affairs and Director-General of Home Affairs v Fourie and Bonthuys* [2005] ZACC 19 at para. 150, per Sachs J). In contrast, some organizations actively seek separate provisions as an alternative to marriage: in Australia, lesbian and gay organizations have successfully sought de facto recognition as a preferable alternative to marriage. More recently, organizations in the UK and the US have been created to actively promote alternative forms of relationship recognition in addition to same-sex marriage (see Beyond Marriage, 2006; Equal Love, 2011).

In Chapter 4, I discuss the symbolic significance of the name 'marriage' to those who advocate for same-sex marriage, but it is not my intention to contribute more directly to this separate but equal literature here. Instead, the purpose of this chapter is to explore how different these provisions actually are from marriage. It is undeniable that they are separate in the sense that they have been created and are governed through different legal provisions and have a different name but the question remains as to whether they can nevertheless be said to follow the marriage model. To the extent that these separate provisions might create a new *model* of relationship recognition, they are potentially a radical development in the legal recognition of relationships.

Kees Waaldijk categorizes these separate provisions as either 'quasi-marriage' as in the case of the more comprehensive registered partnership provisions or as 'semi-marriage' as in the case of those which require registration but confer only some of the legal rights of marriage, such as domestic partnership or the *pacte civil de solidarité* (PaCS) (Waaldijk, 2004, p. 570). Yuval Merin (2002, p. 57) goes further to suggest (in the context of domestic partnerships) that the extent to which provisions could be described as marriage-like depends on their scope; that is, how similar the legal consequences of entering into the provision are to those of marriage. Waaldijk's distinction is useful to highlight the different scopes of the provisions but, while the legal rights, obligations, benefits and burdens contribute to a *perception* of a provision as marriage-like, as I argued in Chapter 1, this forms only a part of the marriage model.

I suggest that whether a provision is marriage-like depends largely on the extent to which the parameters of and access to the provision are regulated in the same way as marriage: does the provision have the same structure of marriage in terms of it being a committed, sexually monogamous relationship between two people who are not within the prohibited degrees of relationship? This would include not only the strict legal requirements of marriage, but also the assumption that the relationship will be one of love, mutual support or interdependence. In other words, the test I am using is how closely the provision adheres to the marriage model, encompassing not only its legal consequences, but also (and more significantly) its structure and ideology.

I argue that though there are some provisions that move away from the marriage model in some significant respects (most notably the French PaCS and Australian de facto provisions), this model nevertheless remains central to the ways in which same-sex relationships are legally recognized.

Domestic partnership

Domestic partnership provisions are the most difficult to characterize because, unlike the other provisions, they are localized, being made available either by city councils (municipalities) or individual employers in the United States. They are the result of political advocacy for same-sex relationships at the municipal level (Leonard, 2001, p. 147) or employers being persuaded to extend spousal benefits to employees who sign a domestic partnership declaration (Kohn, 1999; Human Rights Campaign WorkNet, 2007). As such, each municipality and employer offering domestic partnership provisions may define it and its provisions differently. One definition of domestic partnership is 'local or state ordinances or acts that accord same-sex couples a limited set of enumerated rights' (Merin, 2002, p. 57). However, even this is not sufficiently broad because this does not include domestic partnership provisions offered by private employers. Furthermore, some domestic partnership provisions are also available to unmarried heterosexual couples or any two people (including those within the prohibited degrees of relationship for marriage) who share a home, although these are unusual (Kohn, 1999, p. 9).[2]

Some domestic partnership registries offered by municipalities are purely symbolic, conferring no legal effects on the registered domestic partners (for example, the provision in the City of Cleveland Heights, Ohio (2007)). Others confer a few non-economic protections, such as the right to visit a domestic partner in hospital (for example, the provision in the City of Minneapolis, Minnesota). Despite the minimal (or absent) protections of marriage, these provisions use a marriage-like definition. For example, the Ohio provision requires that: the parties must live together in a 'relationship of mutual interdependence'; they must not already be married, in a civil union or in a domestic partnership with a third person; they must be over 18 years old; they must not be within the prohibited degrees of relationship; and they must both sign a 'Declaration of Domestic Partnership'.

There are also some state-wide domestic partnership provisions. For example, California's provision confers most of the state-level spousal provisions

---

2 There is even one School District in Pennsylvania that created a domestic partnership which explicitly *excludes* same-sex couples. This is currently being challenged in the courts as a violation of the 1st and 14th amendments to the US Constitution and the Equal Rights Amendment of the Pennsylvania Constitution: *Wiessmann and Resko v State College Area School District* (see ACLU, 2011).

and was passed in the wake of wide-spread publicity of the situation of Sherry Smith who was unable to sue for wrongful death after her partner, Dianne Whipple, had been killed by two dogs in her apartment building (Callan, 2003, p. 432). It is the first comprehensive state-wide provision to originate entirely from the legislative process as opposed to being necessitated by a court ruling (Blumberg, 2004, p. 1556). It requires a common residence, the parties must agree to be jointly liable for living expenses during the relationship, and the partnership is registered with the California Secretary of State (Blumberg, 2004, p. 1559). The California Domestic Partner Rights and Responsibilities Act 2003 significantly extended the benefits available and the Supreme Court of California recognized that the 'chief goal of the [Act] is to equalize the status of registered domestic partners and married couples' (*Koebke v Bernardo Heights Country Club* (2005) 36 Cal 4th 824, at 839), though it is worth noting that in *In Re Marriage Cases* the majority subsequently considered that this 'historic achievement' (per Corrigan J, concurring and dissenting at 880) violated the constitutional right to privacy and the equal protection clause. The 2003 Act provides that the requirements for terminating a domestic partnership are the same as divorce and that domestic partnerships will have the same legal consequences as marriage, with the exception of state income tax provisions (Blumberg, 2004, p. 1562). The states of Nevada, Oregon and Washington have also passed comprehensive state-wide domestic partner provisions, while Wisconsin, Colorado and Maine have state-wide provisions that provide some spousal benefits (Human Rights Campaign, 2011b).

However, the most common form of domestic partnership provision is that made available by employers (whether private or public), which confers employee spousal benefits to employees who register (either with the state or municipality, where available, or by signing an affidavit) as domestic partners. For example, 57 per cent of Fortune 500 companies now offer domestic partner benefits (Human Rights Campaign, 2010a). The National Gay and Lesbian Task Force (NGLTF) categorizes the types of benefits available through domestic partnership provisions with the terms 'hard benefits' ('generally insurance benefits' such as employee family health insurance) and 'soft benefits' ('lower cost, non-health benefits' such as employee family discount schemes) (Kohn, 1999, p. 11). The Human Rights Campaign (2011a) asserts that by 2008, 9375 employers in the United States offered domestic partnership health benefits, and undoubtedly there are more that offer soft benefits.

Because of the limited (and employment-based) nature of the rights in question, Merin (2002, p. 57) argues that domestic partnership provisions are not based on the marriage model. Similarly, lesbian and gay advocacy organizations tend to describe them as an equal pay issue rather than a provision analogous to marriage in their literature. This is probably because most domestic partnerships are registered with employers rather than with the state and the most useful provision for many people is the extension of employee health insurance. It is rarely, if ever, analogized to marriage. However, although domestic partnerships do generally confer only a fraction of the rights and obligations associated with marriage, this does not necessarily lead to the conclusion that it is therefore not based on the marriage model.

Examination of the entry requirements of domestic partnership reveals that they are usually based on the same requirements as marriage (that is a relationship between two people who are not already married or in a domestic partnership with a third party, who are both over the age of 18 and not within the prohibited degrees of relationship).[3] It is noteworthy that the entry requirements of domestic partnerships are often more stringent than those of marriage through the imposition of minimum periods of cohabitation and/ or the requirement to demonstrate financial interdependence. The assumptions that are implicit within marriage ideology are, thus, made an explicit requirement in domestic partnership provisions: for example, the California provision requires the partners to agree to be responsible for each other's basic living expenses (David Chambers, 2001, p. 1351). Similarly, though domestic partnerships are dissolved simply by written notification to the employer or municipality, they were created in order to allow access to spousal employment benefits for long-term partners and there is generally an expectation that, as the Minneapolis provision states, the parties 'are committed to one another to the same extent as married persons' (City of Minneapolis, 2007).

The references to intimacy and marriage (and the existence of the prohibited degrees of relationship in most provisions) imply a sexual relationship, though they could also be taken to refer to non-sexual 'core characteristics' of marriage such as mutual dependency and emotional intimacy. As such, this definition does not necessarily exclude the minority of domestic partnership provisions that also include any two people who share a household. Domestic partnerships must be monogamous in the sense that a person who is already in a domestic partnership cannot also contract one with another person. Likewise, being married is a bar to contracting a domestic partnership. Therefore, they are like marriage in that there is an expectation of commitment, financial interdependence and in most cases there appears to be an assumption of a sexual relationship. Like marriage, the terms of the domestic partnership are usually set by a third party, though this is not necessarily the state in the context of employee domestic partnership provisions.

---

3 Some provisions do allow those within the prohibited degrees of relationship but, although the NGLTF describes these provisions as the 'most ideal' (Kohn, 1999, p. 9), they are uncommon.

The most significant difference between domestic partnership and marriage is that the resulting legal protections are fewer and they are easier to dissolve. Therefore, domestic partnership is more accurately described as a *limited version* of the marriage model. I would argue that Stamps' definition of domestic partnership is appropriate: 'Domestic partnerships are contracts between two parties asserting that their relationship exhibits the core characteristics of an intimate association like a marriage.' (1992, p. 451) The NGLTF definition of domestic partnership also illustrates its close definitional link with marriage:

> In general, 'domestic partnership' has been defined as an ongoing relationship between two adults of the same- or opposite-sex who are: sharing a residence; over the age of 18; emotionally interdependent; and intend to reside together indefinitely. (Kohn 1999)

The next two provisions that I will discuss are also from the United States. Unlike domestic partnerships, which (with the exception of California's) were created primarily to remedy injustices of unequal access to employment benefits, reciprocal beneficiary and civil union provisions were created following claims for same-sex marriage in the state Supreme Courts. In Hawaii, this claim was successful but made moot by a constitutional amendment (the legislature enacted reciprocal beneficiaries as a compromise: Burnett, 1998–1999, p. 85), while in Vermont the legislature created civil union as an equivalent provision to marriage in order to satisfy the court's ruling that same-sex couples must have access to the legal rights, responsibilities, benefits and burdens of marriage.

Reciprocal beneficiary

The Reciprocal Beneficiaries Act in Hawaii (Hawaii Revised Statute §572C Supp 1997) was created in anticipation of the successful passage of a constitutional amendment that gave the legislature the power to define marriage as a 'unique social institution based upon the commitment of one man and one woman' (Burnett 1998–1999, p. 87; see Chapter 3 for discussion of the preceding events). The reciprocal beneficiary provision is, therefore, described as a compromise: in prohibiting same-sex marriage, the legislature recognized that those excluded from marriage may also form 'significant personal, emotional and economic relationships with another individual' that should receive some protection (Reciprocal Beneficiaries Act, in Coolidge, 2002, p. 80). Though the reciprocal beneficiary provision resulted directly from the controversy created by the prospect of same-sex marriage (see also Burnett, 1998–1999, pp. 83–5) the provision differs from the marriage model in a number of significant ways, whilst nevertheless bearing a relationship to it and retaining some of its key features.

Reciprocal beneficiary is available to any two people over the age of 18 who are prohibited from marrying each other (Lambda Legal and The Center Hawai'i, 2007, p. 7), meaning that it includes those within the prohibited degrees of relationship. This was said to be intended to 'make the law more palatable to conservatives' (*Washington Post*, 1997), undoubtedly because such a provision makes the distinction between it and marriage unmistakable (a strategy also attempted by conservatives in the UK, see: Baroness O'Cathain, HL Hansard, 24 June 2004, c. 1363; Edward Leigh MP, HC Hansard, 9 November 2004, c. 731). The absence of sexual relationship criteria in the provision (a consummation requirement) means that it is available to friends who are not in a sexual relationship with each other, as long as they would be prohibited from marrying (in other words, friends of the same sex) and are not already married or a reciprocal beneficiary with another person. The parties need not cohabit, nor even both live in Hawaii (Lambda Legal and The Center Hawai'i, 2007, p. 7). The level of commitment is significantly less than marriage in that reciprocal beneficiaries are easily dissolved through payment of $8 and filing of a notarized declaration (Hawaii State Department of Health, 2011) and there are no post-separation 'spousal' support obligations (Burnett, 1998–1999, p. 93).

However, though it departs from the marriage model in terms of the inclusion of prohibited degrees of relationship, absence of sexuality, and its level of commitment in terms of exit requirements, it does share some aspects of the marriage model. Like marriage, the terms and legal consequences of reciprocal beneficiaries are set by the state. It is a dyadic institution, meaning that only two people may enter into a reciprocal beneficiary together and a person may not enter into a reciprocal beneficiary if they are already married or party to a reciprocal beneficiary with someone else. This is a peculiar restriction if the provision is not supposed to be marriage-like, particularly with regard to the inclusion of those within the prohibited degrees of relationship. As the provision is explicitly intended to protect 'a widowed mother and her unmarried son' (Reciprocal Beneficiaries Act, in Coolidge, 2002, p. 80), it is anomalous to exclude the widowed mother with two unmarried sons, or one who also lives with her 'spinster sister'.[4] There is a requirement that the parties must be willing to financially support each other (Coolidge, 2002, p. 81) and there is also an assumption of economic interdependence in some of its legal consequences:

> The Act protects an individual impoverished by the death of a
> same-sex partner by providing him or her with such benefits as

---

4 Spinster sisters are a recurring trope in debates about the extension of marital benefits to same-sex couples, particularly in relation to inheritance tax. In the Canadian context, see, for example, Loek, 2001.

the right to sue for the wrongful death of a deceased partner; the right to elect a statutory share of the deceased partner's estate; and the right to be considered an heir of the deceased partner. (Burnett, 1998–1999, p. 94)

Interestingly, although reciprocal beneficiary is available to a potentially large cohort of those within the prohibited degrees of relationship who could now claim some rights of marriage, the number of 'couples' forming reciprocal beneficiaries has been low: less than 300 had registered by the end of the first year (see Hawaii Department of Health, 2006). In 2011, the state of Hawaii enacted a civil union provision which came into force in January 2012 and allows same-sex (and heterosexual) couples access to the same state-level benefits as married couples (SB232, A Bill for an Act Relating to Civil Unions s. 9). At the time of writing it does not appear that the reciprocal beneficiary provision has been repealed as a result of this legislation, which excludes some of those who would be eligible to register as reciprocal beneficiaries, most notably those within the prohibited degrees of relationship (SB232, s. 3).

Civil union

The civil union provision in Vermont resulted from a ruling of the state Supreme Court that same-sex couples could not be excluded from the legal provisions of marriage (discussed in Chapter 3). However, rather than striking down the definition of marriage, it held that it was for the legislature to decide whether to allow same-sex marriage or enact 'a parallel "domestic partnership" system or some equivalent statutory alternative' (*Baker v State of Vermont* 744 A 2d 864 at 867). The legislature opted for an equivalent alternative in the form of civil unions. During a heated public debate, the state's politicians were targeted by a group of right-wing Christians whose presence both reflected and fuelled public opinion against not only same-sex marriage but also the parallel 'civil union' that was eventually adopted: 'Many House members faced formidable pressure from their home districts to vote against civil unions, and the list of members endangered by a yes vote was long.' (Moats, 2004, p. 208) Following the adoption of civil unions, many legislators who voted in favour did lose their seats in the next election (Coolidge 2002, pp. 83–4). Nevertheless, a decade later Vermont became the first US state to enact same-sex marriage through the legislative process rather than the courts (Gay and Lesbian Advocates and Defenders (GLAD), 2011).

Civil unions have subsequently been adopted in New Jersey (following *Lewis v Harris* 908 A2d 196), Connecticut (now replaced by same-sex marriage), New Hampshire (now replaced by same-sex marriage), Delaware, Illinois and Hawaii. They have also been adopted in a number of Latin

American countries, including Colombia, Uruguay and Brazil (see Amnesty International, 2011; Barnes, 2011), as well as New Zealand. It is noteworthy that beginning with New Hampshire several of these provisions were adopted by the legislatures in the absence of any court proceedings (GLAD, 2007).

The 'parallel and equivalent' direction given to the Vermont legislature by the court indicates that civil unions were necessarily based on the marriage model. They confer all of the same legal rights and responsibilities as marriage at state level (though the state legislatures have no jurisdiction over the substantial number of federal legal consequences of marriage). For example, the New Hampshire legislation states that parties to a civil union:

> shall be entitled to all the rights and subject to all the obligations and responsibilities provided for in [New Hampshire] law that apply to parties who are joined together [in a marriage]. (Civil Union Law, NH Revised Statutes, Chapter 457-A, §6; GLAD 2007, p. 3)

They are thus more analogous with the European-style registered partnership (discussed next) than the domestic partnership. Civil union is quite clearly analogous to marriage in that its consequences, as well as its entry requirements and structure, mirror those of marriage. This is also evidenced by the fact that, at the time of writing, two states (Connecticut and New Hampshire) have subsequently merged civil unions into their new same-sex marriage provision, whilst Vermont still recognizes existing civil unions but has closed the provision to new applicants following the enactment of its same-sex marriage provision (GLAD 2011).

Registered partnership

The Danish Registered Partnership Act 1989 created the most comprehensive and marriage-like model of the separate forms of relationship recognition available to same-sex couples. The provisions that followed in other European countries were based on the Danish model so my description focuses on this provision as a starting point, although I will note some differences between jurisdictions.

The registered partnership was created as an 'inevitable' political compromise because the National Association for Gays and Lesbians (LBL) in Denmark anticipated that the public and the Danish Parliament would reject claims for marriage (Merin, 2002, pp. 62–3). This context suggests that it is intended as a marriage substitute (see also Sloane, 1997, pp. 191–2) and the structure of the institution, in terms of its entry and exit requirements, is marriage-like.

Registered partnerships are only available to same-sex couples (Registered Partnership Act 1989 s. 1), which is generally the case across the jurisdictions that have these provisions (Merin, 2002, p. 70; Waaldijk, 2005, p. 38), with the exception of the Netherlands (Waaldijk, 2001, p. 444). The requirements for registration are the same as those for marriage (with the exception that this is for same-sex rather than different-sex couples): those within the prohibited degrees of relationship cannot enter into a registered partnership; both parties must be over the age of 18; and neither party must already be married or in another registered partnership (Nielsen, 1990, p. 300; see also Waaldijk 2005, p. 38). Furthermore, the registration vow that partners must make 'has strong ceremonial marriage overtones' (Partners Task Force, 2005) and asks the partners to pledge that they will 'live together in mutual affection, helpfulness and tolerance' (replicated in full in Partners Task Force, 2005); so the registered partnership is not distinguishable from marriage in terms of the ceremony.[5] However, there is often an additional entry requirement for same-sex registered partnerships that does not apply to marriages: registered partners must usually be citizens or residents of the country in which they wish to register (in the Danish context, see Baatrup and Waaldijk, 2005, p. 68), although this has been relaxed in some countries. For example, Finland allows citizens of any country with registered partnership provisions to register in Finland, whereas Denmark, Norway, Sweden, and Iceland specify that only citizens of each other's countries (and the Netherlands and Finland) be permitted to register (Merin, 2002). Germany and the Netherlands have the same rules for non-residents and non-nationals entering into registered partnerships as for marriages (Waaldijk, 2005, p. 38). The registered partnership is dissolved in the same way as marriage (s. 5; see also Nielsen, 1990, p. 302).

The scope of the registered partnership is also marriage-like: it confers all of the legal benefits, obligations and protections of marriage (s. 3) except the right to marry in the state church (Henson, 1993, pp. 284–5) and some parenting rights. For example, the partner does not automatically become a legal parent of a child born to her spouse during the partnership (Barrtrup and Waaldijk, 2005, p. 69). This is the case for all registered partnership provisions and same-sex marriage in the Netherlands and Belgium (Waaldijk, 2005, p. 43). Previously, access to reproductive services was legally restricted to married or cohabiting different-sex couples, thus excluding registered partners in Denmark, but this was repealed as of January 2007 (Laursen, 2010). While there was no such restriction in Finland (Hiltunen and Waaldijk, 2005, p. 82), other countries still prevent same-sex couples from accessing assisted

---

5 In contrast, the ceremony creating a registered partnership in Norway differs from that of civil marriage; it uses the 'technical' language of law and 'the partners do not promise each other eternal fidelity' (Merin, 2002, p. 91).

reproduction (see, for example, Ytterberg and Waaldijk, 2005, p. 171 in relation to Sweden). The original Danish Registered Partnership Act also prevented joint adoption and custody, but an amendment in 1999 reversed this provision except where the child was adopted from a foreign country (Lund-Andersen, 2001, p. 417). Similarly, the registered partnership provisions in Iceland, the Netherlands, Norway and Sweden, which originally excluded adoption, were subsequently amended (see Waaldijk, 2005).

In addition, although all provisions referring to 'marriage' or 'spouses' apply to registered partners, those that are defined by the sex of the partner (for example, referring to 'husband' or 'wife') are not extended to registered partners (s. 4(3); see also Nielsen, 1990, p. 299). For example, the presumption that the husband is the father of any children born during the marriage does not apply to registered partners (Merin, 2002, p. 73).

Other restrictions arose from a fear that Denmark would provoke controversy abroad; the registered partnership was originally restricted to Danish citizens and residents (although that has now been relaxed, see above and Waaldijk, 2005, p. 38), and registered partnerships are not recognized for the purposes of international treaties unless the parties to the treaty agree (Merin, 2002, p. 78).

Other than these exceptions, the Danish registered partnership is the same as marriage, from the wedding day to the divorce (International Lesbian and Gay Association, 2000). The Danish registered partnership model also mirrors divorce in its dissolution procedure (Registered Partnership Act s. 5). The exception to this is in the Netherlands, where it is possible to end a registered partnership by mutual agreement without court proceedings (Schrama, 1999, p. 322). This option is not available to spouses, although they could convert their marriage to a registered partnership before dissolving it by mutual agreement (Waaldijk, 2005, p. 152).

While the later Scandinavian registered partnership provisions followed the Danish model of stating that all legal consequences of marriage were applicable to registered partners with the stated exceptions, the Netherlands instead attempted to amend all the statutes relating to marriage by inserting 'or registered partner' after the word 'spouse' (Waaldijk, 2003). This led to mistaken omissions and the necessity for late adjustments and subsequent amendments (Schrama, 1999, p. 322). Nevertheless, this approach was also taken in France (in relation to the PaCS, discussed further below) and Germany (Waaldijk, 2003). The UK's Civil Partnership Act 2004 (CPA) (discussed further below) and Ireland's Civil Partnership and Certain Rights and Obligations of Cohabitants Act 2010 also took this latter approach.

The differences between registered partnership and marriage were considered by the European Court of Human Rights in *Schalk and Kopf v Austria* [2010] ECHR 995. The applicants' primary claim was that exclusion from marriage violated Article 12 (right to marry), but they also argued that the differences between registered partnership and marriage constituted a violation of Article 14 (prohibition of discrimination) in conjunction with Article 8 (right to private and family life). The differences between registered partnership and marriage in Austria are: no possibility of becoming engaged; no entitlement to compensation for a partner's wrongful death; partnerships are formalized at a separate office to marriage; and it is unclear whether certain rights relating to families would be granted to registered partners and their children (at para. 78). The court had previously held that differences in treatment based on sexual orientation must be justified by 'particularly serious reasons' in order to avoid falling foul of the European Convention on Human Rights (*Karner v Austria* [2004] 2 FCR 563 at para 37). However, the court considered that, in the absence of consensus amongst the 47 member states, each state enjoyed a margin of appreciation in relation to whether or not it recognized same-sex marriage and whether or not, by which means, and to what extent it recognized same-sex relationships through a registered partnership provision. This decision leaves open the possibility that the result would be different at a future time when such a consensus could be established. Moreover, the three dissenting judges[6] noted that Austria failed to advance any justification for the difference in treatment, relying only on the margin of appreciation. Unlike the majority, the dissenting judgment considered that a separate provision that did not offer 'at least to a certain extent' the same rights as marriage would require 'robust justification' (at para. 9). There is no doubt that the court unanimously considered the Austrian registered partnership to be marriage-like.

Civil partnership

The CPA follows the Danish registered partnership model, although it took the Dutch approach in that Parliament attempted to amend every reference in other legislation to 'spouse' or 'marriage' to include civil partners rather than simply stating that civil partners had the same rights of marriage with some exceptions. Nevertheless, as I explain below, the CPA largely mirrors marriage in terms of its scope as well as its entry and exit requirements (see also Stychin, 2006a). Like the registered partnership provisions, it is colloquially referred to as (and confused with) marriage. For example, in a qualitative study about same-sex commitment ceremonies and civil partnerships, Shipman and Smart

---

6 While the court unanimously held that there had been no violation of Article 12, the judgment that there was no violation of Article 14 in conjunction with Article 8 was a 4:3 majority decision. The court did, however, recognize that a same-sex couple can be considered a family for the purposes of Article 8 (para. 94).

found that many of the same-sex couples they interviewed 'slipped easily into the terminology of marriage"' (2007, para. 4.14).

Prior to the CPA, same-sex couples had been recognized through incremental changes in certain laws, including: tenancy succession following *Fitzpatrick v Sterling Housing Association* [2001] 1 AC 27 and *Ghaidan v Godin-Mendoza* [2004] 2 AC 557; joint adoption under the Adoption and Children Act 2002; and same-sex couples were also recognized for the purposes of immigration if certain requirements were met (Immigration Rules Part 8 s.1). In the 2001–2002 parliamentary session, two private members' Bills introduced same-sex relationship recognition provisions (the Relationships (Civil Registration) Bill introduced by Jane Griffiths MP; and the Civil Partnerships Bill 2002 introduced by Lord Lester: see Shaw, 2002, pp. 33–42 for a detailed comparative analysis of the Bills). Both Bills would have extended recognition not only to same-sex couples, but also to different-sex couples choosing not to marry. As such, a key objection made to each of these Bills during the parliamentary debates was their potential for undermining marriage through the inclusion of different-sex couples. These two private members' Bills prompted the government to review the issues and it introduced its Civil Partnership Bill in 2004 following an overwhelmingly positive consultation process, with 83 per cent of respondents in England and Wales supporting the proposal (Women and Equality Unit, 2003b, p. 9). The government's Bill, which became the CPA, excluded heterosexual relationships and mirrored marriage much more closely than the previous Bills would have.

The CPA, according to the government, provides 'a measured and proportionate response' to the exclusion of same-sex couples from marriage (per Baroness Scotland, HL Hansard, 22 April 2004, c. 387). The government emphasized that its intention was to provide 'parity of treatment' (Baroness Scotland, HL Hansard, 22 April 2004, c. 322) between registered same-sex couples and spouses in terms of legal protections and the focus of those speaking in support of the Bill during the parliamentary debates was very much on access to financial provisions and formal equality arguments (see also Stonewall, 2003; 2004abc; discussed further in Chapter 4). The CPA is a 'parallel but different legal relationship' to marriage, which is the 'template for the processes, rights and responsibilities' of civil partnerships (Jacqui Smith, HC Hansard, 9 November 2004, c. 776). As such, there are few differences between civil partnership and the structure, consequences or ideology of the marriage model:

> it is the Government's intention that those people who enter into a civil partnership will receive the same rights and take on the same responsibilities as those that we expect of those who enter into civil marriage. (per Jacqui Smith, HC Hansard, 12 October 2004, c. 177)

In terms of structure and legal consequences, the only significant differences are that a civil partnership is contracted by signing the register rather than speaking vows (s. 2), there is no consummation requirement and adultery is not a specific ground for dissolution of a civil partnership (see Barker, 2006; Stychin, 2006a). There are also some differences in language. For example, instead of divorce, the Act provides for dissolution under s. 44. There is also no reference to bigamy. Instead, s. 80 amends the Perjury Act 1911 s. 3(1) to include making a false statement with reference to a civil partnership. This carries a maximum seven-year prison sentence and/or a fine. The first criminal conviction under CPA s. 80 was, despite the offence being perjury, widely reported as a bigamy conviction (see, for example: Barnett, 2007; Walker, 2007). In terms of ideology, the CPA is very clearly intended to mirror marriage: for example, the Bill is intended to 'promote and support stable relationships' (Women and Equality Unit, 2003a).

In the Act as originally passed, there was no provision for a civil partner to be assumed to be the father (or legal parent) of a child born to her partner during the relationship, unlike spouses. This has now been amended by the Human Fertilisation and Embryology Act 2008 ss. 42–7, which extended provisions relating to husbands and unmarried male partners to female civil partners and female partners not in a civil partnership, who will be termed 'female parent' rather than father. Another difference in the original Act was that registration of a civil partnership must not take place in religious premises (s. 6(1)(b)) or during a religious ceremony (s. 2(5)). This appears to be repealed by the Equality Act 2010 s. 202, although at the time of writing this section was not yet in force and the new Coalition government had issued a consultation on this issue (Government Equalities Office, 2011).

The Act attracted opposition from some who claimed that it was 'gay marriage in everything but name' (per Gerald Howarth MP, HC Hansard, 9 November 2004, c. 769; see also Edward Leigh MP, ibid. c. 731), prompting pressure on the government during both the Commons and the Lords debates to specify the exact differences between civil partnership and marriage. In the House of Lords, Baroness Scotland's response referred to the formation of civil partnerships: 'a civil partnership is formed when the second partner signs the civil partnership document, a civil marriage is formed when the couple exchange spoken words' (HL Hansard, 16 July 2004, c. WA160). In the House of Commons, Jacqui Smith MP replied that there are very few differences between civil partnership and civil marriage:

> The whole point, however, is that civil partnership is not civil marriage, for a variety of reasons, such as the traditions and history—religious and otherwise—that accompany marriage. It is not marriage, but it is, in many ways—dare I say it?—akin

to marriage. We make no apology for that. (HC Hansard, 9
November 2004, c. 776)

Jacqui Smith acknowledges that civil marriage was the template for civil
partnerships, a fact that is evident in its provisions. Therefore, there is little
doubt that the CPA follows the marriage model.

Ireland has recently enacted a provision of the same name, which is similar to, but less comprehensive than, the UK provision. The Civil Partnership
and Certain Rights and Obligations of Cohabitants Act 2010 provides that
same-sex civil partners will be treated in the same way as spouses for a number of purposes including: protections in relation to a shared home (part 4);
maintenance obligations (part 5); succession (part 8); and access to domestic
violence prevention (part 9). However, there are notable exceptions, including in relation to children of the family (Mullally and O'Donovan, 2011). In
this sense, the Irish provision follows the lead of the Danish registered partnership as it was first enacted in 1989.

Civil solidarity pact

The French PaCS is less obviously marriage-like than the registered/civil
partnership provisions. It is defined in the Civil Code as a 'contract entered
into by two natural persons of age, of different sexes or of the same sex, to
organize their common life' (Borrillo and Waaldijk, 2005, p. 94). While the
phrase 'common life' would not necessarily require a sexual relationship, 'the
Conseil Constitutionnel upheld the PaCS law as constitutional subject to its
interpretation of "life in common" as meaning "life as a couple" ' (Borrillo,
2001, p. 484). Therefore, the PaCS is only available to couples rather than
any two people sharing a household (Steiner, 2000). Despite this, some
commentators argue that, unlike the Danish model registered partnership,
the PaCS does not attempt to imitate marriage (see, for example: Merin,
2002, p. 139; Richards, 2002, p. 324; Borrillo, 2005, p. 90). This is perhaps
due to both the different political and cultural context of France compared
with Denmark – the French republican values of equality and universal-
ity rather than group rights would make the creation of a separate but
parallel legal provision for same-sex couples politically difficult (Stychin,
2001, pp. 351–2, 354) – and its very contentious political evolution (this
is discussed by Martin and Théry, 2001; Stychin, 2001). In order to avoid
the PaCS being compared to marriage (Martin and Théry, 2001, p. 149),
there is a significant structural difference between them: rather than the
legal consequences being solely imposed by the state, the PaCS is an agreement between the couple to organize their common life, so they can largely
create the terms of their contract themselves (Barlow and Probert, 1999;

Stychin, 2001, p. 350), although the state requires certain minimum rights and responsibilities (Richards, 2002, p. 317; discussed below). This provision is criticized because there is no requirement for the provisions of the PaCS to be verified by any state authority or a lawyer. As such, Martin and Théry argue that many provisions will be illegal:

> For example, many people believe that a Pacs is a means for bequeathing money or property to the other, but it is not. They might then illegally include some dispositions for inheritance in their convention, causing serious problems for the future survivor. (2001, p. 152)

It is also worth noting that as originally enacted, the PaCS meant that the parties remained single after contracting a PaCS rather than changing their legal status to married (Borrillo, 2001). However, this was subsequently changed so that the PaCS will be included on the record of birth meaning that, 'the *pacsé* is no longer regarded as single' (Godard, 2007).

However, despite the structural differences between the provisions, Eva Steiner (2000) describes the PaCS as 'a replica of marriage' because:

> Like marriage it originates from an agreement between two persons wishing to regulate their relationship. As in marriage it is subject to a set of pre-conditions that apply to the parties, independently of their consent.... Furthermore, in the same vein as the duties imposed on spouses, PACS provides for mutual emotional and material assistance between partners, as well as joint liability to third parties for household debts. Finally, similarities occur as well in the management and distribution of assets [on separation]. (Steiner, 2000)

The set of pre-conditions for entering into a PaCS are that both parties are adults and competent to enter a contract, they are not within the prohibited degrees of marriage, and they are not already married or in a PaCS (Martin and Théry, 2001, p. 150). These conditions clearly evoke marriage (Richards, 2002, p. 316) but, nevertheless, there remains some doubt about how marriage-like the entry requirements of this provision are. First, the absence of conjugality in the PaCS (Stychin, 2001, p. 350) may suggest a departure from marriage. However, there is some disagreement on whether a sexual relationship is required under the PaCS (see Borrillo and Waaldijk, 2005, p. 100: 'parties have a duty to have sexual contact'). Furthermore, the exclusion of siblings and other biological and adoptive family members from entering into a PaCS together and the prohibition of multiple PaCS relationships would suggest that it was created with sexual relationships in mind. Richards also argues that the Conseil Constitutionnel based its definition of '*vie commune*' on 'the parliamentary debates in which the Government had stated that the PACS concerns couples who have a shared "roof" and "bed"' (2002, p. 315). Similarly, Daniel Borrillo refers to 'life in common' to mean 'a common residence and a sexual relationship' (2005, p. 91).

A second area of doubt about whether the pre-conditions or entry requirements are marriage-like is in relation to the formalities of registration: unlike marriage, registration takes place at a court rather than a town hall (Steiner, 2000; Martin and Théry, 2001, p. 150). Eva Steiner (2000) argues that, despite the different venue, the formalities for contracting a PaCS have the same legal significance as a marriage ceremony in providing a public record for the couple, for third parties and the state, though Daniel Borrillo undermines this argument when he suggests that there is no obligation to publicize the PaCS (2005, p. 91). Nevertheless, in terms of the ceremonial formalities, while the PaCS can be contracted as a bureaucratic necessity without any ceremony (Martin and Théry, 2001, p. 152), there is also some suggestion that same-sex couples are using the PaCS as a tool of recognition far beyond that which the legislature intended:

> For some couples, specifically among homosexuals, to conclude a Pacs is often an occasion for a ceremony and a feast very like a marriage, despite the fact that the '*tribunal d'instance*' is very different from the Town Council in French republican symbolism ... (Martin and Théry, 2001, p. 152)

As I argued in Chapter 1, because the particular legal consequences of marriage differ between jurisdictions and are more easily amended over time, they form a less significant part of the marriage model. One aspect of the legal consequences that I would argue is consistent across time and jurisdiction and does form part of the structural definition of marriage, however, is that the legal provisions are set by the state rather than the couple themselves. Family law scholars routinely identify this as part of the unique legal character of marriage, as either a status or a contract whose terms are set by a third party and unalterable by the parties themselves (see, for example, Diduck and Kaganas, 2006, p. 57). However, the legal consequences of the PaCS, while there are some requirements imposed by the law, are largely a matter for the parties themselves to decide. This is a significant structural difference from marriage.

The final structural difference is that the PaCS is also dissolved much more easily than marriage; it is terminated immediately through the death or marriage of one partner or by a joint notification to the court clerk if both parties consent, or, for a unilateral termination by one party, three months after they notify the court clerk and the other party (Merin, 2002, p. 139; Richards, 2002, p. 320). The division of assets is carried out by the parties themselves rather than by a court unless they are unable to agree (Richards, 2002, p. 320).

The few legal consequences of the PaCS that are required by the state are, while far from comprehensive, marriage-like in the obligations that they impose on the couple. As Stychin argues, the consequences of PaCS in relation to the state 'resemble, but are not identical to, the package of benefits historically available to married couples' (2001, p. 350). The partners are required to live together (Godard, 2007) and to 'provide each other with "mutual and material aid" as specified in the contract' (Merin, 2002, p. 139). Additionally, while the partners can establish the terms and conditions of the PaCS, there remains an obligation of 'spousal support' on relationship breakdown (Borrillo and Waaldijk, 2005, p. 97). The partners are jointly liable for debts to third parties (Richards, 2002, p. 317) and, unless they agree otherwise in the PaCS, co-ownership of property will apply (Martin and Théry, 2001, p. 150; Borrillo and Waaldijk, 2005, p. 97). They are treated as spouses for social security, succession of tenancy (Richards, 2002, pp. 318–19), wrongful death compensation, and statutory protection against domestic violence (Borrillo and Waaldijk, 2005, pp. 97, 100). However, the PaCS does not provide any parenting rights, or access to reproductive technologies or adoption (Merin, 2002, p. 140; Borrillo, 2005, p. 92). Other rights were delayed, such as joint taxation, which occurred after three years, and tax exemption on gifts between partners, which is a smaller allowance than that for married couples and only available after two years (Borrillo and Waaldijk, 2005, p. 94). However, subsequent legislative changes mean that these now take effect when the PaCS is registered (Godard, 2007).

From the multiple paths of its evolution (see Martin and Théry, 2001) to its structure and legal consequences, the PaCS is characterized by contradiction and uncertainty (Martin and Théry, 2001, p. 152). Despite this, its structure does make it a marriage-like provision in that it is a relationship between two people who live together and are mutually responsible for emotional and financial support. The ease with which a PaCS can be dissolved and the significant differences in legal consequences, particularly that the parties can contract their own provisions, could weaken the marriage analogy (and this was almost certainly the intention behind these provisions, see Martin and Théry, 2001), but the key characteristics of marriage are present in the PaCS so, as Stychin (2001, p. 350) argues, the PaCS, 'both resembles and dissociates itself from the marriage model'.

The provisions discussed so far are all 'opt-in' forms of relationship recognition where partners must register in order to access the legal provisions. The next provisions, while one additionally enables couples to opt-in by registering (the Tasmanian Relationships Act 2003), are characterized by the automatic recognition they give to marriage-like relationships. This usually, but not exclusively, means cohabiting relationships.

De facto relationships

While several jurisdictions recognize same-sex cohabitants for some purposes, I am focusing on the de facto provisions available in some Australian states and territories because, unlike in other jurisdictions, local gay and lesbian organizations and scholars have not sought same-sex marriage (Millbank and Sant, 2000, p. 185) and have argued *against* a proposal for same-sex marriage and in favour of this type of provision (see Gay and Lesbian Rights Lobby (GLRL), 2005). Although the same-sex marriage proposal was only at the state level and so would not have provided access to the federal provisions relating to marriage, such as social security, taxation, and immigration, this marks a different approach to other jurisdictions where the emphasis has been on the symbolic value of marriage as much as the legal provisions associated with it (see further Chapter 4). Instead, Millbank and Morgan (2001, p. 316) argue that the key sites of struggle for same-sex couples in Australia are around the meanings of 'spouse' and 'de facto relationship' rather than marriage. Similarly, a suggestion of seeking a marriage-like opt-in registered partnership scheme was rejected after a public consultation with members of the gay and lesbian communities by their lobbying organization (see Lesbian and Gay Legal Rights Service, 1993; 1994). Graycar and Millbank explain the different approach in Australian jurisdictions (compared to those discussed above) by locating same-sex relationship recognition within the context of the existing framework giving recognition to unmarried heterosexual relationships through de facto provisions (2000, pp. 230–54). They suggest that, 'the path of the current reforms was smoothed by the past fifteen years of reform [in relation to heterosexual relationships]' (2000, p. 276). The other key factors that they note are the involvement of the lesbian and gay communities in the law reform process through the discussion and consultation papers produced by the GLRL (Graycar and Millbank, 2000, pp. 254–61), and the absence of an equality guarantee in the Australian constitution upon which to base an 'equal marriage' claim (2000, p. 229). The preference of the Australian lesbian and gay communities was, it seemed, for de facto rather than marriage recognition: though the Lesbian and Gay Legal Rights Service acknowledges that it could not claim any 'real community consensus' and that it was unable to consult as widely as it would have liked due to lack of time and resources, it, nevertheless, based its approach on 'what we perceive to be a general trend within the communities with which we have consulted' (1994, p. 2).

However, it appears that public opinion on this has now changed, with the most recent GLRL consultation on federal recognition of same-sex relationships revealing that there was significant support for a multi-faceted approach to relationship recognition, which included marriage, civil unions and de facto relationships (GLRL, 2007, p. 24). Ironically, it seems that there was very little support for same-sex marriage within the lesbian and gay communities until the federal government introduced the Bill that would eventually become the Marriage Amendment Act 2004. This Act, which introduced a definition of marriage into Australian federal law for the first time (Nicholson, 2005) prohibits same-sex marriage. This change in attitudes is perhaps also partly a result of lesbian and gay Australians' awareness of marriage gains in other jurisdictions: '*On the basis of the aspirations of the community alone*, marriage as a model of relationship recognition must be pursued' (GLRL, 2007, p. 27, emphasis added). This acknowledgment appears somewhat reluctant, perhaps because the GLRL takes the feminist critiques of marriage seriously (Graycar and Millbank, 2000, p. 275; see Chapter 5), and there remains a contrast with other jurisdictions in that the emphasis of the report is still very much on choice, flexibility and (legal) coverage rather than focusing on a more symbolic recognition.

Therefore, despite this more recent attention to marriage, the de facto model is firmly entrenched in Australian jurisprudence and social consciousness, having developed partly in response to the inadequacies of marriage as an opt-in provision: they were originally created to give unmarried heterosexual couples access to the law 'in times of crisis and dispute' (Millbank, 1999, p. 16). They have since been expanded in all jurisdictions to include same-sex relationships and in some cases also non-sexual relationships. I will argue that, despite the absence of a formal registration procedure and the extension of the de facto provisions to non-sexual relationships in some jurisdictions, the criteria for identifying whether a de facto relationship exists are based on the marriage model. Nevertheless, this provision has the most potential to move away from the marriage paradigm.

For the purposes of this discussion, I will begin by focusing on New South Wales (NSW) because its De Facto Relationships Act 1984 (subsequently renamed the Property (Relationships) Act 1984) was the first of its kind in recognizing cohabiting (heterosexual) relationships as spousal for a number of purposes (Graycar and Millbank, 2000, p. 230). The Act (as amended)[7] provides that a de facto relationship is 'a relationship between two adult persons who live together as a couple and who are not married to one another or related by family' (Property (Relationships) Act, s. 4(1)). This new definition of de facto relationships implies, perhaps unintentionally, that unmarried

---

7 Originally, the De Facto Relationships Act 1984 defined de facto relationships as between those who were 'living together as husband and wife on a bona fide domestic basis' (in Graycar and Millbank, 2000, p. 232). The Property (Relationships) Legislation Amendment Act 1999 inserted the gender-neutral definition.

relationships are not 'family'. This has been criticized: 'While it is simply intended to exclude blood relatives...it reinforces the notion that lesbians and gay men do not form families and that such relationships are appropri-. ately excluded from the concept of family.' (Millbank and Sant, 2000, p. 190)

The existence of a de facto relationship is evidenced by a set of criteria that are clearly based on marriage, including: a long-term, cohabiting, sexual relationship; financial dependence or interdependence; 'mutual commitment to a shared life'; and 'the reputation and public aspects of the relationship' (s. 4(2)). However, none of these factors except cohabitation, which is required under s. 4(1)[8], is to be regarded as necessary and 'a court determining whether such a relationship exists is entitled to have regard to such matters, and to attach such weight to any matter, as may seem appropriate to the court in the circumstances of the case' (s. 4(3)). Couples can apply for recognition as a de facto relationship: if they have lived together for two years; if they have a child together; or if excluding them would cause hardship (Pawlowski, 2001, p. 30).

In 1999 the NSW Act was amended to include same-sex couples as de facto relationships. The impetus for this reform came not from court challenges but the GLRL, which wrote discussion and consultation papers before drafting legislation based on the responses of lesbians and gay men (Graycar and Millbank, 2000, p. 254). The 1999 Act, while differing in some ways from the legislation proposed by the GLRL (see Millbank, 2000a), did adopt the suggestion that it should also include non-sexual relationships (see Lesbian and Gay Legal Rights Service, 1993, pp. 83–4; 1994, p. 4) by introducing the category 'close personal relationships' (Sch. 1[9], s. 5). A close personal relationship is, 'between two adult persons, whether or not related by family, who are living together, one or each of whom provides the other with domestic support or personal care' (Sch. 1[9], s. 5(1)(b)).

This separation of sexual (de facto) and non-sexual (close personal) relationships was also adopted in Tasmania where the Relationships Act 2003 names them 'significant' (s. 4(1)) and 'caring' relationships (s. 5(1)), respectively. The Australian Capital Territory (ACT), in contrast, does not distinguish between sexual and non-sexual relationships, having only one category of 'domestic relationship'. This is: 'a personal relationship between 2 adults in which one provides personal or financial commitment and support of a domestic nature for the material benefit of the other and includes a domestic partnership but does not include a legal marriage' (Domestic Relationships Act 1994 s. 3(1)). Unlike NSW, the Tasmania (s. 4(3–4) and s. 5(5–6)) and ACT (s. 3(2)(a)) provisions do not require cohabitation. All three jurisdictions

---

8 The cohabitation requirement is criticized as being under-inclusive: Millbank and Sant, 2000, p. 208.

exclude caretaking (close personal, caring, or domestic) relationships where that care is provided in commercial, state or charitable contexts or on behalf of a third party (NSW Sch. 1[9], s. 5(2); Tasmania s. 5(2); ACT s. 3(2)(b)).

The de facto (NSW) and significant (Tasmania) relationships are clearly marriage-like and derive from a heterosexual marriage template (see, for example, Lesbian and Gay Legal Rights Service, 1993, p. 97; Graycar and Millbank, 2000, p. 229). The factors identified in the legislation as relevant to establishing the existence of a Tasmanian personal relationship illustrate the similarities with marriage (see above for the NSW factors). The Tasmania provision is similar to that in NSW in that both significant and caring relationships can be evidenced by *some* or all of the following: cohabitation; a long-term relationship; financial interdependence; and 'mutual commitment to a shared life' (s. 4(3)(f) and s. 5(5)(e)). In addition, a significant relationship may be evidenced by the existence of a sexual relationship (s. 4(3)(c)) and the 'care and support of children' (s. 4(3)(g)). For caring relationships, 'the level of personal care and domestic support provided by one or each of the partners to the other may be taken into account' (s. 5(5)(h)). Sex and children are not listed as factors to look for as evidence of a caring relationship. This indicates that significant relationships are expected to be marriage-like, while caring relationships were created for relationships that are non-sexual but nevertheless deserving of recognition because of the level of interdependence in the relationship. However, it is emphasized in the Act that the courts must consider *all the circumstances* of the relationship and that the existence (or not) of any or all of the factors listed is *not conclusive* (s. 4(4) and s. 5(6)).

The close personal (NSW) and caring (Tasmania) non-sexual relationships move further away from a marriage framework than the de facto and significant relationships in that they are based on recognizing financial and emotional interdependencies that occur outside of a sexual and, in Tasmania, cohabiting relationship. Millbank and Sant argue that:

> The concept of a domestic relationship is in some senses a radical departure from traditional laws about the family, because it redefines family obligations around love, interdependence and choice, rather than blood and marriage or 'marriage-like' relationships. In doing this it arguably destabilizes heterosexuality and the hetero-nuclear family. (2000, p. 203)

However, preserving a distinction between sexual and non-sexual (and in NSW, cohabiting and non-cohabiting) relationships could be argued to be reinforcing the primacy of marriage especially where the presumptively sexual, marriage-like, de facto relationship attracts more legal consequences. Even the language of the Tasmanian provision preserves a special symbolic status for the marriage-like relationship: 'significant'. Its name suggests that caring, non-sexual, relationships are by implication less significant. It is also noteworthy that though some federal rights and responsibilities have now been extended to de facto relationships through recent legislation (Family Law Amendment (De Facto Financial Matters and Other Measures) Act 2008), the non-sexual caring relationships were excluded at the recommendation of the Human Rights and Equal Opportunity Commission (2007). The commission recommended that the federal government should retain a clear distinction between sexual relationships and interdependent (or caring) relationships in order to 'contain the scope of entitlements available to people who are not in a couple' (2007, para. 4.3.4).

However, in NSW the lesbian and gay communities argued for the separate statuses and different legal consequences for de facto and close personal relationships for two reasons. First, while they wanted to be as inclusive as possible, they did not want 'their own partner relationships identified by law as "other" than partner relationships' (Millbank and Sant, 2000, p. 197). In other words, they wanted to be recognized on the same terms as heterosexual de facto couples and not in a group of 'other' relationships. Second, on a practical level, it may be argued that including relationships that are not in fact analogous to marriage within a framework that was modelled on marriage and intended for (heterosexual) marriage-like relationships may be problematic. Graycar and Millbank put forward the GLRL's position that it was necessary to recognize that financial dependency, interdependency and emotional ties, while not restricted to sexual relationships, are all more likely to be present in these relationships. In non-sexual relationships, such ties 'may not be so predictable nor so wide-spread' (2000, p. 261). However, in Tasmania, where the legal consequences of personal relationships are virtually the same as the (state-level) provisions of marriage for a range of purposes (Donna Cooper, 2004, p. 46), significant and caring relationships attract the same legal consequences except in relation to a partner's child. Moreover, the ACT provision does not distinguish between sexual/couple and non-sexual relationships at all. The provisions only become operational in the absence of any private arrangements and when one of the parties invokes it (Millbank, 1999, p. 19). As such, concerns about preventing non-sexual relationships being subsumed within a marriage framework may be overstated. Millbank implicitly acknowledges this when she contests claims that de facto recognition for same-sex couples would require assimilation (1999, p. 11).

While the NSW and Tasmanian provisions do move away from marriage in recognizing relationships that would not be described as marriage-like and shifting the emphasis from sexual relationships towards ones based on interdependence, they do so under a separate category of relationship, thus preserving the special status of marriage-like relationships. In contrast, as it does not set apart a sexual relationship either symbolically (as in Tasmania) or by attaching greater legal consequences to it (as in NSW), the ACT provision could be said to be the most subversive of the marriage model:

> in moving to emotional and financial interdependence as the key indicators of a legally recognized relationship, [it] rejected sex and cohabitation as the only criteria for a 'real' relationship. In doing so, it left behind the state of marriage and 'marriage-like' relationships as the only recognized relationships in Australian law, and was in that sense truly revolutionary. (Millbank, 2000b, p. 50)

While the Tasmanian provision mirrors the NSW definitions of significant (de facto) and caring (close personal) relationships, it is unique in that it additionally allows couples to 'opt in' by registering their significant or caring relationship. While registration with the state may suggest a marriage model, unlike the opt-in provisions discussed above it departs from the marriage model in that it was made available to *any* two people who have a 'personal relationship' (that is, either a significant or a caring relationship: Relationships Act 2003, s. 6). The registration does not change the status of the relationship in that registered personal relationships in Tasmania attract exactly the same legal consequences as non-registered ones. The only difference is that registered relationships avoid having to provide evidence that their relationship met the indicators in the Relationships Act s. 4(3) and s. 5(5) in order to access the law, which means that they could have a less normative relationship. In addition, there is no requirement for the relationship to have subsisted for a particular period of time if it is registered (Donna Cooper, 2004, p. 49): registration is taken as evidence of the relationship and its level of commitment. If the relationship is registered, there are no questions on the application form as to the nature of the relationship, other than to ask whether it is a significant or caring relationship,[9] and, following registration, no other evidence is required that such a relationship exists (s. 4(2) and s. 5(4)). Therefore, although there *may* have been an expectation from the legislature that significant relationships will be similar to marriage, there is no legal reason why they need to be in order to register as such.

Initially, the legal consequences of de facto relationships were much less comprehensive than the European registered partnership model in that they were not given the same legal benefits, protections and obligations as marriage. In Australia, marriage is a federal issue and states do not have jurisdiction to legislate on issues such as pensions, income taxation, social security and immigration (Millbank and Morgan, 2001, p. 307). Until the Family Law Amendment (De Facto Financial Matters and Other Measures) Act 2008, the distribution of property on relationship breakdown of unmarried couples was

---

9 'Application To Register a Deed of Relationship' available at: www.justice.tas.gov.au/bdm/appldeedregoform.htm.

a state matter, and (as discussed above) this is where the origins of de facto relationships lie. The 2008 Act attempts to address criticisms of inconsistency and complexity resulting from the variety of de facto provisions across the jurisdictions and create parity for same-sex couples by providing access to the federal family law framework (see further Kovacs, 2009).

The de facto model of relationship recognition is the least marriage-like of all the provisions discussed in this chapter. It is much more flexible than the European model of registration in that it recognizes relationships based on their need for recognition rather than by whether they opt in to a formal marriage-like structure. Furthermore, some provisions have moved beyond an emphasis on sexual and cohabiting relationships to focus on financial and emotional ties, though the 2008 Act has somewhat undermined this by excluding caring relationships from the federal regime and relocating de facto relationships as part of the family law framework. Nevertheless, despite its origins being clearly within a marriage framework these provisions have the most potential to move beyond the marriage model.

Conclusion

In the previous chapter, I argued that the marriage model could be characterized by a framework that assumes a committed, sexual, monogamous and interdependent relationship. I also noted that the legal framework of marriage is distinct from other contractual arrangements in that its terms are set by the state rather than the parties themselves and that the parties must opt in to marriage. In this chapter I have demonstrated that so-called 'alternative' or separate provisions to marriage are, to some extent, each based on the marriage model. This is hardly surprising given the context. Each provision was created as either a substitute for 'gay marriage' or, in the case of the Australian de factos, as a property-focused contingency for unmarried heterosexuals, which was later extended to same-sex couples and non-sexual (inter)dependent relationships, with sexual relationships subsequently falling under the jurisdiction of the federal family courts. More surprising and interesting is my second finding: the ways and extent to which some of these provisions depart from the marriage model. This raises interesting questions about how far the marriage model might be stretched and adapted. The stretching of the marriage model demonstrates the necessity both to engage with and develop critiques of marriage in this context and to assess the new 'gaps' that may open up in this context. For example, even the UK CPA, among the most marriage-like of the provisions, potentially provides some scope to transgress the marriage model through its sexual silences, which I return to in Chapter 6.

The most difficult provision to assess is the PaCS. There are some significant ways in which it follows the marriage model, particularly in terms of its preconditions for entering into a PaCS. However, there are also some striking departures from the marriage model, especially in the ability of the parties to set their own contractual terms (subject to some imposed minimum obligations) and the ease of dissolution. Domestic partnerships are also difficult to characterize because there are several different varieties. The most common form, however, is a limited version of the marriage model in that the entry requirements and expectations of mutual financial support are marriage-like, while the dissolution procedure is very simple and the legal consequences are minimal. The evolution of the California provision demonstrates that, as the legal consequences get more extensive, the dissolution procedure similarly becomes more marriage-like.

The civil union, registered partnership and civil partnership provisions all very clearly map onto the marriage model. The Hawaii provision, reciprocal beneficiary, was extended to those prohibited from marriage through consanguinity or affinity in order to emphasize the difference between same-sex couples and (heterosexual) marriage. Nevertheless, this move away from conjugality and towards care (or dependency) as a basis for recognizing relationships would constitute a significant departure from the marriage model. The Australian de facto provisions, though (perhaps inevitably) similar to marriage in some ways, go the furthest towards reconfiguring the basis of relationship recognition. The Tasmanian provision provides comprehensive recognition of non-sexual 'caring' relationships on the same basis as sexual 'significant' relationships, though the language used and federal recognition suggests primacy for sexual relationships. The effect of implementing a shift from conjugality to care would have to be assessed separately but it demonstrates both the need for a feminist analysis of these developments (some of this work has already been done in the Australian context, for example, Graycar and Millbank, 2000; Millbank and Sant, 2000; Millbank and Morgan, 2001) and the need to develop feminist critiques of marriage in light of the changes in the institution, as I do in the second part of this book.

Where the provisions are clearly within the marriage model (civil union, registered partnership, civil partnership and domestic partnership), the arguments that I will make in relation to same-sex marriage in Part II would also apply to these provisions. Many of the same arguments could still be made about PaCS and de factos but these would have to be made separately and contextually, rather than by analogy and this is outside the scope of this book. In Chapter 3, I return to marriage to explore the evolution of same-sex marriage provisions.

3
Same-Sex Marriage Litigation

Introduction

The world's first legally recognized same-sex marriage took place in the Netherlands in 2001 after the legislature amended the definition of marriage to include same-sex couples. In contrast, there has been a highly contentious and visible battle for same-sex marriage in the United States, through both the courts and the political arena. This chapter outlines the different evolutions (or in some cases perhaps revolutions) that resulted in same-sex marriages in some of the jurisdictions where it is currently available.[1] The purpose of this is to identify the broad themes that have emerged in terms of the legal arguments that have been made for same-sex marriage rather than to provide a detailed analysis of each jurisdiction. I argue that these common themes are: sameness and formal equality; access to the legal consequences of marriage; the symbolic importance of access to the label 'marriage'; and the ways in which same-sex marriage would support the institution more generally. Another common theme is the existence of a backlash against same-sex marriage.

The chronologies of the Netherlands and the United States represent opposite ends of the spectrum. While courts in both jurisdictions were considering same-sex marriage claims in the early 1990s, the outcomes of these cases and subsequent paths to marriage differed significantly. In the Netherlands, the marriage statute was challenged on two grounds: that its language was gender-neutral and thus did not preclude same-sex marriage, and that denying same-sex couples marriage licences infringed same-sex couples' rights to marry and found a family and was discriminatory under Articles 8, 12 and 14 of the European Convention on Human Rights and Articles 23 and 26

---

1 At the time of writing, same-sex marriage is available in the Netherlands, Belgium, Spain, Canada, South Africa, Portugal, Sweden, Norway, Iceland, Argentina and Mexico City. In the United States, it is available in Massachusetts, Connecticut, Iowa, Vermont, New Hampshire, Washington DC and New York (see National Gay and Lesbian Task Force, 2011; Human Rights Campaign, 2011b).

of the International Covenant on Civil and Political Rights (Maxwell, 2001, pp. 143–4). These arguments were heard in two cases, both of which failed as the Dutch courts were reluctant to be more liberal than the other signatories and the European Court of Human Rights in their interpretation of the treaties. To do so was considered to be within the remit of the legislature but not the courts (Maxwell, 2001, pp. 145–6). In the United States, the courts are much less deferential to the legislature in interpreting constitutional provisions and, unlike the Netherlands' courts, have the authority to strike down legislation (Maxwell, 2001, p. 201). Additionally, voter referenda have played a significant role in the United States. For example, in Maine same-sex marriage legislation was passed but subsequently overturned by voter referendum (Human Rights Campaign, 2011b). Likewise, in California the Supreme Court had held that prohibiting same-sex marriage was unconstitutional (*In Re Marriage Cases* 43 Cal 4th 757) but this was subsequently overturned by a constitutional amendment passed by a referendum in 2008, which defined marriage as being between a man and a woman (Proposition 8). The federal District Court then struck down the amendment to California's constitution in *Perry v Schwarzenegger* 704 F Supp 2d 921 (ND Cal 2010) as violating the Due Process and Equal Protection Clauses of the US Constitution but this was stayed pending appeal to the federal Court of Appeal (*Perry v Schwarzenegger* 2010 WL 3212786 (CA 9 (Cal)).

The courts also played a significant role in Canada and South Africa, while Belgium, Spain, Norway, Sweden, Iceland, Portugal and Argentina followed the Netherlands' legislative route, as did some jurisdictions in Mexico and the United States (Mexico City, Vermont, New Hampshire, Washington DC and New York). In this chapter, I focus on the litigation in order to highlight some of the legal bases for same-sex marriage claims. This provides part of the basis for my analysis of the arguments for same-sex marriage in Chapter 4, which draws on both these arguments and those employed by activists and academics.

The United States

In 1993, the Hawaii Supreme Court ruled in the case of *Baehr v Lewin* 74 Hawaii 530. The applicants had sought a declaration that the Department of Health's refusal to issue a marriage licence to same-sex couples was unconstitutional and an injunction to prevent licences from being withheld in the future. The court upheld the claim that the state's interpretation of the marriage statute (HRS§572-1) violates the right to equal protection and due process under Article I s. 5 of the Hawaii Constitution. This provides that there should not be discrimination on the grounds of race, religion, sex or ancestry. The court held that denial of access to marriage denies couples access to 'a multiplicity of rights and benefits that are contingent upon that status' (per Levinson J at 560). The equal protection clause was implicated because the exclusion of same-sex couples from these rights and benefits was prima facie discriminatory on the basis of sex (at 561). The basis for finding sex discrimination was that marriage is restricted to one male and one female but it is not restricted to heterosexuals:

> 'Homosexual' and 'same-sex' marriages are not synonymous; by the same token, a 'heterosexual' same-sex marriage is, in theory, not oxymoronic... Parties to 'a union between a man and a woman' may or may not be homosexuals. Parties to a same-sex marriage could theoretically be either homosexuals or heterosexuals. (per Levinson J at 544)

This was a groundbreaking judgment because it was the first time a United States court had 'understood that a sexual orientation classification is sex discrimination' (Levi, 2004, p. 843). As sex was a 'suspect category' under the state's constitution, the same-sex marriage prohibition was presumed to be unconstitutional unless the state could show a 'compelling interest' (per Levinson J at 571). The case was referred back to the first instance court to determine whether such an interest existed and it was held that one did not (*Baehr v Miike* 1996 WL 694235; see also Wolfson, 2001, p. 172). However, this was a temporary success as the right-wing backlash began even before this case was finally determined on further referral back to the Supreme Court (Wolfson, 2001, p. 170); a constitutional amendment made the matter moot by giving the legislature power to prohibit same-sex marriage (*Baehr v Miike* 92 Hawaii 634; see also Wolfson, 2001, p. 174; Levi, 2004, p. 844). In addition to the constitutional amendment in Hawaii, this case prompted a flurry of Defense of Marriage Acts (DOMAs) in the United States, including one at the federal level (DOMA 1996). Section 3 of the federal legislation, which defines marriage as between one man and one woman for all federal purposes, has recently been successfully challenged at first instance by a group of plaintiffs who were legally married in Massachusetts (*Gill v Office of Personnel Management* 699 F Supp 2d 374 D Mass, 2010, appeal pending) and the Obama administration has indicated that it considers DOMAs to be unconstitutional (United States Department of Justice, 2011). Nevertheless, a total of 12 states now have such provisions, while 29 have constitutional amendments prohibiting same-sex marriage. Of these, 18 have broader provisions that could include prohibition of any form of same-sex relationship recognition (see Human Rights Campaign, 2010b).[2]

---

2 An amendment to the United States Constitution that would define marriage as between a man and a woman was also proposed though ultimately unsuccessful (see Bush, 2004a; 2004b).

In 1999 the Vermont Supreme Court held that it was unconstitutional to exclude same-sex couples from the benefits and protections of marriage (*Baker v State of Vermont* 744 A 2d 864). Under the 'common benefit and protection' clause of the Vermont Constitution (Chapter I, Article 7), the state must demonstrate that the exclusion of same-sex couples from marriage 'bears a reasonable and just relation' to a governmental purpose (per Amestoy CJ at 878–9). The state argued that the purpose of privileging marriage was to encourage the link between procreation and child-rearing by promoting 'a permanent commitment between couples who have children' (per Amestoy CJ at 216–17). The court rejected this argument, noting the many different-sex married couples without children and that same-sex couples with children were unable to marry. Therefore, the court concluded that the state had not provided 'a reasonable and just basis for the continued exclusion of same-sex couples from the benefits incident to a civil marriage license under Vermont law' (per Amestoy CJ at 224).

However, this court did not hold that the exclusion of same-sex couples from *marriage* was unconstitutional but rather their exclusion from the *legal consequences* of marriage:

> It is important to state clearly the parameters of today's ruling. Although plaintiffs sought injunctive and declaratory relief designed to secure a marriage license, *their claims and arguments here have focused primarily upon the consequences of official exclusion from the statutory benefits, protections, and security incident to marriage* under Vermont law. While some future case may attempt to establish that – notwithstanding equal benefits and protections under Vermont law – the denial of a marriage license operates per se to deny constitutionally-protected rights, that is not the claim we address today. We hold only that plaintiffs are entitled under Chapter I, Article 7, of the Vermont Constitution to obtain the same benefits and protections afforded by Vermont law to married opposite-sex couples. (per Amestoy CJ at 224, emphasis added; see also *Lewis v Harris* 908 A 2d 196, per Albin J)

The court thus left it to the legislature to 'craft an appropriate means of addressing this constitutional mandate' (per Amestoy CJ at 226) and the legislature created the civil union. The focus on the legal consequences of marriage enabled the legislature to create this separate provision that was nevertheless modelled on marriage. Subsequent cases have avoided this result by also emphasizing the need for access to the label 'marriage' in order to confer equal protection and dignity.

The first successful litigation for same-sex marriage to actually result in same-sex marriage in the US was *Goodridge v Department of Public Health*

440 Mass 309. The Massachusetts Supreme Court held that refusing a marriage licence to same-sex couples did not have a rational basis and contravened the equal protection principle in the state constitution. In contrast to *Baker*, the *Goodridge* decision focuses on 'dignity and equality' (per Marshall CJ at 312) in addition to legal consequences:

> Barred access to the protections, benefits, and obligations of civil marriage, a person who enters into an intimate, exclusive union with another of the same sex is arbitrarily deprived of membership in one of our community's most rewarding and cherished institutions. That exclusion is incompatible with the constitutional principles of respect for individual autonomy and equality under law. (per Marshall CJ at 313)

Once again, the state's rationales for prohibiting same-sex marriage focused on procreation and child-rearing by a male and female parent. In *Goodridge*, the state additionally claimed that prohibition was necessary to preserve state and private financial resources (at 331). Chief Justice Marshall rejected the first two grounds, noting that such arguments transform the one 'unbridgeable difference' between same-sex and different-sex couples into 'the essence of marriage' (at 333; see also Chapter 1). The court found that:

> The [state] has offered purported justifications for the civil marriage restriction that are starkly at odds with the comprehensive network of vigorous, gender-neutral laws promoting stable families and the best interests of children. It has failed to identify any relevant characteristic that would justify shutting the door to civil marriage to a person who wishes to marry someone of the same sex. (per Marshall CJ at 341)

With regard to the issue of preserving resources, the court held that there is no rational relationship between prohibiting same-sex marriage and 'the goal of economy' (per Marshall CJ at 336). It also rejected a further claim by the state (and some amici briefs) that same-sex marriage would trivialize or destroy the institution of marriage. In doing this, it employed the type of argument made by conservative supporters of same-sex marriage (see further Chapter 4):

> If anything, extending civil marriage to same-sex couples reinforces the importance of marriage to individuals and communities. That same-sex couples are willing to embrace marriage's solemn obligations of exclusivity, mutual support, and commitment to one another is a testament to the enduring place of marriage in our laws and in the human spirit. (per Marshall CJ at 337)

Like the Hawaii and Vermont rulings, *Goodridge* prompted a right-wing backlash and claims that 'activist judges' had violated the separation of powers (see Baird and Rosenbaum, 2004, pp. 10–11; Bush, 2004b, pp. 63–4). This claim was taken to the federal Court of Appeals in *Largess v Supreme Judicial Court for State of Massachusetts* 125 S Ct 618, where it was unsuccessfully argued that by redefining marriage (and ignoring the separation of powers) the Massachusetts court had violated the guarantee in the federal constitution of a republican form of government in every state. The backlash culminated in failed attempts to put a constitutional amendment defining marriage as being between a man and a woman to a state-wide referendum on the November 2008 ballot.

Despite the backlash in Massachusetts, three other states have subsequently legally recognized same-sex marriages as a result of litigation: in California, *In Re Marriage Cases* did result in a state-wide referendum in November 2008 (Proposition 8), which over-ruled the court's finding that the same-sex marriage prohibition was unconstitutional.[3] There were also successful cases in Connecticut (*Kerrigan v Commissioner of Public Health* 289 Conn 135) and in Iowa (*Varnum v Brien* 763 NW 2d 862), which mirror the themes already identified in the earlier cases.

The California litigation began with an act of 'civil disobedience' by the San Francisco mayor who began issuing marriage licences to same-sex couples in 2004. In *Lockyer v City and County of San Francisco* 33 Cal 4th 1055, the California Supreme Court ruled that he did not have the authority to do so and declared the marriages invalid. However, the court reserved judgment on the issue of whether the same-sex marriage prohibition was constitutional as that was not at issue in the case: *Lockyer* concerned only the power of the mayor to act in contravention of legislation that had been passed by both the ordinary legislature (an amendment to the Family Code in 1977) and by voter referendum (the Knight Initiative, or Proposition 22, in 2000). *In Re Marriage Cases* is a combined appeal of several cases brought by same-sex couples seeking a declaration that a same-sex marriage ban is unconstitutional and by the proponents of Proposition 22 and others who sought to 'protect' heterosexual marriage.

The California case differed from the earlier cases discussed above because the state of California already had a comprehensive domestic partnership provision in place. This meant that the focus in this case was firmly on access to the word 'marriage' rather than the more pragmatic arguments of exclusion from legal protections made in Vermont.

---

3 Marriages that took place before the voter referendum remain legally valid. The amendment was successfully challenged in the federal District Court (*Perry v Schwarzenegger*, appeal pending).

The California Supreme Court held that access to the constitutional right to marry in California is not limited to access to the same legal protections as marriage (cf. Vermont Supreme Court in *Baker*) but rather includes access to 'dignity and respect equal to that accorded other officially recognized families' (per George CJ at 783). In other words, access to the label 'marriage' *is part of* the nature and substance of the constitutional right; it would be insufficient to grant access to the provisions of marriage under a different name. Using the different language of domestic partnership 'poses at least a serious risk of denying the family relationship of same-sex couples such dignity and equal respect' (ibid.). In this reasoning, the California court is echoing the dual concern of the Massachusetts Supreme Court about access to dignity and equality in addition to legal protections.

The California Supreme Court went on to find that recognition through the separate domestic partnership provision also violates the state's equal protection clause. In doing so, the court rejected the Hawaii Supreme Court's finding that prohibiting same-sex marriage constitutes sex discrimination but instead considered it to be discrimination on the basis of sexual orientation (see 837). The California court held that sexual orientation is a 'suspect class' requiring 'strict scrutiny' rather than the more deferential 'rational basis' review that the Massachusetts court held was violated in *Goodridge*.[4] The strict scrutiny standard was applied for two reasons. First, the rationale for holding that a characteristic belongs to a suspect class 'clearly applies' to differential treatment on the basis of sexual orientation:

> The most important factors in deciding whether a characteristic should be considered a constitutionally suspect basis for classification are whether the class of persons who exhibit a certain characteristic historically has been subjected to invidious and prejudicial treatment, and whether society now recognizes that the characteristic in question generally bears no relationship to the individual's ability to perform or contribute to society. (*In Re Marriage Cases* at 843)

Second, the differential treatment in the (marriage and domestic partnership) statutes impinges upon a 'fundamental, constitutionally protected privacy interest' because by revealing their relationship status in 'numerous everyday social, employment, and governmental settings' they would

---

4 Unlike rational basis review, which requires only that the decision meets a 'rational, constitutionally legitimate interest that supports the differential treatment at issue' and that the different treatment is rationally related to this state interest, strict scrutiny requires the state to establish that it has a 'constitutionally compelling' interest that justifies the different treatment and that this different treatment is *necessary* to further the state interest (*In Re Marriage Cases* at 847).

also necessarily reveal their sexual orientation (at 847). It also impinges upon the right of same-sex couples to 'have their family relationship accorded respect and dignity equal to that accorded the family relationship of opposite-sex couples' (at 845). The domestic partnership was considered to lack the dignity and respect of marriage because of the 'long and celebrated history of the term marriage' and the symbolic importance of this term; because 'in light of the historic disparagement of and discrimination against gay persons' it is likely that the new parallel institution would be viewed as inferior to marriage and a 'mark of second-class citizenship'; and finally, that lack of familiarity with the term 'domestic partner' is likely to pose difficulties for same-sex couples and their children for a considerable period of time (at 845–6).

The state was not able to demonstrate that excluding same-sex couples from marriage was *necessary* to protect a 'compelling state interest' for three reasons. First, limiting marriage to opposite-sex couples was 'not necessary to preserve the rights and benefits of marriage' enjoyed by heterosexuals: allowing same-sex marriage will not restrict heterosexual marriage in any way (at 854). Second, same-sex marriage will not alter the substance of the institution of marriage because same-sex couples will be subject to the same legal framework and consequences as heterosexual spouses: the California Supreme Court agreed with the plaintiffs' contention that it was not being asked to create 'a new constitutional right – the right to "same-sex marriage"' (at 812) but rather to find that the existing right to marry should properly include same-sex couples. Finally, the religious freedom of any organization or person will be protected because those who object will not be required to solemnize a same-sex marriage (at 855). The court concluded that same-sex marriage would not impact upon the rights and benefits of heterosexual couples but that excluding same-sex couples from marriage does create 'a real and appreciable harm' for same-sex couples and their children (at 855).[5]

Interestingly, the court considered that the remedy for this violation of the state's equal protection principles could be to either extend marriage to same-sex couples or to withhold marriage from *both* same-sex and different-sex couples (at 856). However, they found that due to the history and importance of marriage there could be 'no doubt that extending the designation of marriage to same-sex couples' was the appropriate remedy (at 856).

In the *Kerrigan* and *Varnum* cases, the Supreme Courts of Connecticut and Iowa both follow very similar reasoning to that of *In Re Marriage Cases*, particularly in their finding that the respective marriage statutes violate each

---

5 There were dissenting and concurring judgments in this case, which dealt with constitutional issues of the separation of powers, including judicial powers in relation to voter referenda, but these discussions are outside the scope of my analysis here.

state's equal protection clause. However, these courts used an intermediate level of scrutiny rather than the strict scrutiny of California or the rational basis test used by Massachusetts: as the Iowa Supreme Court notes, once it has concluded that the marriage statute cannot withstand intermediate scrutiny, there is no need to decide whether sexual orientation classifications are subject to a higher level of scrutiny (*Varnum*, per Cady J at 896). Heightened scrutiny, applied to 'quasi-suspect' classifications, requires the law to 'not only further an important governmental interest and be substantially related to that interest, but the justification for the classification must be genuine and must not depend on generalizations' (*Varnum* at 880). They both also follow the California Supreme Court rather than Hawaii in basing their decisions on sexual orientation discrimination rather than sex or gender discrimination. In *Kerrigan*, as in *In Re Marriage Cases*, the court rejected a comprehensive civil union provision as constituting a 'cognizable harm' to same-sex couples because it lacks the 'status and significance' of the institution of marriage (at 141).

The Connecticut and Iowa Supreme Courts held that sexual orientation is a quasi-suspect class, entitled to heightened scrutiny under each state's constitution based on a four-part test developed by the US Supreme Court:

1 that there is a history of invidious discrimination against the group;
2 that the impugned characteristic bears no relation to the group's ability to contribute to society;
3 that the characteristic is immutable; and
4 that the group is a minority or politically powerless.

Both courts considered the third and fourth parts to be subsidiary (*Kerrigan*, per Palmer J at 169) or supplemental rather than 'critical to the analysis' as the first and second are (*Varnum*, per Cady J at 889). However, it was the issue of political power that was the most controversial in each case. In *Kerrigan*, whilst the majority had no doubt that gays and lesbians constitute a minority and thus satisfy criteria four in the absence of political powerlessness, there is extensive discussion in the judgment on this issue. The dissenting judges conclude that the 'politically powerless' criterion should have equal weight and the general legislative trend, particularly the recent enactment of civil unions, in the state demonstrates that gays and lesbians do have political power (Borden J joined by Vertefeuille J at 273–304). However, the majority found that the existence of anti-discrimination statutes was evidence not of the political power of gays, but instead of the legislature's recognition that legislative protection of gays and lesbians was *necessary*. Followed by the unanimous Iowa court in *Varnum*, the majority in *Kerrigan* considered the test did not require absolute powerlessness, but rather that 'the group lacks sufficient political strength to bring a prompt

end to the prejudice and discrimination through traditional political means'
(per Palmer J at 197).

Having concluded that gays and lesbians meet this test, the courts next
consider whether the prohibition of same-sex marriage is substantially related
to an important governmental objective. In *Kerrigan*, the state of Connecticut
put forward two reasons. The first reason was to maintain uniformity with
the laws of other states, the vast majority of which had civil union provisions
rather than marriage. This was quickly dismissed by the court: 'beyond the
mere assertion that uniformity and consistency with the laws of other jurisdictions represent a truly important governmental interest, the defendants
have offered no reason why that is so, and we know of none' (at 253–4). It
was instead 'abundantly clear' that the second reason, maintaining marriage
as heterosexual, was the 'overriding reason' for the prohibition of same-sex
marriage (at 254). This was also one of the reasons offered by the defendant
county in Iowa, along with support for 'the optimal procreation and rearing
of children' (at 897) and financial considerations. In these arguments there
are again similarities with the previous cases and these courts also found
them to be unconvincing.[6]

Both courts rejected the 'empty analysis' (*Varnum* at 898) and circular reasoning of the protecting marriage argument:

> When tradition is offered to justify preserving a statutory scheme
> that has been challenged on equal protection grounds, we must
> determine whether the *reasons* underlying that tradition are
> sufficient to satisfy constitutional requirements. Tradition alone
> never can provide sufficient cause to discriminate against a
> protected class... (*Kerrigan* at 256)

The Iowa court also considered and unanimously rejected the claim that
the same-sex marriage prohibition promotes child-raising in an optimal environment, noting that in failing to exclude other non-optimal parents (such as
violent felons and child abusers) and by including same-sex couples who had
no children, the same-sex marriage ban is both under- and over-inclusive in
attempting to achieve this. Furthermore, the state of Iowa does not prohibit
same-sex parenting, which suggests that this provision is 'less about using
marriage to achieve an optimal environment for children and more about
merely precluding gay and lesbian people from civil marriage' (at 901). The
procreation claim that the Iowa court considered was also central to Justice
Zarella's dissenting judgment in *Kerrigan*, though it was framed in slightly
different terms. In Iowa, the court framed the question as 'whether *exclusion*

---

6 Some of these arguments have, however, been successful in other courts, which have
upheld same-sex marriage prohibitions. See, for example: *Hernandez v Robles* 7 NY 3d 338 at
359–61.

of gay and lesbian individuals from the institution of civil marriage will result in *more* procreation?' and found the link between same-sex marriage prohibitions and increased procreation to be 'far too tenuous to withstand heightened scrutiny' (at 901–2). In contrast, Justice Zarella's dissent criticizes the majority in *Kerrigan* for failing to consider the *purpose* of marriage laws, which he considers is to privilege and regulate procreative sexual conduct, and for failing to explain why the state would have an interest in 'promoting or regulating committed and loving relationships that have no potential to result in the birth of a child' (at 335).

Finally, the Iowa court (as had the Massachusetts court in *Goodridge*) considered the issue of the conservation of state resources: 'The [defendant's] argument is based on a simple premise: couples who are married enjoy numerous governmental benefits, so the state's financial burden associated with civil marriage is reduced if less people are allowed to marry.' (at 902) The unanimous court noted several problems with this reasoning, including that 'sexual orientation is a flawed indicator of resource usage' (at 903) and that if the true goal was to save resources, the state would better achieve it by excluding a much larger group than same-sex couples (such as those marrying for a second time). As a result, this does not substantially further a legitimate governmental interest such that it meets the heightened scrutiny test.

Therefore, in both the *Kerrgian* and *Varnum* cases, the defendant state and county failed to put forward 'adequate reason' (*Kerrigan* at 260) to justify the statutory prohibition of same-sex marriage according to the equal protection requirements of each state:

> We are firmly convinced the exclusion of gay and lesbian people from the institution of civil marriage does not substantially further any important governmental objective. The legislature has excluded a historically disfavoured class of persons from a supremely important civil institution without a constitutionally sufficient justification. (*Varnum* at 906)

Perhaps anticipating the 'judicial activism' claims that followed the earlier cases, the Connecticut and Iowa courts explicitly address the issue of separation of powers:

> These Iowans, believing that the law is inconsistent with certain constitutional mandates, exercised their constitutional right to petition the courts for redress of their grievance. This court, consistent with its role to interpret the law and resolve disputes, now has the responsibility to determine if the law enacted by the legislative branch and enforced by the executive branch violates the Iowa Constitution. (*Varnum*, per Cady J at 875)

The Connecticut court also rejected claims that it should not interfere with the democratic decision to recognize same-sex relationships under a separate provision: '[if] the intended effect of a law is to treat politically unpopular or historically disfavored minorities differently from persons in the majority or favored class, that law cannot evade constitutional review under the separate but equal doctrine' (*Kerrigan*, per Palmer J at 153).

In Canada and South Africa, the road to same-sex marriage began in the courts but also involved the legislatures. Both countries constitutionally prohibit discrimination on the grounds of sexual orientation: in Canada it is an analogous ground in the Canadian Charter of Rights and Freedoms (the Charter), meaning that while statutory distinctions based on sexual orientation are not explicitly and automatically prohibited, such distinctions would be discriminatory if they impaired 'human dignity' (Hogg, 2006, p. 713); and South Africa was the first country in the world to specifically outlaw discrimination on the basis of sexual orientation in its post-apartheid constitution (Lind, 2001, p. 279).

Canada

In Canada, a series of cases that extended specific forms of spousal recognition to same-sex couples and prohibited sexual orientation discrimination (*Egan v Canada* 1995 CarswellNat 6; *Vriend v Alberta* [1998] 1 SCR 493; *M v H* [1999] 2 SCR 3; and *Little Sisters Book and Art Emporium v Canada* [2000] 2 SCR 1120) made same-sex marriage 'more or less inevitable' (Hogg, 2006, p. 713), or at least 'a logical next step' (Loosemore, 2002, p. 47; see also L'Heureux-Dubé, 2001, detailing developments in Canadian equality law regarding sexual orientation). These developments are attributed to both the functional approach to family law taken in Canada, where the courts treat unmarried different-sex couples in the same ways as married couples for many purposes, and the substantive approach taken to the equality guarantees in s. 15 of the Charter (Radbord, 2005, pp. 102–3). Joanne Radbord makes this argument through a sequence of cases from *Miron v Trudel* [1995] 2 SCR 418, where the Supreme Court of Canada held that unmarried different-sex couples must be included in the definition of spouse for the purposes of the Insurance Act 1980, to *M v H*, 'Over time, and across the country, marriage largely lost its status as a privileged marker of [legal] entitlement' (2005, p. 106; see also Lahey, 2001, pp. 237–9). As in the other jurisdictions that now recognize same-sex marriage, an incremental approach is evident: there was a conscious strategy 'to pursue incremental equality by developing the jurisprudence in relation to unmarried cohabitants, and only turning to marriage once that victory was in hand' (Cossman, 2002a, p. 236; see also Cotler, 2006, pp. 64–5).

M v H is the first case in which it was held that same-sex relationships were spousal. M and H were a cohabiting couple for 10 years and when the relationship broke down M sought spousal support from H. She was successful in arguing that the exclusion of same-sex relationships from the spousal support provisions under the Family Law Act 1990 was unconstitutional. The court held that the different treatment of same-sex and different-sex couples was based on sexual orientation and 'discriminates in a substantive sense by violating the human dignity of individuals in same-sex relationships' (per Cory and Iacobucci JJ at para. 3). There was no justification because the objectives of the Act, which were 'providing equitable resolution of economic disputes' at the end of relationships and 'alleviating the burden on the public purse', are not furthered but instead undermined by excluding same-sex couples (para. 4). It is interesting that whereas the earlier cases would have allowed same-sex couples access to rights as against employers or the state, *M v H* allows them access to rights as against each other. The consequent savings to the public purse featured prominently in the judgment:

> Providing for the equitable resolution of economic disputes when intimate relationships between financially interdependent individuals break down, and alleviating the burden on the public purse to provide for dependent spouses, are to my mind pressing and substantial objectives. These objectives promote both social justice and the dignity of individuals. (per Iacobucci J at para. 106)

As Cossman argues, this ruling is entirely consistent with a politics of privatization; expanding the scope of spousal support obligations would reduce reliance on the state for economically vulnerable ex-partners (2002a, pp. 237–8; this politics is discussed further in relation to marriage in Chapter 5). Conversely, in *Egan*, Justice Sopinka (agreeing with the majority) referred to limited public funds in holding the discriminatory treatment to be justified (at para. 104).

Following *M v H* several provinces legislatively extended some of the legal consequences of marriage to same-sex couples but they did so by creating separate registered partnership status. This led Kathleen Lahey to argue that while the courts have 'tended to extend full equality' to same-sex couples, legislatures have only extended partial equality by segregating lesbian and gay relationships and/or extending only *some* spousal rights to same-sex couples (2001, p. 238). The title given to the legislation in Ontario underlines the grudging nature of the provision: Amendments Because of the Supreme Court of Canada Decision in M v H Act 1999. It is unsurprising, then, that the courts played a key role in the process of legally recognizing same-sex marriages in Canada; same-sex marriage cases were successful despite sustained opposition from the federal government in the Courts of Appeal of British Columbia, Ontario and Québec. Although Irwin Cotler, Minister of Justice and Attorney General of Canada, has written of the later development of same-sex marriage at the federal level in Canada in positive terms of 'constructive debate' and 'respect for diversity' (2006, p. 60), the view from the litigants in the provinces was somewhat different: 'In all provinces, the applicant couples faced formidable opposition from the federal government. The government spent almost half a million dollars on expert evidence, scouring the nation, and indeed the globe, for academics opposed to equal marriage.' (Radbord, 2005, p. 115) This is not to say that all of the governments in Canada were either hostile or politically cautious as to same-sex marriage claims: the British Columbia government challenged the prohibition of same-sex marriage in court, though its petition was subsequently withdrawn following the election of a Liberal government in 2001 (Casswell, 2001, p. 235).

The first same-sex marriage case to be decided was *EGALE Canada Inc. v Canada* (Attorney General) 2001 CarswellBC 2071 in British Columbia. At first instance, the petitioners were unsuccessful. Citing *Hyde v Hyde and Woodmansee* [1866] L Rev 1 P&D 130 and *Corbett v Corbett (Otherwise Ashley)* [1971] P 83, Justice Pitfield held that the common law definition of marriage was 'a legal relationship between two persons of opposite-sex' (para. 8). Although the court had the power to change the common law, this should be done only in incremental steps and, as 'change would affect a deep-rooted social and legal institution' (para. 93), changing marriage to include same-sex couples would be 'much more than incremental' (para. 92). As such, it must be up to Parliament rather than the courts to make such a change. However, Justice Pitfield then considered whether it would be within the authority of Parliament to do this and concluded on the basis of the division of powers in the Canadian Constitution that it would not. After discussing whether the federal or provincial legislatures had jurisdiction, he concluded that, as the word 'marriage' was used in the Constitution Act 1867, its meaning was entrenched so that only a constitutional amendment could change it. I do not intend to digress into a detailed discussion of Canadian constitutional jurisprudence, other than to say that Justice Pitfield's reasoning here was unanimously rejected by the Court of Appeal, which held that the use of the word 'marriage' in the Constitution Act does not entrench its definition (at paras 69–71, per Prowse JA). In *In Re Same-Sex Marriage* 2004 CarswellNat 4422, the Supreme Court of Canada also dismissed this:

> The 'frozen concepts' reasoning runs contrary to one of the most fundamental principles of Canadian constitutional interpretation: that our Constitution is a living tree which, by way of progressive interpretation, accommodates and addresses the realities of modern life. (para. 22)

The strongest legal basis for the petitioners' claims in all of the same-sex marriage cases was the Charter. Although the petitioners in *EGALE* also claimed violation of other Charter rights (freedom of expression and association (s. 2), mobility rights (s. 6), liberty and security of the person (s. 7), and equality between males and females (s. 28)), they were only successful with regard to the claim of violation of equality under s. 15. Justice Pitfield concludes that: the common law prohibition of same-sex marriage constituted differential treatment for same-sex couples; that this difference was based on sexual orientation, an analogous ground in the Charter; and that the differential treatment discriminated against same-sex couples in a substantive sense in that (among other things):

> Canadian courts accept the fact that gays and lesbians have been disadvantaged by stereotyping and prejudice. There is a need in the gay and lesbian community to have society acknowledge the value and reality of same-sex unions. The distinction between opposite-sex and same-sex relationships in the marriage context excludes the latter from a social and legal institution of considerable importance and tends to perpetuate the stereotypical and frequently critical community view of gays and lesbians. (at para. 174, per Pitfield J)

The first instance and Court of Appeal judges in Ontario and Québec agreed with this part of Justice Pitfield's judgment, as did the British Columbia Court of Appeal (see para. 82, per Prowse J). However, unlike the subsequent judgments, Justice Pitfield went on to find this discrimination was *justified* under s. 1 of the Charter. There were two bases for this justification. The first is that:

> The Constitution, itself, expressed an intention that marriage was an issue of pressing and substantial national importance and differentiation and discrimination inherent in the fact that marriage was then, and still is, an opposite-sex relationship would be permitted. (para. 199, per Pitfield J)

The second justification refers to what Justice Pitfield considers to be the undeniable fact that marriage is the way in which 'humankind perpetuates itself in our society' (at para. 207):

> While, in the recent past, same-sex couples have been accorded many of the rights and obligations previously reserved for married couples, the one factor in respect of which there cannot be similarity is the biological reality that opposite-sex couples may, *as between themselves*, propagate the species and thereby perpetuate humankind. Same-sex couples cannot....The state

has a demonstrably genuine justification in affording recognition, preference, and precedence to the nature and character of the core social and legal arrangement by which society endures. (paras 205–7, per Pitfield J, emphasis added)

Finally, Justice Pitfield concludes that the necessity to preserve the 'opposite-sex core' of marriage 'far outweighs' the negative effect that lack of public recognition has on same-sex couples (para. 214).

The first instance cases in Ontario and Québec delivered their judgments shortly after *EGALE*, but had very different results. The Ontario Divisional Court in *Halpern v Toronto* 2002 CarswellOnt 2309 held that the common law definition of marriage violated the equality guarantees under s. 15 of the Charter and that this violation could not be justified under s. 1. Finding that the procreation justification had no rational basis (see LaForme J para. 249), the court held that:

> The restriction against same-sex marriage is an offense to the dignity of lesbians and gays because it limits the range of relationship options available to them. The result is they are denied the autonomy to choose whether they wish to marry. This in turn conveys the ominous message that they are unworthy of marriage. For those same-sex couples who do wish to marry, the impugned restriction represents a rejection of their personal aspirations and the denial of their dreams. (per LaForme J at 261)

The court gave Parliament two years to amend the definition of marriage, failing which the common law definition would automatically be amended to include same-sex couples. In Québec, the Superior Court held in *Hendricks v Québec (Procureure Générale)* 2002 CarswellQue 1890 that the provision in the Civil Code of Québec that marriage is only between a man and a woman would be declared inoperative, though this declaration was also suspended for two years. In the meantime, all three cases were appealed to their respective Courts of Appeal.

The British Columbia Court of Appeal unanimously rejected the procreation justification for different-sex-only marriage (*EGALE Canada Inc. v Canada (Attorney General)* 2003 CarswellBC 1006). Prowse JA held that procreation had been displaced as the central purpose of marriage within an evolving view of the institution and its role in society:

> It is on this basis that I find that procreation (including the rearing of children), resulting from sexual intercourse between a husband and a wife, can no longer be regarded as a sufficiently pressing and substantial objective... (para. 124)

Furthermore, she agrees with the view of LaForme J in Halpern (2002) that there is no rational connection between the importance of procreation and restricting marriage to heterosexual relationships (paras 126–7). As such, procreation arguments could not justify the breach of s. 15 rights and the Court of Appeal declared the common law bar against same-sex marriage to be of no force or effect on the grounds that it unjustifiably violates the equality guarantee under s. 15 of the Charter. The court reformulated the common law definition of marriage to mean 'the lawful union of two persons to the exclusion of all others' (paras 158–9). However, like the first instance decisions in Ontario and Québec (above), relief was suspended, 'solely to give the federal and provincial governments time to review and revise legislation to bring it into accord with this decision' (para. 161).

The case in the Ontario Court of Appeal, *Halpern v Toronto* 2003 CarswellOnt 2159, was decided just one month after the *EGALE* appeal in British Columbia. Its facts, reasoning and outcome are similar but there are two differences that are worth noting: one in relation to the facts, the other in relation to the remedy. The facts of this case differ slightly in that one of the *Halpern* parties was the Metropolitan Community Church of Toronto (MCCT), using a religious freedom argument *for* same-sex marriage. The MCCT had married two same-sex couples after publishing the banns of marriage but the city's registrar refused to register the marriages on the grounds of an alleged federal prohibition against same-sex marriage (paras 13–14). Though the first instance court had found that the couples' equality rights under s. 15 of the Charter were unjustifiably infringed, it had not accepted the MCCT's argument that its freedom of religion had been infringed (para. 16). The Court of Appeal also rejected this argument:

> In our view, this case does not engage religious rights and freedoms. Marriage is a legal institution, as well as a religious and social institution. This case is solely about the legal institution of marriage. It is not about the religious validity or invalidity of various forms of marriage. We do not view this case as, in any way, dealing or interfering with the religious institution of marriage. (para. 53)

The second difference was in relation to the remedy. While the Ontario Court of Appeal also reformulated the common law definition of marriage to include same-sex couples, rather than suspending the remedy it gave it immediate effect:

> There is no evidence before this court that a declaration of invalidity without a period of suspension will pose any harm to the public, threaten the rule of law, or deny anyone the benefit of

legal recognition of their marriage. We observe that there was no
evidence before us that the reformulated definition of marriage
will require the volume of legislative reform that followed...*M v H*.
In our view, an immediate declaration will simply ensure that
opposite-sex couples and same-sex couples immediately receive
equal treatment in law in accordance with s. 15(1) of the *Charter*.
(at para. 153)

As a result, Ontario became the first province to legally celebrate same-sex
marriages. The litigants in *EGALE* returned to the British Columbia Court
of Appeal to request that the suspension be lifted on the grounds that marriages were already taking place in Ontario (*EGALE Canada Inc. v Canada
(Attorney General)* 2003 CarswellBC 1659). As neither the federal nor provincial governments intended to appeal, nor did they oppose the request,
the court assumed that a suspension of remedy was not necessary for any
consequential amendments that might be required to various laws (para. 6).
Furthermore, any delay would result in unequal application of the law
between Ontario and British Columbia (at para. 7). As such, the suspension
was lifted in British Columbia.

The Canadian federal government decided not to appeal these decisions
and instead proposed legislation that would define marriage in a gender-neutral way for the whole of Canada (Hogg, 2006, p. 716).[7] The Proposal For
an Act Respecting Certain Aspects of Legal Capacity for Marriage for Civil
Purposes (Proposed Act) would provide that 'Marriage, for civil purposes, is
the lawful union of two persons to the exclusion of all others' (s. 1) and that
religious officials may 'refuse to perform marriages that are not in accordance
with their religious beliefs' (s. 2). In 2003, amid heated political debate, a
Standing Committee held hearings on the proposal: 'No fewer than 362 briefs
were presented and 444 witnesses appeared....Of those witnesses, 265 supported same-sex marriage, 163 opposed it, and 16 took no position.' (Young
and Boyd, 2006, p. 226) It was perhaps these debates that encouraged the
legislature to refer questions about the Proposed Act to the Supreme Court of
Canada (SCC) for advice on its constitutionality in *In Re Same-Sex Marriage*.
The Governor in Council asked the court three questions: first, whether
the proposed legislation was 'within the exclusive legal authority of the
Parliament of Canada'; second, if so, whether it is consistent with the Charter
to extend the capacity to marry to same-sex couples; third, whether religious officials are protected under the Charter's freedom of religion provision
from having to perform same-sex marriages if it is contrary to their beliefs

---

7 This decision was taken after a standing committee had recommended this action with a
   margin of only one vote (Young and Boyd, 2006, p. 235).

(para. 2). It subsequently added a fourth question: whether the opposite-sex requirement of marriage was consistent with the Charter (para. 3).

The first question addresses the issue of the division of powers between the federal and provincial legislatures with regard to marriage that was raised in the cases. Parliament has competence with regard to capacity to marry, whereas the provinces have competence in relation to the performance of marriage ceremonies (para. 18). The SCC concluded that 'in pith and substance, s1 of the Proposed Act pertains to legal capacity for civil marriage' and therefore s. 1 was within the exclusive legal authority of Parliament (para. 19). However, s. 2 was not because it concerned the solemnization requirements, which are allocated to the provinces (para. 37). The second question asks whether recognizing same-sex marriages would violate the Charter on the basis of discriminating against religious groups that do not recognize the right of same-sex couples to marry religiously and opposite-sex couples (para. 45). The court dismissed this claim on the basis that the Proposed Act is a response to findings from several courts that to *not* allow same-sex marriage is a violation of the Charter (para. 41). Furthermore, 'the mere recognition of the equality rights of one group cannot, in itself, constitute a violation of the rights of another' (para. 46).

In response to the third question, the court concluded that the Proposed Act was concerned with civil marriages (para. 55) but that any 'state compulsion on religious officials to perform same-sex marriages contrary to their religious beliefs would violate...the Charter' (para. 58). The court refused to answer the fourth question on the grounds that it would be 'unwise and inappropriate' to do so (para. 64) because:

> The government has stated its intention to address the issue of same-sex marriage by introducing legislation regardless of our opinion on this question. The parties to previous litigation have relied upon the finality of their judgments and have acquired rights which in our view are entitled to protection. Finally, an answer to Question 4 would not only fail to ensure uniformity of the law, but might undermine it. These circumstances, weighed against the hypothetical benefit Parliament might derive from an answer, convince the Court that it should exercise its discretion not to answer Question 4. (para. 71)

Shortly after the reference was sent to the SCC, in *Hendrick v Québec* (Procureure Générale) 2004 CarswellQue 1927, the Québec Court of Appeal rejected an application to appeal from the Catholic Civil Rights League on the grounds that it did not have standing absent a 'genuine interest' (para. 39) and that the issue was moot since the refusal of the Attorney General to appeal had 'created a new legal context' (para. 38). The court also noted that the reference to the SCC had commenced and had a broader scope than this appeal, with more interveners. This attempt to appeal by an organization that was not party to the first instance decision (though had been an intervener in it), and after same-sex marriages were already taking place in other provinces and the federal government had sent a reference on the issue to the SCC, perhaps attests to the controversy that the issue of same-sex marriages was causing. Though vehement opposition also came from Canadian organizations, the American Christian right attempted to influence the debates through a Canadian chapter of Focus on the Family and the US Knights of Columbus, which paid for newspaper adverts and postcards opposing same-sex marriage (International Lesbian and Gay Association, 2005, p. 21).

The federal Parliament passed the Civil Marriage Act, which provides a uniform gender-neutral definition of marriage across Canada, in 2005. Conservative politicians continued to challenge same-sex marriage until December 2006, when a final motion in Parliament against same-sex marriage was defeated by 123 votes in favour to 175 against; the leader of the Conservative Party, which proposed the motion, has said that he will not reopen the issue again (Bourassa and Varnell, 2006).

South Africa

Beth Goldblatt notes that an incremental, 'step-by-step' approach was also taken in South Africa, beginning with challenges to sodomy statutes and eventually culminating in same-sex marriage (2006, p. 265). Craig Lind describes the political strategy towards relationship recognition in South Africa as subtle because of a fear that it would not receive public support:

> Instead of pursuing marriage and thereby acquiring all at once, the Coalition set out to acquire so many of the attributes of marriage for lesbians and gay men that the acquisition of marriage itself would ultimately be rendered irrelevant, or would be easy (since it would involve only a slight material gain for lesbians and gay men beyond what they had already achieved by that stage). (2001, p. 284)

By the time the Constitutional Court heard the case of *Fourie (Minister of Home Affairs and Director-General of Home Affairs v Fourie and Bonthuys* [2005] ZACC 19, below), same-sex partners could be registered as each other's dependents, the sodomy law had been successfully challenged, a same-sex partner of a South African citizen could apply for permanent residency, a same-sex partner could receive spousal pension benefits, and both partners could be registered as parents of adopted children (Goldblatt, 2006, pp. 265–6). These gains were far from comprehensive when compared to marriage so the acquisition of marriage was not yet 'irrelevant' in terms of legal consequences but they clearly had paved the way to some extent (see also De Vos, 2007b).

In *Fourie*, Sachs J (writing for the unanimous court) explicitly referred to the five consecutive decisions that had resulted in these gains as highlighting the evolving family forms in South African society and the inappropriateness of entrenching 'any particular form as the only socially and legally acceptable one' (at para. 59). This decision is made with South Africa's history clearly in mind. Noting the long history of 'marginalisation and persecution' of lesbians and gay men and the exclusion of same-sex couples from any comprehensive family law regulation, Sachs J states:

> our Constitution represents a radical rupture with a past based on intolerance and exclusion, and the movement forward to the acceptance of the need to develop a society based on equality and respect by all for all. Small gestures in favour of equality, however meaningful, are not enough. (at para. 59)

The Constitutional Court held that excluding same-sex couples from marriage was an unjustifiable violation of the rights of equal protection and non-discrimination under s. 9 of the constitution and the right to dignity under s. 10 (para. 114). The judgment of the court strongly emphasized the need for recognition of same-sex relationships, demonstrating that it was as concerned with the symbolic aspects of (exclusion from) marriage as with the practical effect. For example:

> The exclusion of same-sex couples from the benefits and responsibilities of marriage...represents a harsh if oblique statement by the law that same-sex couples are outsiders, and that their need for affirmation and protection of their intimate relations as human beings is somehow less than that of heterosexual couples. It reinforces the wounding notion that they are to be treated as biological oddities, as failed or lapsed human beings who do not fit into normal society, and, as such, do not qualify for the full moral concern and respect that our Constitution seeks to secure for everyone. It signifies that their capacity for love, commitment and accepting responsibility is by definition less worthy of regard than that of heterosexual couples. (per Sachs J at para. 71)

However, rather than 'reading in' same-sex couples to the marriage law, the Constitutional Court gave the legislature one year to remedy the defect via legislation (para. 156). If Parliament failed to do so, the words 'or spouse' will automatically be read into the Marriage Act 1961 (para. 161). The only dissent in this case involved the remedy, with O'Regan J arguing that the court should both read in the words 'or spouse' to the Marriage Act and develop the common law definition of marriage to include same-sex couples rather than waiting for the legislature (para. 169).

Despite this strong unanimous decision in the Constitutional Court, there was an organized, though unsuccessful, opposition lobbying for a constitutional amendment which would have read: 'The constitution shall be interpreted to mean that a marriage is the voluntary union between a man and a woman only' (Constitutional Marriage Amendment Campaign, 2006). The Constitutional Marriage Amendment Campaign argued that:

> This ruling undermines respect for marriage, confuses the line between moral and immoral sexual conduct, and makes moral people more vulnerable to lawsuits from homosexual activists. By damaging respect for marriage, it will reduce the security of mothers and children to have a caring father at home. In this way the governments social upliftment goals would be undermined. With homosexuality equated with marriage, many more youth may be seduced into this unhealthy lifestyle. Many trapped in it may lose hope of overcoming this deviancy and returning to a straight lifestyle. The judges have made an error and been seriously disrespectful to God in declaring God's creation design for marriage as discriminatory.[8]

Although the court had very strongly directed the legislature that a separate provision would not suffice, analogizing this to the unacceptability of racial apartheid, the first option that the legislature considered was civil partnership (De Vos, 2007b). Same-sex marriage activists then used the *Fourie* judgment and drew on the history of racial discrimination and the symbolism of marriage to oppose this:

> By pointing out that the concept of marriage has a profound symbolic, emotional and political power in our culture that gives it a special status, it became easier to show that by refusing same-sex couples the right to enter into an institution called 'marriage', the Bill would deprive same-sex couples of the right to access the status associated with the term 'marriage' ... [We argued that this] is extremely insulting and humiliating towards those of us who

---

8 James Dobson, the American preacher, has also written an open letter supporting South African (Christian) opponents of same-sex marriage and offering 'eight powerful arguments that you can use against this untested and unprecedented social experiment' (Dobson, 2003).

might want to marry a member of our own sex...(De Vos, 2007b, p. 459)

However, while the end result is marriage rather than civil partnership, same-sex marriage is administered under the new Civil Union Act 2006 rather than the Marriage Act 1961, which remains heterosexual (International Lesbian and Gay Association, 2006). While only different-sex couples may be married under the Marriage Act, the Civil Union Act is open to both same-sex and different-sex couples. The Civil Union Act is different from the Marriage Act in two ways: first, it gives couples the option of whether they wish their union to be a marriage or a civil partnership (De Vos, 2007b, p. 461); second, the Civil Union Act allows officers to refuse to marry same-sex couples on grounds of belief (De Vos, 2007b, p. 462; Mhlambiso, 2007). This raises interesting questions, which I return to in Chapter 4, of how far a legislatively separate marriage provision, yet, nevertheless, a marriage provision, may be successful in satisfying symbolic recognition demands.

Conclusion

The most striking theme that arises across the jurisdictions is the almost universal backlash against same-sex marriage. The inevitability and strength of the backlash does perhaps influence the types of argument that were made for same-sex marriage.[9] This can be seen in both the emphasis on formal legal (usually constitutional) provisions and the ways in which same-sex couples were argued to fit within rather than challenge the marriage model, particularly its ideologies (see Chapter 1).

The arguments made by both advocates and opponents of same-sex marriage in these cases reflect the marriage model. However, the ideologies of marriage invoked by the opponents of same-sex marriage are, I suggest, inaccurate in relation to the claims that (heterosexual, biological) procreation is central to marriage. These interpretations of marriage go against the contemporary judicial understandings that I identified in Chapter 1. However, the litigants did not always reject the premise of this claim by arguing that procreation is not central to contemporary understandings of marriage. Instead, they attempted (generally successfully) to overcome the issue by demonstrating that same-sex couples also have children and perform the same societal functions as heterosexual couples. For example, Joanne Radbord, the co-counsel in the Ontario same-sex marriage case, refers to her own pregnancy as challenging

---

9 It also served to silence dissent on the marriage issue within the lesbian and gay communities in Canada (and probably elsewhere): 'It became progressively more difficult to argue against same-sex relationship recognition when the law's reasons for doing so were so profoundly conservative.' (Cossman, 2002a, pp. 230–1)

this conservative discourse in that case: 'the lesbian lawyer said "we" want to marry with a massive pregnant belly, my body exploding the government's lie that we cannot procreate' (2005, p. 99).

The sameness of same-sex couples to heterosexual couples, then, is a key theme that implicitly or explicitly underpinned the constitutional claims that were being made on the basis of formal equality. Though they varied depending on the scope and language of the constitutional provisions, these claims primarily focused on access to the legal consequences of marriage on the basis of equal protection and non-discrimination; and the equality and dignity of same-sex couples through marriage recognition. In Vermont, a focus on access to the legal consequences of marriage resulted in the creation of a separate provision. However, the later cases in Massachusetts, California, Connecticut, Iowa, Canada and South Africa placed much more emphasis on arguments about the symbolism of recognition through marriage.

There were also arguments made, largely in response to conservative opposition, that same-sex marriage would support the institution as a whole. Furthermore, preservation of limited state resources was both an argument *against* same-sex marriage that had to be countered with equality discourse (in *Goodridge*) and an argument *for* relationship recognition in that it would encourage partners to take financial responsibility for each other (in *M v H*). I consider these issues further in the remaining chapters, focusing first on these themes of sameness, legal consequences and recognition, along with academic and activist arguments for same-sex marriage in Chapter 4. In Chapters 5 and 6, I then explore and develop the feminist critiques of marriage in this context.

Part II

4
Arguments for Same-Sex Marriage

Introduction

As illustrated in the previous two chapters, the case for same-sex marriage has been increasingly successful over the last decade with the introduction of legal marriage for same-sex couples in some jurisdictions and the creation of marriage-like provisions, such as civil partnerships, in many more. In this chapter, I classify and assess the merits of the arguments in favour of same-sex marriage. I contend that the strongest factors from a feminist perspective are those that emphasize the need for positive state recognition of same-sex relationships, particularly when marriage is framed as a demand for positive recognition of *difference* rather than sameness. This is because recognition of difference within marriage might provide opportunities to transform the institution by challenging inequalities within it, or even transgress (or queer) it. Although arguments are based on conservative family values rhetoric, access to the legal consequences of marriage and formal equality are strong in terms of their appeal to mainstream audiences (and, as demonstrated in the previous chapter, probably the most successful type of argument) but are the weakest from a feminist perspective because they simply reinforce the existing marriage model.

Although the primary focus of this chapter is on the views that have been expressed in favour of *marriage*, I also draw on examples of the discourses surrounding marriage-like provisions, particularly the UK's Civil Partnership Act 2004. I do this because, as I demonstrated in Chapter 2, civil partnerships follow the marriage model. Furthermore, the points made in favour of these provisions (particularly those that are very closely modelled on marriage) are generally the same as those that are made for marriage, notwithstanding that those advocating for separate marriage-like provisions tend to additionally put forward reasons that emphasize their separateness in order to forestall claims that it will undermine heterosexual marriage. For example:

> [The legal protections of the Civil Partnership Act] will come without undermining, in any way, the institution of marriage. Civil partnership is a separate legal structure, designed for same-sex couples. There is no overlap in any way with marriage. (Stonewall, 2004a, p. 2)

As noted in the previous chapter, the key arguments deployed by the litigants in the same-sex marriage cases were the practical need for access to the legal consequences of marriage and the symbolism of such recognition from the state. These were sometimes combined with more conservative arguments claiming that same-sex marriage will strengthen the institution and promote stable relationships. These arguments are also the most prominent amongst mainstream activists and academic supporters of same-sex marriage. Additionally, however, academics and (to a lesser extent) activists have also been engaged in debate within the gay and lesbian communities. Some arguments for same-sex marriage that have been made in this context move away from formal equality and sameness to emphasize difference and diversity. The reasoning put forward tends to be more equivocal about the institution of marriage but nevertheless claims that access to it is important for same-sex couples.

Civilizing gays and strengthening marriage: the conservative case for same-sex marriage

Conservative discourses are most frequently deployed in (often homophobic) opposition to same-sex marriage. Conservatives argue that marriage needs to be protected from gays and lesbians, 'who seek to force their agenda upon the vast majority...who reject the homosexual lifestyle' (Helms, 1997, pp. 21–2). For example, Robert Knight draws not only on the familiar right-wing arguments of marriage as the site of heterosexual, biological reproduction and the circular logic of 'marriage should continue to be heterosexual because it always has been' (a claim disputed by scholars including Eskridge, 1996; and Bonthuys, 2007) but also refers to gay male promiscuity. He argues that: 'The very act of obtaining recognition for same-sex relationships on a par with marriage would transform the notion of "family" entirely.' (Knight, 1994, p. 110) Such discourses appear to have the most support in the United States, but are also found in other jurisdictions.

What I call the conservative arguments for same-sex marriage respond to these homophobic arguments on their own terms, employing two strands of argument. The first is that marriage is necessary to 'civilize' gay men (Eskridge,

1996) in that it will discourage 'promiscuity' and encourage 'responsible' behaviour. Lesbians are almost entirely invisible in this discourse (this is not unusual, see also Herman's analysis of Christian Right discourse: 1997, p. 92). The second is that it will strengthen marriage and 'family values'.

There are a number of prominent examples of the former approach, particularly from the US context. For example, William Eskridge argues that:

> It should not have required the AIDS epidemic to alert us to the problems of sexual promiscuity and to the advantages of committed relationships. ... To the extent that males in our culture have been more sexually venture-some (more in need of civilizing), same-sex marriage could be a particularly useful commitment device for gay and bisexual men. ... Whatever its source, sexual variety has not been liberating to gay men. In addition to disease costs, promiscuity has encouraged a cult of youth worship and has contributed to the stereotype of homosexuals as people who lack a serious approach to life. ... A self-reflective gay community ought to embrace marriage for its potentially civilizing effect on young and old alike. (Eskridge, 1996, pp. 9–10; see also Rauch, 2004a, pp. 66–7)

Similarly, in response to claims that same-sex marriage would remove the principled grounds on which the law denies polygamous marriages (see Arkes, 1996; Bennett, 1996), Andrew Sullivan argues that rather than opening up possibilities for multiple-partner relationships, same-sex marriage would actually act as an incentive for 'responsible behaviour, monogamy, fidelity' (1996, p. 280). Although the more hard-edged family values rhetoric of the American conservatives is largely absent from UK mainstream political discourse on civil partnerships, a more liberal version of this argument is framed in terms of formal equality and *rewarding* the commitment that those in same-sex relationships have made to each other by giving them the same legal rights. However, while the UK Civil Partnership Act 2004 was publicly framed in these terms by Stonewall and the government, Carl Stychin suggests that similar principles underlie New Labour's Third Way rhetoric in that the Civil Partnership Act 2004 provides 'a disincentive for "irresponsible" behaviour ... [such as] promiscuous sex, relationship breakdown at will, and the selfishness of living alone' (Stychin, 2006b, p. 30). This discourse imbues marriage with the capacity to control the sexual behaviour of gay men and assumes that this would be a positive outcome.

The second strand of the conservative case for same-sex marriage attempts to appeal to family values rhetoric as a reason for same-sex marriage. This is linked to the arguments above, bringing 'uncivilized' gay men back to 'traditional' family values. However, this discourse argues that marriage is not only 'good for gay people' (Eskridge, 1996, p. 8), it is also good for the institution of marriage itself. For example, in response to the call for a constitutional amendment in the United States that would 'define and protect' marriage as heterosexual (Bush, 2004b, p. 64), Jonathan Rauch argues that:

> Children, parents, childless adults, and marriage itself are all better off when society sends a clear and unequivocal message that sex, love, and marriage go together. Same-sex marriage affirms that message. It says that...marriage is the ultimate commitment for all: the destination to which loving relationships naturally aspire...And marriage, like voting and other core civic responsibilities, is strongest when universal. It best serves the interests of all when all are eligible and welcome to serve...(2004b, pp. 65–6)

This argument is, perhaps more than the others, a strategic one. It pre-empts (or maybe responds to) the right-wing claim that same-sex marriage would undermine the institution of marriage by responding that recognizing (and thus encouraging) committed, stable relationships strengthens the institution as a whole. This approach is evident in the strategies of gay and lesbian advocacy organizations. For example, in the UK, 'civil partnership arguably strengthens marriage, by recognising and valuing the importance of committed relationships to society generally' (Stonewall, 2004a, p. 2). Groups advocating for same-sex marriage in the US have particularly emphasized these arguments in the public debates. For example, the Human Rights Campaign published an advert that appeared in the *Boston Globe* and the *New York Times* on 4 December 2003, which pictured a married lesbian couple and their daughter with the text: 'When Americans like the Goodridges have access to marriage, it makes their family stronger and more stable. And it makes society stronger and more stable as well.' The headline was: 'A marriage license: Good for this family. Good for *every* family.' Furthermore, in their publication *Why Marriage Matters*, Gay and Lesbian Advocates and Defenders (GLAD) (2006) stated that:

> Far from undermining marriage, the struggle for full equality for gay and lesbian couples is *an acknowledgement of the importance marriage has in society and the power it has over all our lives.* Increasing access to marriage for adults in committed relationships will strengthen the institution, not weaken it...(emphasis added)

While these conservative discourses constitute a strong argument for same-sex marriage in terms of their appeal to conservative and mainstream politics and their persuasiveness to the courts,[1] they are the weakest from a feminist

---

1 See, for example, *In Re Marriage Cases* 43 Cal 4th 757, at 817, per George CJ: 'Although persons can have children and raise them outside of marriage, the institution of civil marriage

perspective. In fact, as I argue in the next two chapters, the resort to (among others) family values, responsibility and anti-promiscuity discourses at best posits same-sex marriage as being the same (and having the same problems from feminist and queer perspectives) as heterosexual marriage. For example, Jonathan Rauch (1997, p. 288), describing marriage as 'society's most stabilizing, civilizing institution', claims that 'I don't ask to break the rules that we all depend on. I just want to be allowed to follow them.' These conservative arguments for same-sex marriage suggest that lesbians and gay men are different from heterosexuals only (or largely) because they are unable to marry. They rest on the premise that ideally they *should* be the same as heterosexuals but will not be until marriage is available. At worst, they suggest that same-sex marriage would strengthen the institution by making it universal: every responsible citizen, gay or straight, could (and would be expected to) marry. Additionally, there would no longer be a reason to allow legal reform that does erode the institution by recognizing relationships outside of marriage:

> Allowing *and expecting* marriage for all Americans would show respect for the welfare and equality of all Americans, and it would *protect the institution of marriage from the proliferation of alternatives* (civil unions, domestic-partner benefits, and socially approved cohabitation) that a continued ban on same-sex marriage will inevitably bring – is, in fact bringing already. (Rauch, 2004b, pp. 66–7, emphasis added)

These are anti-feminist arguments and so do not have any merit from feminist perspectives.

Snakes and ladders: access to the legal benefits of marriage

> The need for the [Civil Partnership] Bill is obvious to any one who has seen and felt some of the heart-rending injustices that can occur when a committed gay couple are denied the basic rights that a married heterosexual couple would take for granted. (Alan Duncan (Con.) HC Hansard, 12 October 2004, c. 183)

Access to legal benefits is one of the primary mainstream arguments for same-sex marriage and its combination of pragmatism and appeals to formal equality and justice have meant that it is frequently successful in gaining some form of legal recognition for same-sex couples. Legal benefits arguments

---

affords official government sanction and sanctuary to the family unit, granting a parent the ability to afford his or her children the substantial benefits that flow from a stable two-parent family environment...'

are generally central to claims for same-sex marriage in most jurisdictions, though the emphasis of the arguments concerning legal benefits does shift according to national context. For example, while the primary concerns of American marriage advocates are next-of-kin rights and access to the federal benefits of marriage (see Human Rights Campaign, 2007a), in the UK context, access to spousal pensions and inheritance tax exemptions featured most heavily in the Civil Partnership Bill 2004 debates:

> Many same-sex partners face significant problems in their day-to-day lives because there is currently no mechanism to secure legal recognition of their relationships.... We think the Bill, if passed, will remedy many of the injustices that committed same-sex couples face in a number of areas. These include inheritance, pensions, next of kin, and the right to make key medical decisions. (Stonewall, 2004a, p. 2)

The legal consequences of marriage can be grouped into two categories: *economic*, by which I mean those that have financial implications for either party or the couple as a whole, such as tax exemptions and provisions relating to the welfare state and pension systems; and *status* benefits, that is those provisions that ascribe a special status to spouses, giving them legal protections that are either not given to or take priority over those of other family members and friends. I will begin by considering and problematizing the discussions around economic benefits before considering the status benefits and the extent to which claims of access to legal benefits in general might provide a strong argument for same-sex marriage.

Economic benefits

Economic benefits, although they also contain responsibilities such as spousal maintenance, usually focus on tax exemptions. For example, in the US the following list of reasons why same-sex couples need marriage is heavily dominated by tax concerns:

> [Same-sex couples] receive no Social Security survivor benefits upon the death of a partner, despite paying payroll taxes. They must pay federal income taxes on their employer's contributions toward their domestic partner's health insurance, while married employees do not have to pay such taxes for their spouses. They must pay all estate taxes when a partner dies. They often pay significant tax penalties when they inherit a 401(k) [a retirement savings plan] from their partner. They are denied family leave under the Family and Medical Leave Act. All American families deserve these crucial protections. (Human Rights Campaign, 2007a)

Similarly, inheritance tax, along with access to survivor pensions, dominated the civil partnership debates in the UK. For example, in its parliamentary briefing, Stonewall recounts Rex's story:

> Rex is 76. His partner, John, died after they had spent 45 years together. Their house was in both names and John left everything to Rex in his will. Rex faced a huge tax bill in order to be able to stay in his own home. He also lost John's pension. Had he married a woman for just one day, no tax would have been payable and Rex would have had a survivor pension. (Stonewall, 2004c, p. 2)

These situations are clearly unjust when viewed in isolation and compared with different-sex couples, particularly when there is a risk that elderly people may lose their homes. However, the other side of the economic rights coin are the economic responsibilities:

> Government policy-makers, of course, knew full well that there were snakes as well as ladders involved in applying the same legal rules to same sex couples as were applied to opposite sex couples. So too did those in the lesbian and gay community [sic] who were campaigning for the change. (per Baroness Hale, *Secretary of State for Work and Pensions v M* [2006] UKHL 11 at para. 101)

Baroness Hale refers to 'snakes as well as ladders', yet in the claims for same-sex marriage there is little acknowledgment of the snakes; the financial responsibilities of marriage are rarely mentioned, except in the context of presenting reasons *for* same-sex marriage that would appeal to fiscal conservatives in saving the state welfare system money:

> The taxpayer would actually save money in the area of benefit and tax credit payments. Same-sex partners currently claim benefits as two individuals, meaning that they will receive more money than if their needs had been assessed as a couple. This Bill will treat same-sex couples in the same way as heterosexual couples. (Stonewall, 2004c, p. 4)

Stonewall emphasizes that same-sex couples should be advantaged and disadvantaged in exactly the same ways as similarly situated heterosexuals. For example, in relation to income-related benefits: 'We support the proposal that registered partners should be liable to maintain each other in the same way as married couples.' (2003, p. 5); and in relation to taxation: 'All other aspects of the tax system which deal with the concept of spouses should be extended to registered partners.' (2003, p. 8) This is, perhaps, a strategic (and necessary) concession, particularly appealing to the New Labour government's emphasis on linking rights with responsibilities (Stychin, 2006b, p. 26). For example:

> It is important to recognize that these rights and responsibilities come together as a package – it would not be appropriate to give registered partners rights in some areas but not others, unless there was a good reason, or to pick and choose rights without the attendant responsibilities. (Women and Equality Unit, 2003a, p. 30)

However, the provision must be read in the context of its wider class-based and gendered consequences. While there are some non-economic provisions, in terms of its economic consequences the Civil Partnership Act 2004 will have a differential impact depending on the income and assets of the partners concerned, particularly where one or both of them are claiming state benefits. Higher-income lesbians and gays will primarily encounter ladders in the form of the tax breaks they were previously excluded from (unless/until their relationship ends and they become liable for, among others, spousal support and pension-sharing in the same way as divorced heterosexuals), while those who are claiming state income benefits will immediately be bitten by snakes, seeing their income reduced, *whether or not they choose to register their relationship* (Civil Partnership Act 2004, Sch. 24). This has also been the case in relation to marriage and marriage-like provisions in other jurisdictions. For example, in the Canadian context, Boyd and Young (2003, p. 774) note that, as a result of being treated as spouses (again, even where they do not marry), those with lower incomes are likely to see a reduction in their income, while those with higher incomes are likely to be advantaged by paying less tax through being jointly assessed under the Income Tax Act 1985.

Therefore, where 'snakes' are acknowledged by same-sex marriage advocates (and often they are de-emphasized), the discourse of accepting responsibilities along with rights obscures the gendered and classed differential impact of these responsibilities (see also Boyd, 2004, p. 215). Priya Kandaswamy also argues in the US context that these discourses are racialized in that property rights, rooted in racial domination, primarily benefit white Americans and that 'social rights' (such as insurance programmes) are 'material manifestations of white privilege' (2007, p. 9). Thus:

> the politics of gay marriage is more materially entangled in the project of racialized state austerity than it would at first seem. Nowhere is this more apparent than in an examination of the benefits gay and lesbian couples seek to obtain through marriage, benefits that are perhaps better understood as privileges of a racially stratified welfare state. (2007, p. 7)

It could be argued that same-sex marriage would help lower-earning individuals within a same-sex relationship through requiring spousal maintenance during the relationship and division of assets via a court process on relationship breakdown. Christopher Carrington recounts one story that illustrates the vulnerability of those providing a 'housewife' role in same-sex relationships. Henry and Joe had been together for 14 years, with Joe as primary wage-earner and Henry doing most of the domestic labour. Their home was financed by Joe and Henry did not have any savings or pension scheme of his own. When the relationship ended, 'Henry had invested his energy, his labor, and his time into creating a family for Joe and himself, and now he had little or nothing to show for that effort.' (1999, p. 209) This might provide a strong argument for same-sex marriage but Carrington argues *against* it on the basis that legal marriage 'would not reduce the economic risks involved in pursuing domesticity' (1999, p. 222). He argues instead that:

> In fact, legal marriage might well encourage caregiving individuals to take those risks, to invest more in domestic life without providing substantive resources (time and/or money) to create that domestic life. (ibid.)

The problem with relying on spousal support to create parity at the end of a relationship is that it is dependent on there being substantial assets. Carrington argues that many couples would end a marriage with debt rather than assets and not enough resources to compensate a partner who focused on domestic work rather than a career (1999, p. 221).

As this example illustrates, the 'responsibilities' of marriage have implications in terms of privatizing care and dependency within the family (see, for example, Boyd, 1997; Cossman and Fudge, 2002; Fineman, 2004). These issues are central to the socialist feminist critiques of marriage and I return to them in Chapter 5.

Status benefits

In contrast to economic benefits of marriage, status benefits are much more difficult (though not impossible) to argue against on the grounds of gendered and classed differential impact. Status benefits give spouses a status in relation to each other above that of other family members and friends. Examples include decision-making power when a spouse is incapacitated, immunity from being required to give evidence against a spouse, and the right to register a spouse's death. Interestingly, the two status examples given by Stonewall in the quote at the beginning of this section, next of kin and the right to make key medical decisions, are much more directly relevant in the US context, where these are key issues due to the different legal arrangements in relation to medical decision-making and next-of-kin status, than in the UK. Rosemary Auchmuty notes that there is no such thing as a legal next of kin in UK law, nor does anybody have a right to make 'key medical decisions' on behalf of their spouse (2004, p. 114).[2]

However, the underlying argument is that the status of marriage is a universally understood and powerful symbol in signifying the importance of a relationship so that, for example, when a partner is in hospital, medical staff should give a same-sex spouse the same courtesies as they do a different-sex spouse. Here, same-sex marriage is seen as a way to tackle bad practice, rather than discriminatory law: it is hoped that same-sex marriage would dull the edges of homophobia in such situations in that a same-sex spouse could not be ignored in favour of a biological family member. The spectre of the long-lost, homophobic relative re-emerging to assert priority over a long-term partner when a lesbian or gay man is ill or dies is frequently present in same-sex marriage advocacy, particularly (though not exclusively) in the US (see, for example, Buseck, 2004, p. 497). In the UK, these themes were also present in the campaign for civil partnerships. For example, Stonewall highlighted the 'real problems' experienced by same-sex couples, 'both in their day-to-day lives and also at times of great stress' due to the lack of legal recognition, telling the following story at the beginning of their response to the government's consultation paper:

> My partner was knocked over by a car and rushed to hospital. When I went to be by his side, I found the hospital was under no obligation to let me see or talk to my partner. They didn't ask my view on his treatment and said that if anything happened, they would only want to talk to his 'legal' next of kin, a sister who lived on the other side of the world and who he has not seen in over 15 years. (Stonewall, 2003, p. 2)

Such stories are compelling and even those who view marriage as a deeply problematic institution would be sympathetic to these types of cases and acknowledge that these *are* real problems. However, the question of whether access to legal benefits is sufficiently important to justify same-sex marriage despite wider problems with the institution assumes that same-sex marriage is the only possible way to access the legal consequences of marriage, whereas many feminists would argue that this is not the case (see Auchmuty, 2004, p. 114). For example, in contrast to the marriage advocates cited above, Paula Ettelbrick refers to the Sharon Kowalski/Karen Thompson case (*In Re*

---

2 That these arguments were used by Stonewall perhaps indicates the extent to which UK organizations were influenced by arguments from the US.

Guardianship of Kowalski 478 NW 2d 790 (Minn Ct App 1991)),[3] in arguing that legal provisions should be 'decoupled' from marriage:

> Legal marriage would probably not have saved Karen from the years of expensive and debilitating legal battle she fought to retain contact with Sharon. Karen and Sharon were desperately closeted.... They certainly would not have risked the public declaration required by marriage. Yet, regardless of whether they could or would have married, their relationship should have been accorded greater respect, and Sharon's desire to retain contact with Karen should have been inferred. (1996, p. 125)

Symbolic recognition[4]

Symbolic recognition arguments treat marriage as both an end in itself and a means to an end. It is argued that same-sex marriage is necessary against a background of 'historic' homophobia on the part of the state and discrimination against lesbians and gay men. It would both remove the negative symbolism of the absence of same-sex marriage and make a positive statement about the equal worth of same-sex relationships and heterosexual marriages. Additionally, it is a means to an end in that it is also argued that it would provide social support for same-sex relationships in creating what I will refer to as secondary recognition from (among others) families of origin and employers. I end this section by returning to the South African 'separate but same' marriage provision to problematize some of the assumptions made in recognition arguments.

From condemnation to celebration: the symbolism of state recognition

In the UK context, Celia Kitzinger and Sue Wilkinson sought marriage recognition both as a way of gaining protection from a 'previously' homophobic state and also as a signal of wider social acceptance:

> The key meaning of our marriage, for us, is that our continuing (and reaffirmed) centrality in each other's lives now stands some

---

3 Kowalski, a closeted woman who was incapacitated by a car accident, was separated from her partner by her parents who refused to believe that she was a lesbian.

4 I am using the term 'symbolic recognition' to distinguish it from legal recognition in the sense of access to the substantive legal protections discussed above. This also emphasizes the focus of these arguments on the 'messages' that (absence of) recognition sends to wider society. This is not intended to suggest that recognition is 'merely' symbolic, nor that symbolic recognition does not also have substantive material implications (see further Fraser, 1997b).

chance of being protected – even facilitated – by governments and states that have previously marginalized and condemned us for loving women. More broadly, we also experience it as a powerful symbol of the gradual erosion of prejudice and discrimination against lesbians and gay men and of the slow progress towards social justice. (Kitzinger and Wilkinson, 2004, p. 139)

The first part of this statement emphasizes the importance of protection from the state not only as valuable in itself but also as a signal that the state is no longer homophobic. This involves removing negative symbolism of exclusion as well as positively recognizing same-sex relationships (see also Radbord, 2003, pp. 21–2). Similarly, for the litigants in the *Halpern* cases in Ontario (*Halpern v Toronto* 2002 CarswellOnt 2309; *Halpern v Toronto* 2003 CarswellOnt 2159) the key goal of same-sex marriage was to 'overcome the stigma of exclusion, and to overcome the legal barriers to equality as a precondition to overcoming social inequality' (Nicol and Smith, 2007, p. 16). In California and Connecticut, the provision of a separate institution (domestic partnership), though comprehensive, would be 'viewed as an official statement that the family relationship of same-sex couples is not of comparable stature or equal dignity to the family relationship of opposite-sex couples' (*In Re Marriage Cases*, per George CJ at 855; see also *Kerrigan v Commissioner of Public Health* 289 Conn 135).

However, arguments of the positive symbolism of recognition from the state are more common. For example, Bruce MacDougall argues that by the year 2000 attitudes of the Canadian state to lesbians and gay men had gone from condemnation (criminalization) through to condonation and compassion but, in order for 'real equality' to exist, the state must *celebrate* same-sex relationships through marriage: 'It is the institution that accords to a union the profound social stamp of approval and acceptance of the relationship as being of the highest value.' (2000, p. 242) The celebration of same-sex relationships by the state does, in itself, potentially challenge legal heteronormativity (Young and Boyd, 2006, p. 213) by giving non-heterosexual relationships this stamp of approval:

> For the state to be involved in celebration means that what is celebrated is not just *acceptable* but in fact is *good*. In the context of a group like gays and lesbians, celebration means that society not only accepts or condones this group but *approves* of it. The members of the group are not inferior; they may be different, but of a difference that merits celebration. This celebration is public, unlike compassion and condonation which are, at most, only partly public and mostly or entirely private. (MacDougall, 2000, p. 256, original emphasis)

Interestingly, and perhaps surprisingly, considering that the government created a separate legal institution, symbolic recognition arguments were made in relation to civil partnerships in the UK:

> In addition, the [Civil Partnership] Bill will have a significant impact in terms of valuing lesbian and gay couples and treating their relationships with respect. It will ensure that young gay people grow up knowing that as adults they will be entitled to exactly the same respect as everyone else. If it becomes law, the Bill will have huge cultural and social significance. (Stonewall, 2004a, p. 2)

However, the symbolism in relation to separate provisions is highly contested. Some marriage advocates argue that rather than a positive symbolism, the denial of access to the term 'marriage' has a negative symbolic effect. This also brings practical difficulties. For example:

> One of the main protections that come with marriage is the word *marriage*, and the security, clarity, and dignity it brings to families. To be denied the vocabulary of marriage and its meaningful, resonant, and readily understood statement of love and commitment – and instead, have to fumble for 10 documents, explain a new term that doesn't even have a verb, and, possibly, retain a lawyer just to protect your family in a time of crisis – is not fair and not equal. (Wolfson, 2005, original emphasis; see also *In Re Marriage Cases*, at 845–6)

In addition to the cases discussed in Chapter 3, the issue of access to the *language* of marriage was considered in the UK High Court in *Wilkinson v Kitzinger* [2006] EWHC 2022. Wilkinson and Kitzinger refer to the 'downgrading' of their Canadian marriage to a civil partnership. They claim that:

> This symbolic status of marriage as a fundamental social institution is, in many ways, as important as its formal legal status. It provides for social recognition of key relationships, and to have our relationship denied that symbolic status devalues it relative to the relationships of heterosexual couples. (Wilkinson's testimony at para. 5.21)

This claim was rejected by the court, with Sir Mark Potter ruling that: 'Abiding single sex relationships are in no way inferior, nor does English law suggest that they are by according them recognition under the name of civil partnership.' (at para. 121) He emphasized that UK law *had* provided recognition of same-sex couples through the Civil Partnership Act 2004. The reason for withholding the label 'marriage' was, he suggested, not that same-sex relationships are inferior to marriage, merely that, 'as a matter of objective fact and common understanding' as well as the legal definition of marriage, same-sex relationships are *different* from marriages.

However, for marriage advocates it appears to be the title 'marriage', as much as the comprehensiveness of the legal provisions, which holds significance in terms of the symbolism of both negative and positive state recognition. Marriage advocates criticize separate provisions on the basis that they are segregationist, or even that they are a form of apartheid:

> For the first time in modern British legal history, instead of repealing discrimination parliament has reinforced and extended it. Civil partnerships are for same-sex couples only. Straights are excluded. Conversely, marriage remains reserved for heterosexuals, to the exclusion of gays. The differential treatment of hetero and homo couples is enshrined in law. Welcome to segregation, UK-style. ... By legislating a two-tier system of relationship recognition Labour has, in effect, created a form of legal apartheid based on sexual orientation. (Tatchell, 2005; see also Kitzinger and Wilkinson, 2004, p. 133)

Similar arguments have also been made in the US (Partners Task Force, 2006), South Africa (De Vos, 2007a) and Canada (MacDougall, 2000, p. 263).

The second part of Kitzinger and Wilkinson's statement (2004, above) focuses on the positive symbolism of state recognition in signalling to wider society the need to respect (committed, married/registered) same-sex partners. The symbolism of legal recognition is, then, expected to have a wider impact providing a signal for society that homophobia is no longer acceptable (see, for example, MacDougall, 2000, pp. 238–9). Alternatively, access to marriage is a *prerequisite* for changing social attitudes, in that it will not automatically and immediately have that effect but is a necessary step towards it. For example, the litigants in the Ontario same-sex marriage case state that:

> When we eventually have in all provinces and territories in this country, the right to go to your City Hall, the right to get married, that will not end the ostracism in the community. It's cold comfort for a couple out in [small-town Alberta] ... 'Oh great, we can go get married now. Does that mean our neighbours are going to treat us any differently and not have our windows smashed?' No, that's not going to end that. *But until that legal barrier falls, we can't start to work on the second piece.* (Bourassa and Varnell in Nicol and Smith, 2007, p. 17, emphasis added)

These are important issues and there is a huge negative symbolism in the state denying access to marriage to same-sex couples. However, for reasons that I discuss below in relation to the South African context, I would suggest that marriage may not be enough to remove this negative symbolism and may not provide a corresponding positive symbolism. First, though, I discuss one way in which state recognition may impact on the ways in which other parties, such as families of origin or society more generally respond to lesbian and gay relationships.

Secondary recognition

Those who seek same-sex marriage not only seek recognition from the state but also from members of families of origin, religious institutions and private (as well as public) employers. In fact, the expected value of legal status in prompting what I will refer to as a secondary recognition (that is, social recognition that is expected to result from legal status) from birth families in particular has been found to be one of the key reasons for lesbians and gay men supporting the marriage-like civil partnerships in the UK (Shipman and Smart, 2007). The Massachusetts-based organization GLAD provides an example of this type of argument:

> Marriage is a major building block for strong families and communities. Weddings are an opportunity for friends, family and neighbors to come together to recognize a couple's lifelong commitment to one another. This occasion strengthens a couple's bond and marks their inclusion as a family into the communities of which they are a part. (GLAD, 2006)

Linked to this secondary recognition are the social supports that flow from it. As Mari Matsuda argues, the public commitment of marriage is a demand for support in the endeavours of mutual caretaking, monogamy, and family (2005, p. 193). Furthermore, several of the interviewees in Nancy Nicol and Miriam Smith's research on the same-sex marriage movements in Canada and the US referred to its potential for 'changing attitudes' (Rev. Dr Brent Hawkes of the Metropolitan Community Church Toronto in Nicol and Smith, 2007, p. 15) and for being 'a great issue for public education' in challenging the assumption of 'homosexuality as being about sex', and in emphasizing long-term, stable relationships (Richard North in Nicol and Smith, 2007, p. 14).

Ambiguous symbolisms: separate but same in South Africa

There is undoubtedly a negative symbolism in the exclusion of same-sex relationships from marriage, which the law *can* resolve but (leaving to one side for now other reasons why this may not be a satisfactory strategy) the South

African context provides an example of where marriage might nevertheless leave some negative symbolism in place. Recognition through a separate provision may be, at the very least, an ambiguous symbol. Furthermore, the complex marriage regime of South Africa, consisting of (in descending hierarchical order) civil, customary and Muslim marriages, highlights that not all marriages will necessarily share the same status.

In South Africa, the law has removed the exclusion of same-sex relationships from marriage: same-sex couples can get married (or enter into civil partnerships) in the same way as heterosexual couples can get married (or enter into civil partnerships) under the new Civil Union Act 2006 (although the inclusion of heterosexual relationships appears to be somewhat ambiguous, in that although the language of the Act is gender-neutral, they are not explicitly mentioned, unlike same-sex relationships: see further Bonthuys, 2007; cf. De Vos, 2007b). However, that a new piece of legislation was introduced instead of simply amending the existing legislation (which remains valid only for heterosexuals) raises questions about what the symbolism is here. Some marriage advocates in South Africa remain unhappy with the 'separate yet same' compromise that their government has made (see De Vos, 2007a), which suggests that for them perhaps marriage itself will not satisfy claims for symbolic recognition in the absence of *sameness* of treatment. Furthermore, marriage in South Africa is not a single status institution, with civil, customary and Muslim marriages each holding a different place in a descending hierarchy of recognition (Bonthuys, 2007). I would suggest that, despite the claims of advocates, same-sex marriage has not eliminated second-class status but merely shifted its boundaries. For example, Bonthuys argues that seeking access to civil (as opposed to customary) marriage re-affirms the 'paramount status' of civil marriage and 'fails to acknowledge and engage with existing same-sex practices within African communities' (2007, p. 541):

> it also implies that customary and Muslim family norms are static, inflexible and incapable of accommodating change. ... The argument rests on an implicit statement that African and Muslim communities will not tolerate radical change or radical ideas, thus obscuring from view the fact that white and African Christians were united with Muslim clergy and African traditional leaders in opposing same-sex marriages. It implies that, in order for family law to meet constitutional demands, it must follow the model of civil marriage, while customary and Muslim family law systems should be left to disappear quietly over time. (Bonthuys, 2007, pp. 532–3)

Therefore, in the South African context of a separate but same provision and a hierarchy of status between civil, customary and Muslim marriages, the symbolism of recognizing same-sex marriages is more ambiguous than the arguments made by same-sex marriage advocates would suggest. Marriage itself can take different forms and within that status some forms of marriage may be more privileged than others (see further Barker, 2011).

Nevertheless, recognition is a powerful argument. Recognition of same-sex relationships by the state is a significant achievement in the context of a history (and present) of homophobia perpetuated by heteronormative or homophobic state policies. Removing the negative symbolism of exclusion and celebrating same-sex relationships on the same terms as heterosexual marriages and the effects this may have in terms of secondary recognition from society more generally are important. The radical potential of recognition arguments is, however, diluted by reliance on discourses of sameness and formal equality, as discussed next. I also return to the issue of recognition in Chapter 6 to explore the question of, among others, *which* types of same-sex relationships would be recognized through marriage.

Formal equality and sameness

Underpinning the two arguments discussed above (legal protections and recognition) is formal equality, which is a recurring theme in mainstream political and legal arguments for same-sex marriage. For example, in Canada, Claire Young and Susan Boyd analysed the arguments made in legislative debates on the legal recognition of same-sex relationships and identified a formal equality approach among supporters of same-sex relationship recognition (2006, pp. 223 and 227). Claims of formal equality in this context involve emphasizing sameness between those who seek equality (same-sex couples) and those whom they want to be equal with (married heterosexuals) (see also Boyd, 2004, p. 212; Harding, 2006, p. 521).

Formal equality carries significant weight in the mainstream political and legal arenas, which respond positively to these arguments. For example, as noted in Chapter 3, constitutional equality provisions have featured in successful claims for same-sex marriage in the US, Canadian and South African courts. Furthermore, its appeal to the (liberal) mainstream is particularly useful to combat anti-gay rhetoric. For example, Lisa Glennon argues that (formal) equality frameworks were useful in Northern Ireland to 'create a more "progressive" political dialogue where anti-gay rhetoric is becoming marginalized' (2006, p. 276).

Formal equality arguments do not engage with the institution of marriage in a critical way, instead seeking access to it for same-sex relationships on the basis that they are the same as heterosexual relationships and thus deserving of the same legal provisions and recognition from the state, whatever their substantive content and effects. Claims of sameness are made, whether implicitly or explicitly, in a number of ways. For example, referring to the functional approach to relationship recognition in Canada, Joanna Radbord argues that:

> We seek to recognize and support the social, economic and emotional interdependencies *that arise in all intimate relationships*, married or not, different-sex or same-sex. This functional approach recognizes that family is forged over time, in love and labour, not in contract, and that *all families may advance true family values*. (Radbord, 2005, p. 100, emphasis added)

This quotation highlights two of the key underlying themes of the sameness claims: that, like heterosexual relationships, same-sex relationships are based on *love* (see also Cox, 1994, p. 112); and that they are *functionally* the same in that they perform the same roles in relation to the private family unit and wider society (see also Hickman, 1997; Mohr, 1997). These roles include supporting dependency and the interdependence of family members and providing a site for reproduction and child-rearing. An additional, third point integral to the sameness claim is that same-sex relationships follow the marriage model in terms of being monogamous and 'stable', or long-term. This claim is often made implicitly through the stories of the litigants in marriage cases, which are frequently cited in the judgments, particularly in those where the claim for marriage was successful (see also Boyd, 2004, p. 213). These discourses are also evident in the arguments that are made for marriage-like provisions. For example, as Jacqui Smith MP stated in her 'Foreword' to the Civil Partnership consultation paper:

> Today there are thousands of same-sex couples living in stable and committed partnerships. These relationships span many years with couples looking after each other, caring for their loved ones and actively participating in society; in fact, *living in exactly the same way as any other family*. They are our families, our friends, our colleagues and our neighbours. Yet the law rarely recognizes their relationship. (Women and Equality Unit, 2003a, p. 9, emphasis added)

Therefore, it is clear that the goal of same-sex marriage for those who engage discourses of formal equality is not to undermine or challenge marriage in any way. Instead, the aim is 'to rectify a perceived unfairness within marriage for an equality-seeking constituency' (Stychin, 2006b, p. 31). This constitutes what Fraser (1997a, p. 23) refers to as an 'affirmative' remedy: one that attempts to remedy unjust outcomes for a specific group but leaves the underlying social structures that generate injustices intact (discussed further in Chapter 6). Therefore, arguments based on sameness and formal equality suggest that either the goal of access to the institution of marriage for same-sex couples is a more pressing need than resolving other inequalities or that both can be tackled simultaneously. For these marriage advocates, gaining the same legal treatment as heterosexual couples trumps wider concerns about the institution of marriage itself:

> Would anyone say that people in love should accept discrimina-tion based on their race or religion until other injustices are recti-fied? Or would we say that *both* the discrimination and the other injustices should be combated and that those... [who claim same-sex marriage] are right to challenge their exclusion from a central social institution? (Wolfson, 1996, pp. 131–2)

Alternatively, Robert Wintemute argues that it is necessary to make arguments of sameness and formal equality in the first instance as a way of challenging homophobia and anti-gay campaigns (see, for example, Glennon, 2006, p. 276, above) but that, once formal equality (sameness) is established, attention will turn to claims of difference, highlighting instances of indirect discrimination and the need for substantive equality:

> In other words, there is a shift from claims that 'we are the same' in all relevant respects (and therefore entitled to formal legal equality) to 'we are different' in some relevant respects that require accommodation (in order to achieve substantive equality). (Wintemute, 2004, p. 1173)

In this way, formal equality is a necessary stage in the path to 'real' equal-ity. However, I would argue that claiming relationship recognition on the basis of sameness does not leave room for subsequent arguments of diffe-rence. Wintemute himself acknowledges that same-sex couples 'can expect an uphill struggle in persuading courts that neutral rules must be invalidated (for the benefit of all) to accommodate their differences or that they must be exempted from such rules' (2004, p. 1174).

There are several more general problems with formal equality approaches. The first, linked to its acceptance of the status quo, is that it reifies traditional marriage and family structures and 'allows advocates... to remain agnostic on the question of whether marriage itself is a normative good' (Feldblum, 2005, p. 182). As such, it leaves existing unequal social structures in place and affirms the existing social order. However, the underlying social structures are a key part of the problem so leaving them intact or possibly reinforcing them is not a way to create equality:

> Formal equality and substantive equality are goals worth seeking. But when formal equality is conferred by inherently misallocative

systems, it is almost impossible to deliver substantive equality as well. (Lahey, 2003, p. 18)

It could be argued that, as noted above, such challenges are not the goal of formal equality, which seeks only that 'likes are treated alike' without commentating on other aspects of the (in)justice of that treatment, and that this approach is vital in ending oppression of gays and lesbians *as* gays and lesbians rather than as members of other disadvantaged groups (this forms the basis of Cheshire Calhoun's argument, discussed below).

The next two critiques of formal equality approaches also highlight these issues. The second critique is that the effect of formal equality arguments is assimilation, particularly in that it is necessary to hide or deny difference, or dismiss people with differences as an unruly minority within the group. Thirdly, formal equality and sameness rely on 'liberal-neutrality arguments' (Feldblum, 2001). This avoids engagement with moral anti-gay arguments and thus misses an opportunity to make a moral case *for* same-sex marriage, claiming the 'moral legitimacy of gay sex' (Feldblum, 1997, p. 1008). This avoidance takes the (potentially) radical edge off same-sex marriage gains:

> Genuine equality for gays and lesbians...requires more than merely coming to be tolerated. It requires that we, as a culture, give up the belief that gays and lesbians are unfit to participate in normatively ideal forms of marriage, parenting, and family. (Calhoun, 2000, pp. 130–1)

Formal equality does not require a fundamental change in attitudes, but merely a toleration of (what may remain) abnormal, deviant or immoral behaviour. The only requirement would be recognition that the law should treat everybody the same, regardless of their flaws, unless there are material differences between them. More importantly, from the perspective of the feminist critiques of marriage, when lesbians and gay men must emphasize sameness with heterosexuals, the ways in which same-sex relationships are different must be hidden and thus the opportunity to positively impact on heterosexual relationships and society is lost (Feldblum, 2005, p. 183).

Nevertheless, formal equality approaches do provide a useful strategy that should not be dismissed completely:

> Once formal legal equality has been achieved, and proves inadequate, there is a tendency among equality-seeking groups to dismiss it as trivial, even insulting. Of course, formal legal equality on its own is not enough.... And full social equality will require education and a substantial change in attitudes among the heterosexual majority.... But formal legal equality on its own

> has tremendous material and symbolic value, which only those who have been denied it for many years can fully appreciate. (Wintemute, 2004, p. 1180)

There is a clear link here between formal equality and symbolic recognition and there is a symbolic value in formal equality. However, by moving away from arguments of sameness, it is possible to make more radical arguments for same-sex marriage.

Recognizing diversity: lesbian difference, egalitarian marriage and political resistance

In this section I examine arguments for same-sex marriage that focus, in various ways, on difference rather than sameness. I examine the ways in which the interests of lesbians and gay men in accessing marriage might differ from those of heterosexual feminists; the argument that same-sex marriages may be more egalitarian than heterosexual marriages and as a result have a positive, transformative, influence on the institution as a whole; and the ways in which same-sex marriage might be a form of political resistance or a way to transgress the institution.[5] These perspectives then, to a greater or lesser extent, seek marriage as a demand for positive recognition of diversity. Emphasizing difference could provide a way for same-sex marriage advocates to seek access to the institution on terms which may challenge unequal social structures more generally, including some of those that underpin marriage. For example, Davina Cooper constructs equality as a more social (rather than individualistic or group-based) construct so that rather than seeking a formal notion of equality where, in the case of same-sex marriage, members of two comparable groups must be treated the same, real equality demands 'the contestation of social relations of inequality more generally' (2001, p. 77).

From a feminist perspective, these may be the strongest arguments for same-sex marriage by claiming to alter it in various ways through the inclusion of same-sex couples. The first perspective I examine, however, does not claim to alter the institution through same-sex marriage. Instead, this argument is a direct response to feminist critiques of marriage, arguing that the subordination of lesbians and gay men is different from that of heterosexual women. As such, though marriage is an oppressive institution for heterosexual women, it is the exclusion from the institution that is central in the

---

5　I use transgression to refer to 'opportunities to challenge, or go beyond, the expected (and assumed) boundaries' of marriage. This is distinct from transformation, which refers 'to the possibilities of creating change through working within the existing legal framework' (Barker, 2006, p. 242).

oppression of lesbians and gay men. On the basis of this, same-sex marriage is argued to be necessary.

'What exactly do you mean when you say "we"?' Lesbian specificity and feminist critiques of marriage

This phrase was used by Hazel Carby (1992, p. 233), arguing that white feminists' pre-occupation with the patriarchal family as the site of women's oppression (see Chapter 5) ignores the experiences of black women for whom the family operates as a site of resistance against racism. Cheshire Calhoun (2000) argues that just as racial oppression is seen as a separate (though linked) axis of oppression in relation to gender, so should the subordination of lesbians and gay men. Instead, theorizing of lesbian oppression has too often been subsumed within that of heterosexual women. By attempting to separate lesbian theory from feminist theory, Calhoun makes a very direct challenge to the feminist critiques of marriage in the context of same-sex marriage. Calhoun's argument is based on the premise that lesbian and gay subordination is fundamentally different to women's oppression (and racial oppression). This premise has been considered and critiqued elsewhere (see Card, 1998; Cuomo, 1998; Ferguson, 1998) and, as it is outside the scope of this research to consider its broader applicability, I will analyse it only as it relates to marriage. In order to present the strongest possible argument for same-sex marriage I will assume for these purposes that its premise is correct.

Calhoun argues that the rejection of sexual relationships with men made lesbianism appear to be 'inherently feminist and anti-patriarchal' (Calhoun, 2000, p. 25). As a result of this perception of lesbianism *as* feminism, lesbian and feminist theories merged to the extent that 'lesbian thought became applied feminist thought' (2000, p. 26). That lesbian and feminist theories inform each other is not surprising and is not the subject of Calhoun's criticism; she accepts that there would be problems with both theories if this were not the case. Instead, her claim, echoing Hartmann's use of the marriage analogy in criticism of Marxism, is that '[l]esbian theory and feminist theory are one, and that one is feminist theory' (2000, p. 26). This merging has occurred to the extent that lesbians and/or lesbian perspectives are not even mentioned in some feminist legal theory. Other lesbian feminist writers have also noted that the specificities of lesbian subordination have been overlooked within wider feminist theorizing. For example, Rosemary Auchmuty argues:

> [F]eminist legal studies have tended to assume the heterosexuality of legal subjects and to ignore or, by representing lesbians as a subset of women distinguished solely by virtue of their sexual

preferences, to misunderstand the situation of lesbians and lesbianism within the law. (Auchmuty, 1997, p. 253)

Similarly, Didi Herman (1994b, p. 510) argues: 'Feminist approaches to law have tended to focus upon an implicitly heterosexual "woman"; most feminist legal theorists do not even begin to take lesbianism seriously.'

Calhoun argues that the subordination of lesbians and gay men is, while related to gender oppression in a number of ways, a separate axis of oppression (2000, p. 10). She makes this claim for two reasons. First, although the elimination of gender oppression is necessary for the elimination of heterosexism, it is not *sufficient* to achieve this: '*Any* society, even a gender-egalitarian one, that makes the male–female couple foundational will be one in which stigmatizing lesbianism and homosexuality has a point.' (2000, p. 7, original emphasis). Furthermore, even if heterosexism is only a 'byproduct of male dominance', there would be pragmatic reasons for treating it as a separate axis of oppression to highlight 'lesbian specificity' so that it does not become obscured within feminist theorizing, in the same way that the necessity of doing so is recognized in relation to racial and class dominance (2000, pp. 13–14).

Calhoun argues that in order to take lesbianism seriously, we must recognize that the lesbians' experience of heterosexuality is very different from a heterosexual woman's. Unlike heterosexual women, who are oppressed through being confined to subordinate, disadvantaged roles within society, lesbian and gay subordination arises from our *displacement* to 'the outside of society' and the exclusion of lesbian and gay identities from both the public and private spheres. This means that lesbians and gay men, Calhoun argues, have no legitimized place in society, not even a disadvantaged one, because of 'the requirement that all citizens adopt at least the appearance of a heterosexual identity as a condition of access to the public sphere' (2000, p. 76). Lesbians and gay men are excluded from the (protected) private sphere through prohibitions on same-sex marriage, and are 'displaced from civil society's future' by, for example, anti-gay educational policies that aim to discourage those in future generations from being gay (Calhoun, 2000, p. 76).

Calhoun argues that lesbian politics should centre access to marriage (despite feminist critiques of it) because of what our exclusion from it represents: prohibitions of same-sex marriage exist because lesbians and gay men are constructed as outsiders to the family, and 'are *for that reason* defective citizens' (2000, p. 110, original emphasis). In a system where lesbians are pressured to closet our desire for women, lesbian experience 'of complete sexual fulfilment, of falling in love, of finding one's soulmate, of committing oneself, of marrying, of creating a home, and of starting a family' are pathologized (2000, p. 47). While heterosexual women's oppression originates *within* the family, from the confines of gender roles and the relegation of women to the private sphere through caretaking responsibilities, lesbian women's oppression results from *exclusion* from the family. Lesbians and gay men are constructed as 'outlaws' to the family; whereas heterosexual women are seen as 'natural' mothers and caretakers, lesbian women and gay men are stigmatized as unsuitable for those roles (2000, p. 132). In short:

> From a feminist point of view, sexual interaction, romantic love, marriage, and the family are all danger zones because all have been distorted to serve male interests. It thus does not behoove feminist politics to begin by championing the importance of sexual interaction, romantic love, marriage, and the (couple-based) family. But it does behoove lesbian politics to start in precisely these places. (Calhoun, 2000, p. 47)

As Calhoun, Auchmuty and Herman all note, there *are* times when lesbian subordination becomes subsumed within heterosexual feminism. As such, I would agree with Calhoun that it is necessary to consider them as distinct *though connected*: heterosexism and homophobia are products of male dominance but also other related (and unrelated) social systems. However, there is a danger that in analysing lesbian and women's subordination separately, lesbian theorists might fail to 'consider lesbians as *women*' with the result that 'institutionalized heterosexuality, and its relation to the construction of gender, are left unquestioned' (Herman, 1994b, pp. 521–2). It is therefore important to adequately consider and theorize the connections between lesbian and women's oppression, but at the same time to not lose sight of the differences that do exist in the way hetero-patriarchal systems of subordination manifest themselves in relation to heterosexual and lesbian women.

In the context of marriage, I would be sympathetic to Calhoun's view that, as lesbian and gay oppression is through displacement from civil society (including our construction as outlaws to the family), then access to marriage would be a significant challenge to such oppression. There is little doubt that a major part of the intention of the rightwing in excluding lesbians and gays from marriage *is* to keep same-sex relationships out of the public sphere, the protected private sphere and away from influencing future generations. However, the question of the extent to which this supports an argument for same-sex marriage despite the feminist critiques of the institution depends upon the points at which lesbian theory and feminist theory *do* converge in relation to marriage. Furthermore, while Calhoun rejects a joint theorizing of lesbian and heterosexual women's oppression, she then theorizes lesbian women's and gay men's oppression together. I would suggest that this is also problematic, particularly in the context of marriage claims where (as has been evident in this chapter) the discourse does generally focus greater attention on the gay male than the lesbian subject. In Chapters 5 and 6, I argue that marriage would mean much more (and in some senses much less) than simply recognition for lesbians and gay men: marriage would have wider social implications, and broader consequences than 'just' recognition (including, for example, the legal provisions – rights *and* responsibilities – discussed above). At the same time, as I argue in Chapter 6, same-sex marriage would not recognize all lesbian and gay families but instead only those that are able to 'pass' in the sense of meeting the heteronormative requirements of the institution of marriage.[6]

Next, I examine the arguments that same-sex marriage might have radical potential in that it could have a subversive or transgressive influence on the institution. In this context I present arguments that same-sex marriage might transform the institution itself. I then examine a further aspect of Calhoun's argument: for her what is at stake in the same-sex marriage debate is the cultural authority to define what family and marriage are.

'The next frontier in democratizing marriage': same-sex relationships as challenging traditional marriage

> Yes we must be aware of the oppressive history that weddings symbolize. We must work to ensure that we do not simply accept whole-cloth an institution that symbolizes the loss and harm felt by women. But I find it difficult to understand how two lesbians, standing together openly and proudly, can be seen as accepting that institution. What is more antipatriarchal and rejecting of an institution that carries the patriarchal power imbalance into most households than clearly stating that *women can commit to one another with no man in sight? With no claim of dominion or control, but instead of equality and respect.* I understand the fears of those who condemn us for our weddings, but I believe they fail to look beyond the symbol and cannot see the radical claim we are making. (Cox, 1994, p. 113, emphasis added)

Some feminists, while being equivocal or even critical about marriage as an institution, nevertheless argue for same-sex marriage. This is either on the basis that individual same-sex relationships will not reproduce the problematic aspects of heterosexual marriages, such as gendered power relations, or (linked to this) because same-sex relationships may have a positive influence on the institution as a whole, leading Nan Hunter to describe same-sex

---

6 One of the reasons why Calhoun distinguishes lesbian and gay subordination from gender and race oppression is that lesbians and gay men are able (expected) to avoid discrimination by 'passing' as heterosexual.

marriage as 'the next frontier in democratizing marriage' (1995, p. 114). In the above statement Barbara Cox makes three interlinking arguments, which I will address in turn.

First, she argues that lesbians and gay men should not accept marriage 'whole-cloth': that is, from within marriage 'we' can make it our own, challenge its patriarchal roots and transform it to fit our needs. This point is also made by Evan Wolfson, arguing that those in the lesbian and gay communities who oppose same-sex marriage are 'ignoring the fact that marriage (like other social institutions we are part of or seek to make our own choices whether or not to be part of) has changed throughout history to meet the needs and values of real people' (1996, p. 131). The argument here is that the ways in which same-sex couples will 'do' marriage may transform the institution. This is partly linked to claims of egalitarianism within same-sex marriages (discussed below) but is also a wider claim. For example, same-sex marriage might provide a good example for *heterosexual* marriages because 'something of the gay relationship's necessary honesty, its flexibility, and its equality could undoubtedly help strengthen and inform many heterosexual bonds' (Sullivan, 1995, p. 130).

The second strand to Cox's argument is that same-sex marriage is a way to increase visibility of lesbians and gay men, which will challenge heteronormativity and patriarchy. Cox describes how the process of getting married led her and her partner to interact with a number of people in ways that challenged the invisibility she had previously felt. For example, it led to conversations with her nephews, where the unspoken knowledge that she was a lesbian was finally spoken, and to another family member to 'question and resolve the discomfort' that he had felt with their relationship for many years (1994, p. 113).

However, the cost of being 'out' in the sense of having public (state) recognition of lesbian and gay relationships may be a loss of the autonomy and imagination that allows us to live and legally organize our relationships differently to the (heterosexual) marriage model:

> The liberal agenda may, indeed, grant us rights to hitherto heterosexual privileges. But unless we are careful, *it will do so on its terms*, naturally assuming that heterosexual values are the norm, if not the best. In so doing, it may lose the opportunity presented by the recognition of lesbian and gay existence to gain two important insights. One is that the ways heterosexuals live may not be the best. The second is that the ways lesbians and gays live might be better. In sum, rather than assimilate us to their preferred relationship models, heterosexuals might do well to look at how gays and lesbians conduct their relationships... (Auchmuty, 2004, p. 124, emphasis added)

Barbara Cox's third point is that same-sex marriages would be egalitarian rather than patriarchal. Nan Hunter (1995) also makes this point, going further to argue that this egalitarianism may have an influence on heterosexual marriage. Hunter argues that the definition of marriage conflates issues of nature, gender and law (that is patriarchal notions of dependence and authority being based on natural differences between the sexes, discussed further in Chapter 5). As such, the continued exclusion of same-sex couples from marriage leaves intact the 'natural', 'gendered definitional boundaries of marriage' (1995, p. 110). Her claim is not that same-sex marriage would *directly* shift the balance of power in heterosexual marriages, but rather that same-sex marriage could change the 'fundamental concept' of marriage: 'Its potential is to disrupt both the gendered definition of marriage and the assumption that marriage is a form of socially, if not legally, prescribed hierarchy.' (1995, p. 112) This is because, since the 'authority/dependence' status of husbands and wives is no longer legally enforceable, the only remaining feature of gender in marriage is the 'foundational constructs' husband and wife. Without their gendered content, Hunter argues that even these would become meaningless (1995, p. 112). This, she goes on to argue, would destabilize the cultural meaning of marriage:

> It would create for the first time the possibility of marriage as a relationship between members of the same social status categories. However valiantly individuals try to build marriages grounded on genuine equality, no person can erase his or her status in the world as male or female, or create a home life apart from culture. *Same-sex marriage could create the model in law for an egalitarian kind of interpersonal relation,* outside the gendered terms of power, for many marriages. At the least, it would radically strengthen and dramatically illuminate the claim that marriage partners are presumptively equal. (1995, pp. 112–13; emphasis added)

Her position is, therefore, that marriage is a social construct (notwithstanding the powerful force of tradition) and that the absence of gender dichotomies in same-sex marriage would play a part in reshaping marriage law.[7] However, she does acknowledge that this would have minimal effect without other feminist reforms (1995, p. 114). In fact, in the Canadian context, Shelley Gavigan argues that while changing the legal *form* of marriage (in that the language of 'husband' and 'wife' was substituted with the gender-neutral 'spouse') has 'inhibited some of the worst linguistic excesses of patriarchy'

---

7   Catherine MacKinnon has also said, almost in passing, that: 'I do think it might do something amazing to the entire institution of marriage to recognize the unity of two "persons" between whom no superiority or inferiority could be presumed on the basis of gender.' (1987, p. 27)

(1999, p. 130), it has also obscured the continued existence of patriarchal principles because it appears to be gender neutral (1999, p. 130). Hunter may well argue that same-sex marriage would have more than an *appearance* of gender-neutrality, although she does not appear to account for the existence of 'gender' in same-sex relationships in terms of, for example, butch/femme roles. These arguments that assume an absence of gender dynamics in same-sex relationships also collapse the distinction between sex and gender.

The central thesis is nevertheless supported by the findings of some empirical research (Dunne, 1997; Weeks et al., 2001; cf. Carrington 1999, discussed in Chapter 5). Despite the existence of factors that could result in power imbalances in lesbian relationships, such as in class and income, Dunne (1997) found in her in-depth study of 60 lesbians that her participants were able to recognize and challenge inequalities of power that might otherwise have surfaced (this finding is supported in relation to gay men as well, see Weeks et al., 2001). That Dunne's research emphasizes the very different organizations of labour in lesbian relationships compared to heterosexual ones suggests that, in the absence of a pre-existing legally supported patriarchy, it might be possible for egalitarian marriages to develop. It is an assumption along these lines that underpins Hunter's (1995) claims that same-sex marriage would destabilize both the operation of gender in marriage and the cultural meaning of marriage itself. In other words:

> it is not home life per se which can represent a drain on women's energies, but rather home life *within heterosexual contexts*. All these differences in the way lesbians negotiate and experience their interpersonal and material lives demonstrate that interpretations of sexuality are the *medium through which we experience* the overlapping nature of public and private worlds. (Dunne, 1997, p. 228, original emphasis)

E J Graff also argues that same-sex marriage is a way to transform marriage itself, claiming that it 'shifts the institution's message' (1996, p. 135) in that it would challenge the link made by the state between marriage and procreation, emphasizing instead sexual choice (see also Halle, 2001, p. 385). Although, as Halle notes, this challenge would be to the link made by the state and not necessarily the way that marriage is conceived extra-legally in society, the recognition of same-sex families would introduce 'new life possibilities' in society, 'diversifying social forms, and providing greater individual choice' (2001, p. 385). Those 'new' life possibilities did, of course, already exist; families are not created by the law but merely recognized (or not) by it. Halle is therefore presumably referring to newly *legitimated* life possibilities.

The arguments presented so far in this section suggest that differences between lesbians (and gay men) and heterosexual women would result in marriage having a different meaning in a lesbian context: first, because lesbians and gay men are oppressed through exclusion from marriage and family rather than within them; and second, because same-sex relationships would do marriage differently and thus potentially challenge gender in all marriages. I return to and problematize these claims in the context of the feminist critiques of marriage in the next chapter. The arguments that I discuss next explore the ways in which same-sex marriage may be a form of political resistance. It is argued that, in addition to the transformative effect discussed above, same-sex marriage may also be transgressive of the heteronormative marriage framework.

'Municipal anarchy': same-sex marriage as political resistance

In the US in 2004, George W Bush's state of the union address included a statement about his support for 'traditional marriage' (Bush, 2004a). This 'galvanized a small-scale movement of civil disobedience' (Nicol and Smith, 2007, p. 5), beginning in San Francisco when the mayor, Gavin Newsom, issued marriage licences to same-sex couples despite California law explicitly defining marriage as being between a man and a woman (Family Code 1977 s. 308.5, passed as a result of the Knight Initiative, Proposition 22, in 2000). Conservative opponents of same-sex marriage filed a petition for an injunction, referring to the mayor's actions as 'municipal anarchy' (Gordon, 2004). In this section, I examine the ways in which same-sex marriage might be a form of political resistance. First, these acts of civil disobedience, the performance of ceremonies in defiance of prohibitions, may challenge compulsory heterosexuality in making same-sex relationships visible. Morris Kaplan (1997) argues that same-sex marriage *itself* is also an act of civil disobedience in its refusal to comply with heterosexist silences and invisibility of same-sex relationships. Second, same-sex marriage could disrupt heteronormative notions of public and private and proper place (Cooper, 2001) and which relationships 'count' as family (Calhoun, 2000). Finally, same-sex marriage could have a subversive influence on the institution of marriage, not only through 'degendering' marriage, as Cox and Hunter suggest (above), but also by transgressing the norms of marriage more broadly.

The same-sex marriages that were performed in San Francisco, New Paltz and other US cities in 2004 were acts of civil disobedience, according to Bedau's definition: 'Anyone commits an act of civil disobedience if and only if he [sic] acts illegally, publicly, non-violently, and conscientiously with the intent to frustrate (one of) the laws, policies, or decisions of his [sic] government.' (1961, p. 661)[8] They were illegal, not only in that they were not

---

8 Although there are other slightly different definitions of civil disobedience, Bedau's definition appears to be generally accepted (see Kaplan, 1997, p. 232).

legally valid marriages (this in itself is not sufficient to meet this definition of civil disobedience: see also Kaplan, 1997, p. 228) but also in some cases resulted in the arrests of those officiating followed by criminal charges of solemnizing a marriage without a licence (Nicol and Smith, 2007). Though the charges were dropped before the cases went to trial (Fisher-Hertz, 2006), the ceremonies were performed in anticipation that arrests would follow. See, for example, Jason West, the mayor of New Paltz:

> We didn't know if I was going to be arrested for doing this right off the bat, so my lawyer and myself and the ACLU lawyers were there kind of watching the police, seeing what they were going to do. We actually had a notary public and all the paperwork there for that first couple, because we figured by the time the cops make it through the crowd, we can at least get one set of paperwork signed and notarized and done, so we have at least one finished wedding...(in Nicol and Smith, 2007, p. 6)

Second, they were performed publicly and non-violently: in San Francisco reporters from the *San Francisco Chronicle* and a documentary film-maker were recording the event (Gordon, 2004) and in New Paltz (and subsequently in New York City) the ceremonies were performed on the steps of City Hall (Nicol and Smith, 2007, para. 6.9). Finally, those who performed the ceremonies did so explicitly as a matter of conscience and to protest a discriminatory law: the New Paltz mayor considered it his 'moral obligation' to do so (Wald, 2004), while the mayor of San Francisco said:

> While some may believe that separate and unequal institutions are acceptable, we will oppose intolerance and discrimination every step of the way. San Francisco is a city of tolerance and mutual respect and we will accept nothing less than full civil rights for all our residents. (in Nicol and Smith, 2007, pp. 5–6)

Following the charges against the New Paltz mayor and the two local Unitarian Universalist ministers who also performed same-sex marriages, a protest rally in New York City culminated in three same-sex marriages being performed by clergy on the steps of New York City Hall (Nicol and Smith, 2007, p. 9). In this context, the significance of asserting the legality of same-sex marriages and publicly performing the ceremonies as a form of political protest is undeniable. Performing same-sex marriages and publicly and defiantly asserting their legality in the context of prohibitions on same-sex marriage is, as Nicol and Smith argue, to engage in civil disobedience (2007, p. 7).

Further, Morris Kaplan argues that same-sex marriage is *in itself* an act of civil disobedience. He draws on Thoreau's theorizing of democracy where resistance to unjust acts is necessary as 'silence results in complicity' (1997, p. 229). This, Kaplan argues, 'lends support to a politics of contestation and an ethical imperative of coming out for lesbians and gay men in heterosexist regimes'. The public ceremony of marriage is a refusal to comply with a heterosexist 'regime of silence' and in this sense is civil disobedience. He argues that same-sex marriage would make lesbians and gay men visible within the 'daily business of government' (1997, p. 234). As such,

> At bottom the demand for legal recognition of same-sex partnerships is a demand to acknowledge the validity of lesbian and gay forms of life. To the extent that lesbian and gay citizens are prepared to assert this claim, and to occasionally break the law publicly in doing so, we are challenging the moral consensus that supports compulsory heterosexuality. (1997, p. 235)

As Kaplan highlights, one of the consequences of same-sex marriage might be to increase the visibility of lesbians and gay men and same-sex relationships, not only in relation to the state but also other third parties (such as hospitals and insurance companies, see above discussion of secondary recognition) who would be required to recognize the relationships. Therefore, in addition to securing access to the protected private sphere of family, as discussed above, same-sex marriage would also bring same-sex relationships 'out of the closet' and into the public sphere (Kaplan, 1997, p. 208; Calhoun, 2000, pp. 159–60; see also Cox, above).

As Calhoun argues (2000, above) lesbian and gay sexualities have been excluded from the public sphere.[9] Same-sex marriage, however, by compelling the state and other third parties to recognize lesbian and gay relationships, re-imagines same-sex relationships as appropriately belonging in the public sphere. As Cooper notes, it is a demand that the establishment recognizes them 'not as they have been traditionally hailed, as sick, sinful or marginal people, but rather as respectable (property-owning) citizens of the polity' (2001, p. 94). It is also a demand that they have access to the 'protected private sphere' (Calhoun, 2000, p. 15). These demands are closely linked with the issues of access to legal provisions and symbolic recognition discussed above. However, here I am interested not in these specific issues, but in the broader picture of how access to them might disrupt heteronormative conceptions of not only what appropriately belongs in the public and private spheres, but also who has access to the language of family.

---

9 Though see Cooper, arguing that conceptions of public and private are a 'partial, contested and contingent' aspect of social organizing principles (2001, pp. 85–6). In other words, what it means to behave properly or appropriately in given (public or private) spaces, what is 'in place' or 'out of place' may change or be redefined, as might the ways in which public and private themselves are constructed.

Cheshire Calhoun argues that lesbian and gay subordination comes from 'requiring gay men and lesbians to adopt pseudonymous heterosexual iden-tities as a condition of access to those public spaces' (Calhoun, 2000, p. 106). Marriage, by giving lesbian and gay identities public recognition, would sig-nal that this is no longer necessary. This may in itself be radical: Calhoun claims that Defense of Marriage Acts are defending the existing social order, where gays are pressured to be closeted (or even ex-gays) and 'family' means heterosexuality. In this context, access to marriage for same-sex couples would mean either that marriage remains a foundational institution in soci-ety (see Fineman, 1995, p. 141) and lesbians and gays are 'fit' to participate in it; or that marriage does not differ from any other type of relationship so there is no reason to continue restricting it to heterosexual relationships, thus disrupting gay and lesbian subordination 'by denying that marriage and family had any special importance in the first place' (2000, p. 129). The latter position would be entirely compatible with the feminist critiques of marriage in that it would, if taken to its logical conclusion, be an argument for the abolition of marriage:

> [This option] would reject the idea altogether that there are any prepolitical, foundational forms of intimacies. We might argue that civil societies depend only in the most general way on its [sic] citizens having the capacities for and interest in casting their personal lot with others and sharing, in voluntary private arrange-ments, sex, affection, reproduction, economic support, and care for the young, the infirm and the elderly. But no one form or set of forms for doing so is foundational to civil society. Nor need all of these activities be consolidated within one relationship, as we standardly consolidate them within couples and couple-based families....Nor need all of these activities be best undertaken through private arrangements, as we have up to this point typi-cally thought to be true of the care of children and the provision of sex....(Calhoun, 2000, pp. 129–30)

However, Calhoun, while agreeing that abolition of marriage would be a desirable goal, endorses the former position on the grounds that it is more likely to challenge lesbian and gay subordination. She likens the second posi-tion to liberal neutrality arguments, discussed above, on the basis that it does not require the state to positively endorse same-sex relationships but merely be neutral with regard to the ways in which people organize their family and sexual lives. What is at stake for her, however, is 'the right to *define* what counts as family' (Calhoun, 2000, p. 132, original emphasis):

> To have familial status is not to have applied to oneself one highly conventional family form. Having familial status means

having the privilege that heterosexuals alone have heretofore had, namely the privilege of claiming that *despite their multiple deviations* from norms governing the family, their families are nevertheless *real* ones and they are themselves naturally suited for marriage, family, and parenting *however* these might be defined and redefined. It also means having the cultural authority to challenge existing familial norms, to redefine what constitutes a family, and to demand that the preferred definition of the family be reflected in cultural and legal practices (Calhoun, 2000, p. 156, original emphasis).

Thus, the right to define what counts as family may provide opportunities to challenge heteronormativity. However, the demand that same-sex relationships be recognized by both the public sphere and the protected private sphere is a demand that necessarily 'looks to, and thereby helps reproduce, the authority and legitimacy of the Establishment' (Cooper, 2001, p. 94). It is perhaps unsurprising, then, that those who seek the radical potential of same-sex marriage remain equivocal about the institution itself and, in most cases, are not actually making an argument for same-sex marriage but rather exploring the possibilities that it may hold.[10]

Nevertheless, as Carl Stychin argues, there may be 'room for subversion and resistance in the ways in which lesbians and gays (and, indeed, others) map on to the law's attempt at categorization' (2005b, p. 572). For Stychin, this room for subversion arises, in the UK context, from the inherent incoherence of the Civil Partnership Act 2004 in creating a provision that is simultaneously marriage and not marriage, and that gives primacy to a conjugal relationship but without the sexual provisions of marriage (discussed further in Chapter 6). Some of the ways in which same-sex relationships map on to marriage in a potentially transgressive way are illustrated through accounts of ceremonies. For example, Ellen Lewin found that same-sex weddings incorporated 'messages of "queerness" at vital points' (2001, p. 47) as a deliberate attempt to mark the ceremony as lesbian or gay and highlight its difference from traditional weddings (see also Weston, 1991, p. 161). Examples included a ceremony 'which combined predominantly Jewish liturgical elements with a country-western theme' (Lewin, 2001, p. 47) and a ceremony that included 'flower fairies': 'two men dressed in matching floral-pattern vests' carrying baskets of flowers. The couple and their attendants 'literally danced down the aisle' and the congregation were asked to 'vow to oppose homophobia wherever it might be encountered' in addition to the usual (Protestant)

---

10 See, for example, Cooper (2001, p. 95) arguing for a 'more equivocal response' to same-sex marriage; and Kaplan (1997, p. 208) arguing that whether same-sex relationships should be recognized through marriage or a new form of relationship recognition 'remains an open question'.

request for them to 'uphold and support the marriage' (Lewin, 2001, p. 48). Lewin found that most ceremonies 'play with both sets of meanings [the traditional and the queer] and overlap them constantly, offering a new twist on the camp aesthetic of incongruity and contradiction' (2001, p. 51).

It is not just the ceremony aesthetic or theme that may be non-traditional. For example, Weston (1991, pp. 161–2) describes same-sex marriage ceremonies in which the couple are situated firmly within a chosen rather than birth family. There certainly is a seemingly irresolvable contradiction here between the claim for legitimacy in the adoption of recognizable traditional symbolism of marriage and the fact that the visibility of same-sex couples within the institution of marriage may in itself be disruptive, particularly when it involves emphasizing families of choice.

There are, then, several ways in which same-sex marriage may provide opportunities for resistance in the form of transformation or transgression of heteronormative marriage and civil disobedience in resisting the invisibility of same-sex relationships. There are problems with some of these, particularly because it is difficult to predict what the result of relationship recognition will be. It is, therefore, equally likely that, rather than transforming or transgressing marriage, same-sex relationships will be transformed through marriage, suffering a reduction in the autonomy and imagination that have resulted in more progressive relationship forms. Nevertheless, these concerns should be taken seriously, particularly in the context of Calhoun's argument that lesbians and gay men are subordinated by exclusion from marriage in contrast to heterosexual women's oppression within it.

Conclusion

While it is impossible to determine the extent to which any of the arguments for same-sex marriage are motivated by strategy considerations and how far they are the genuine beliefs of those making them, the discourses employed suggest that access to marriage is both an end in itself and also a means to an end. Marriage advocates not only seek access to the legal provisions and the state recognition associated with it but also expect that this will send a powerful message to society about the equal value and status of same-sex relationships. Thus same-sex marriage is expected to provide access to specific legal provisions and equally to solve wider social problems of homophobia and heterosexism.

The first set of arguments for same-sex marriage that I discussed were those made on the basis that it would strengthen the institution of marriage and discourage promiscuity in same-sex relationships. Though these conservative arguments may be strong in terms of appealing to the mainstream, they are the weakest in terms of feminist arguments for same-sex marriage.

They do not provide any good reasons for same-sex marriage from a feminist perspective because they are based on conservative family values rhetoric that is anti-feminist and, despite the gay identities of some of its advocates, homophobic.

The mainstream arguments that I discussed have significant strengths and weaknesses. The emphasis on the problems caused by the exclusion from the legal consequences of marriage has been a successful strategy in terms of gaining access to provisions. It is difficult to argue against increasing the protections for a partner at a hospital bedside, for example, whether the vulnerability has been exacerbated by bad practice or a legal requirement to allow access to next of kin only. However, claiming access to legal protections is problematic for a number of reasons. The legal consequences of marriage have class- and gender-based differential impacts, which mean that those with higher incomes and significant assets benefit from tax exemptions, while those who rely on state benefits will see their incomes reduced. They also rely on seeking a higher status for conjugal relationships than for other friends and family members. In contrast, there is a growing movement, particularly in North America, to separate legal benefits from conjugal relationships (see, for example, the Law Commission of Canada, 2001). It is, therefore, difficult to justify a claim based on legal protections from a feminist perspective.

A key theme that recurred in many of the arguments in this chapter is the need to overcome the invisibility of and prejudice against same-sex relationships, whether in law or in the public sphere more generally. The value of state recognition of same-sex relationships and the positive impacts this may have was central to both mainstream liberal arguments of sameness and the more radical arguments that were based on difference. I discussed symbolic recognition first in the context of arguments that were based on an (implicit or explicit) assumption that same-sex relationships are the same as different-sex marriages. I argued that sameness arguments are problematic in a number of ways, including that they reify marriage and heteronormative notions of family, seeking only to be included within it. Furthermore, the discussion of the South African marriage provisions demonstrates that the symbolism of recognition may be ambiguous. Nevertheless, the value of state recognition in removing the negative symbolism of exclusion and positively recognizing same-sex relationships makes it a strong argument for same-sex marriage.

However, emphasizing sameness means that the potential for same-sex marriage to positively impact on the institution as a whole is limited. In contrast, arguments based on diversity and difference may be more palatable from a feminist perspective in seeking marriage as a demand for positive recognition of difference. This, it was argued, may provide opportunities to challenge inequalities *within* marriage and social structures more generally. The first claim that I examined, however, was a direct challenge to feminist critiques of marriage in arguing that they failed to take account of the specific-ity of lesbian, as opposed to heterosexual women's, oppression. For Cheshire Calhoun, the oppression of lesbians arises from exclusion from normative discourses of family so, despite heterosexual women's oppression within it, lesbians and gay men should have access to marriage. This is a difference aspect in terms of claiming lesbian specificity, but it is ultimately a claim for symbolic recognition based on similar reasons to those discussed above. While I agree with Calhoun that it is important not to lose sight of lesbian specificity, I would reject her assumption that lesbians are not oppressed as women. The remaining difference arguments claim that the institution of marriage could be transformed or transgressed by same-sex marriage. From feminist perspectives, these are, therefore, stronger arguments than those merely seeking inclusion in the existing parameters of marriage.

The argument that the institution of marriage could be transformed is based on two, linked, premises. First, that the increasing visibility of same-sex relationships will challenge heteronormativity and patriarchy; and second, that egalitarianism within same-sex relationships will challenge its funda-mental inequality and disrupt gendered norms. The transgression argument is also based on visibility in that same-sex marriage would disrupt the notion that same-sex relationships should be closeted. It is argued that transgression of heteronormative understandings of marriage is possible through queering marriage, a concept that I return to in Chapter 6. These provide the strongest arguments for same-sex marriage. Despite their many flaws, arguments based on symbolic recognition should also be taken seriously because they can shift marital ideology as an aspect of the marriage model.

In the next chapter, I discuss the second-wave feminist critiques of marriage in light of these arguments for same-sex marriage. This discussion demon-strates the context of my scepticism about claims for marriage on the basis of access to legal protections by illustrating the numerous ways in which these 'protections' have operated to the disadvantage of women. However, my aim is also to revisit these feminist critiques in light of the stronger arguments that have been made in this chapter. As such, I return to the issue of whether same-sex marriage might transform the institution as a whole to shift it from its patriarchal basis and make it more egalitarian. I continue this aim in Chapter 6, where I return to recognition and transgression arguments.

5

Second-Wave Theories for Third-Wave Families? Feminist Perspectives on (Same-Sex) Marriage

Introduction

As discussed in Chapter 4, there are some reasons why access to the legal institution of marriage may be important or perhaps even necessary for same-sex couples. In particular, the symbolic value of state recognition for same-sex couples in the context of a history of criminalization of gay male and, to a lesser extent, lesbian sexual activities (see, for example, Weeks 1977; Waites, 2002) should not be underestimated. Further, it is argued that same-sex marriage may provide opportunities to transform or transgress the institution. Marriage and the (heterosexual nuclear) family form that it creates and supports have, however, long been the subject of criticism, most notably from feminists, as well as Marxists and socialists (see, for example, Engels, 1972), and gay liberation groups (see, for example, the Gay Liberation Front, 1971). Despite this history of critiquing marriage within these movements, there has been limited acknowledgment of, and even less engagement with, their ideas that marriage is a problematic institution from those advocating for same-sex marriage and similar forms of relationship recognition (see also Young and Boyd, 2006; Auchmuty, 2007). Indeed, as discussed in the previous chapter, some have made feminist arguments *for* same-sex marriage.

The purpose of this chapter is to revisit the second-wave[1] radical and socialist feminist theories of marriage and examine their arguments in the context of the contemporary marriage model and the arguments for same-sex marriage discussed in the previous chapter. The marginalization of (critical) feminist perspectives from the same-sex marriage debates may imply, among other

---

1 My use of the wave metaphor is not intended to imply that radical and socialist feminisms are frozen in time or that they stopped developing in the 1980s. Instead, I use it as a conceptual tool that illustrates the passing of time whilst emphasizing the connectivity between past and present (see Aikau et al., 2003, p. 400).

things: that marriage and the family have changed sufficiently that second-wave theories are no longer relevant; that it is possible for women to create a 'feminist marriage' through the exercise of agency; and that what is required are changes to the understandings of gender relations rather than changing social reality itself (Nash, 2002, p. 324). By juxtaposing the radical and socialist feminisms of the second wave with the family practices of the third wave, I will argue that these assumptions are mistaken and that second-wave feminist theory does still provide a useful tool to critique both heterosexual and same-sex marriage. I will demonstrate that these theories operate at both the *individual* level (what happens between the parties within a marriage) and at the *structural* level (in terms of the role that the *institution* of marriage plays in society). I will argue that, while there is some debate about what the implications of same-sex marriage could be for the critique at the individual level, at the structural level there is no distinction between same-sex and different-sex marriage. As such, second-wave feminist theories not only remain relevant to contemporary heterosexual marriage but also provide an important critique of same-sex marriage.

I develop this critique in the context of the 'third-wave' family by making two arguments. First, on the individual level, the 'ideal' is no longer the housewife of the second-wave but instead the dual-income family. This does not mean that women are no longer exploited within the family but rather that what Betty Friedan identifies as 'occupation: housewife', becomes 'occupation: superwoman', where the 'ideal' is for women to both work and also take primary responsibility for the household and children.[2] Second, the increasing privatization of care under the neoliberal state makes the second-wave structural critiques of marriage even more important because it means that the status of caring work as unpaid and occurring within the family (and thus feminine *gendered*, regardless of the *sex* of the person who actually does the caring work) is reinforced. The question then remains as to whether there is an overriding argument for same-sex marriage that would provide justification *despite* these critiques. This is addressed in Chapter 6.

I begin by examining the development of the radical and socialist feminist critiques of marriage during the second-wave before I analyse these critiques in relation to contemporary, third-wave families. One difficulty with using second-wave critiques is that while the *legal* meaning of marriage and its importance within family law has remained relatively static, there have been significant changes in *social* understandings of family and the centrality of marriage within these (see, for example, Eichler, 1997, pp. 1–3; Silva and Smart, 1999). As such, while second-wave feminist critiques of 'the family' clearly implicate marriage, it is less clear that there is such a direct link

---

2 Primary responsibility in this context may not always involve actually doing the housework and childcare herself but perhaps hiring other, lower-income, women to do it.

today due to the decline in the statistical significance of marriage compared to cohabitation (see Barlow et al., 2005, p. 16) as the key familial relationship. As the statistical incidence of non-marital family structures increases, the causal link between marriage and women's oppression and exploitation within the contemporary (heterosexual) family becomes less obvious: do women who cohabit rather than marry experience less exploitation than their married counterparts? The unlikelihood of this raises questions about what role marriage as a legal and social institution currently has in the oppression of women, as opposed to cohabitation (or even heterosexuality) as a social practice. This is not to suggest that feminist critiques of the family were ever one-dimensionally focused on marriage: radical feminists in particular indicted heterosexuality itself as central to the oppression of women. However, marriage did always play a very clear central role as constituting the dominant legal and social definition of family (these issues are discussed further below). The statistical decline of marriage potentially makes that role less clear now.

In the penultimate section, I argue that despite the decline in the statistical significance of marriage, it retains its *symbolic* significance as signifier of the ideal family (see also: Deborah Chambers, 2001, pp. 1–32; Diduck, 2003, pp. 20–43). I then argue that feminist critiques of marriage also refer to the marriage *model;* that is, relationships that mirror the legal and social image of marriage as identified in Chapter 1. Having established this, I widen the discussion of contemporary family relationships, problematizing both theoretical assertions of post-modern relationships and women's agency, and assertions of the influence of same-sex marriages.

Following this, in the final section, I set out what I see as the continuing importance of second-wave feminist critiques in relation to third-wave families, arguing that, even if the relations between men and women within marriage *had* changed significantly, the focus of the second-wave critique was not simply individual but also structural. In other words, the key issue is not only that domestic labour is distributed unevenly within the family, but also that responsibility for care and dependency are privatized within the family. I conclude that this privatization has actually *increased* for the third-wave family with the rise of neoliberalism (and neoconservatism), demonstrating the continued significance of its second-wave critiques.

Marriage and patriarchy: radical feminist perspectives

Radical feminist constructions of patriarchy provide an important part of the foundation of the second-wave marriage critique. In this section, I will discuss the two facets of these constructions that have particular relevance to marriage: first, the emphasis on the ways in which women's reproductive biology and the denigration of feminine nurturing traits are used to oppress women; and second, the problematization of (hetero)sexuality as manifesting and perpetuating an unequal balance of power between women and men. I will begin by explaining how I am defining radical feminism and giving a brief overview of radical feminist understandings of patriarchy.

Radical feminism has been described as a collection of 'eclectic theories' (Douglas, 1990, p. 2) as it encompasses several different viewpoints of women's oppression through patriarchy and it is sometimes linked to or used interchangeably with the terms lesbian feminist, separatist, or radical lesbian, though others distinguish between them (see further Douglas, 1990, pp. 9–10). For example, Douglas identifies two main groups of radical feminists: first, the 'classic' radical feminist position, which she refers to as the 'concentrate-on-the-enemy' politics of those such as Shulamith Firestone, Kate Millett, and Ti-Grace Atkinson who (despite differences between them) argue that male domination is based on exploitation of biological differences in reproduction between men and women in order to define women as inferior; and, second, what she refers to as the 'focus on women' position of Mary Daly and others who argue that there are some biological differences between women and men that should be preserved in that women's culture is more nurturing than male culture and women can gain more from being with each other than attempting to eliminate socially recognized differences between women and men (1990, pp. 11–12).

It is not the purpose of this chapter to work through the similarities and differences existing within radical feminism (for such analysis see Douglas, 1990), instead I take a very broad approach to its definition in that I include in this section theories which cite reproductive biology and (hetero)sexuality as the sources of patriarchy. I have, however, primarily used the work of Firestone and Millett as they are two of the most often-cited exponents of radical feminism, particularly in relation to its interaction with socialist feminist theory and the family (see, for example, Eisenstein, 1979, pp. 16–22; Hartmann, 1981, pp. 11–14; Hearn, 1987, pp. 38–9), though this does not mean that they are without criticism from these socialist feminists (for further critiques see also Douglas, 1990, pp. 49–55).

Patriarchy is used by radical feminists to refer to a system of male domination, or male control, not only of women but also of other males; for example, Millett describes the 'principles of patriarchy' as twofold: 'Male shall dominate female, elder male shall dominate younger.' (1969, p. 25) Similarly, the Redstockings (1969) argue that 'men dominate women, a few men dominate the rest'. As this indicates, patriarchy is seen as the root of all other oppressions such as racist or class-based oppressions (see, for example, Bunch, 1972, pp. 8–9), which are an extension of male supremacy. For radical feminists, this hierarchy of domination is rooted in nature, or biological sex differences, specifically reproduction (Firestone, 1970, p. 11), and sexuality

(Leeds Revolutionary Feminist Group, 1981). For example, while Millett identifies patriarchy as multi-faceted (arguing that the following are contributory
factors: ideology; biology; socialization; class; education and economy; force;
religion and mythology; and psychology), she concludes that the tenacity
and power of patriarchy comes through 'its successful habit of passing itself
off as nature' (1969, p. 58). Therefore, while radical feminists, particularly
Millett, do take into account factors other than biological sex differences,
their argument is that this is the root of women's oppression under patriarchy and that all other types of oppression (such as economic) flow from
this (see, for example, Firestone, 1970, p. 35; Bunch, 1972, pp. 8–9). This
emphasis on nature, biology, and reproduction means that radical feminists,
following Simone de Beauvoir (1949, p. 18), do not characterize patriarchy
as something that began with a particular event or at a particular time but
rather has always existed throughout history (Douglas, 1990, p. 47). It is not,
however, nature or biology themselves that oppress women, but the ways
in which these biological differences are exploited by patriarchal ideology to
justify or support male domination. For radical feminists then, patriarchy is a
wide-ranging concept but, as discussed next, the focus on the way in which it
exploits biological reproductive differences and sexuality to oppress women
clearly implicates the family, as defined and idealized by the law of marriage,
as the 'chief institution' of patriarchy (Millett, 1969, p. 33).

Firestone argues that it is not biological differences between men and
women in themselves that created inequality, but the *reproductive functions*
of those differences (1970, p. 8) within the biological family. As such, she
argues that women could be freed by taking control of the means of reproduction; not only by regaining ownership of their own bodies, but also by
seizing control of human fertility 'as well as all the social institutions of
child-bearing and child-rearing' (1970, p. 11). While biological reproduction
could, of course, take place outside marriage in an equally oppressive manner,
Firestone's argument is that marriage 'was organized around, and reinforces,
a fundamentally oppressive biological condition [i.e. reproduction]' so that
as long as marriage exists, the oppressive conditions of biological reproduction will be built into it (1970, p. 202). For example, Firestone notes that at
the time of writing *The Dialectic of Sex* the majority of Americans approved of
scientific developments in artificial reproduction only if it was in the service
of 'family values', such as being restricted to helping infertile married couples
to conceive (1970, p. 179). In the UK, s. 13(5) of the Human Fertilisation
and Embryology Act 1990 (requiring consideration of the need of the child
for a father) also testified to the enduring nature of these beliefs (see further
Thomson, 1997; Sheldon, 2005; Thomson, 2008). This section was replaced
with a requirement for consideration of the need for 'supportive parenting'
by the Human Fertilisation and Embryology Act 2008, s. 14(2)(b), but this

new language has not meant a significant change in the interpretation of the provision in practice (McCandless and Sheldon, 2010).

To free women from biological reproduction would, according to Firestone, also necessitate freeing them from 'the *social* unit [marriage and the biological family] that is organized around biological reproduction and the subjection of women to their biological destiny' (1970, p. 185). So, for radical feminists such as Firestone, patriarchy exploits reproductive differences to oppress women and one of the primary ways in which it does this is through the social ideologies of the marriage model. This explanation of the role that the marriage model plays in even those aspects of patriarchy which are ostensibly 'justified' through biology and nature serves as a useful reminder of both the power and reach of patriarchy and the social significance of marriage in sustaining it. The power of the ideology of the marriage model is discussed further below, while reproduction is explored further through socialist feminist perspectives in the next section.

The second aspect of radical feminist theories of patriarchy that particularly implicates marriage is (hetero)sexuality and love; according to Firestone, 'love, perhaps even more than child-bearing, is the pivot of women's oppression today' (1970, p. 113). Firestone is not arguing that love is inherently destructive, nor that love itself is problematic, but instead that 'it becomes complicated, corrupted, or obstructed by *an unequal balance of power*...love demands a mutual vulnerability or it turns destructive' (1970, p. 116, original emphasis). In patriarchal society, it is not possible for there to be an equal balance of power while women occupy a lower class status to men. For Firestone, however, this unequal balance of power in love again derives from reproduction rather than (hetero)sexuality itself. In contrast, others who fall into the broad category of radical feminism would argue that hetero sex is, *in itself*, a manifestation and root of patriarchy as it constitutes the invasion and colonization of women's bodies (Leeds Revolutionary Feminist Group, 1981, p. 5). There are two parts to this argument. First, in a heterosexual couple, love and sex 'obscure the realities of [women's] oppression' (Leeds Revolutionary Feminist Group, 1981, p. 6), allowing the illusion that the woman is exercising free choice to love rather than it being in exchange for the security that her sex class position denies her independent access to (Firestone, 1970, p. 124; see also Dryden, 1999, discussed further below); and second, that penetration is not necessary for women's (or men's) sexual pleasure, but is:

> an act of great symbolic significance by which the oppressor enters the body of the oppressed....Every man knows that a fucked woman is a woman under the control of men, whose body is open to men, a woman who is tamed and broken in. (Leeds Revolutionary Feminist Group, 1981, p. 6)

Contemporary literatures on masculinities provide a parallel point to be made about the fucked man. A man whose body is entered by another man (or a woman) is perhaps also 'tamed' in the sense that, within the dominant (legal) discourse, 'normal masculinity' is so closely bound to the performance of penetration (Thomson, 2008) that '[the impotent man] is, *like the homosexual,* not really a man at all' (Collier, 1995, p. 150, emphasis added). The gay man is analogized with the impotent man as 'not really a man at all' both because he does not penetrate women *and* because he is (assumed to be) penetrated himself. This penetration of a man is seen as a threat to normal or hegemonic masculinity and the gay man, inevitably imagined as passive, is feminized by the gendered sexual stereotypes of the active and dominant masculine and the passive and submissive feminine. This is evidenced by derogatory attitudes towards 'bottoms' in gay male subcultures (see further Underwood, 2003).

Hetero sex that is not penetrative is also criticized on the basis that the 'emotional accretions' of any form of hetero sex reinforce men's class power (Leeds Revolutionary Feminist Group, 1981, p. 7; the emotional work of women is discussed below). The Radicalesbians argued that until women are free from heterosexuality tremendous energy will go into trying to make a 'new man' in the hope that this will result in the 'new woman', but instead women's emotional energies must 'flow towards our sisters not backwards towards our oppressors' (1970, p. 21). As such, these groups would espouse political lesbianism or even separatism (for discussion of separatism, see Frye, 1977), though this is controversial as a strategy even within radical feminism (see, for example, Leeds Revolutionary Feminist Group, 1981; Hoagland and Penelope, 1988).

Adrienne Rich (1981) presented a similar argument to that of the Leeds group, but attracted less controversy because, though she also argues that heterosexuality is a political system of oppression, her focus is on *compulsory* heterosexuality (discussed further in Chapter 6) rather than heterosexuality *as such* (Jeffreys, 1990, p. 295). Thus, 'heterosexuality is not indicted, only the force necessary to get women to participate' (Jeffreys, 1990, p. 297). Nevertheless, Rich's argument is that male power is maintained through enforcing heterosexuality on women (1981, p. 12), ensuring 'male right of physical, economical, and emotional access' (1981, p. 19).

As discussed next, the legal construction of sexuality through the consummation requirement of marriage provides a significant obstacle to achieving a more positive understanding of (hetero)sexuality in that *penetrative* hetero sex is legally defined *as* sex (Brook, 2001, p. 140).

Marriage is romanticized as a site of (hetero)sexuality, love and reproduction (see, for example, Barrett and McIntosh, 1982, p. 54; O'Donovan, 1993, p. 57; and Geller, 2001). The legacy of women's dependency on men within the institution did not end with the demise of coverture (see, for example, Millett, 1969, pp. 34–5; dependency is discussed further below). In fact, Heather Brook warns that 'vestiges of coverture' are still apparent in the consummation requirement (Brook, 2004, p. 83), which enforces a particularly patriarchal penetrative (hetero)sexuality within marriage. Through consummation, heterosexual penetration becomes the only legally approved form of sexual expression (O'Donovan, 1993, p. 47; see also Brook, 2001, p. 140, above). Thus, hetero sex and marriage are mutually reinforcing: marriage supports and is supported by (compulsory) heterosexuality in providing a legally approved forum whereby men (are expected to) access women's bodies (Pateman, 1988, p. 2). This, according to Pateman (1988, p. 110), makes the sexual contract[3] appear natural and inevitable.

This aspect of the radical feminist critique may not directly apply to same-sex marriage if the consummation requirement is not imposed on same-sex couples. However, its continuing relevance is not only in critiquing heterosexual marriage but also in demonstrating one of the problems with privileging sexual relationships in general (for further problems with this, see Cossman and Ryder, 2001).

Radical feminism is much criticized and has many internal divisions, which are particularly evident on the issue of hetero sex (see further Leeds Revolutionary Feminist Group, 1981; Segal, 1987, p. 97; Douglas, 1990). It is not my intention to provide another general critique of radical feminism in this chapter, as those debates are not the focus of this research. Instead, I will continue to chart the development of the feminist critiques of marriage by exploring the ways in which socialist feminists redefined and built upon this radical feminist notion of patriarchy, returning to issues of reproduction, dependency, emotional labour and privatization, before asking whether these arguments remain relevant to contemporary marriage.

Marriage, patriarchy and capitalism: socialist feminist perspectives

In contrast to the radical feminist focus on the denigration of women's biological reproduction, socialists (or Marxists)[4] explain women's oppression

---

3 That is, Pateman's theory that part of the original social contract (that the legitimacy of state rule comes from its origin in a contract where freedom is exchanged for protection) was also sexual in establishing 'men's political right over women … [and] orderly access by men to women's bodies' (1988, p. 2).

4 I am using these terms interchangeably because different socialist feminists have referred to the same work as both socialist and Marxist. Rather than making any political or ideological point about the sameness or difference of these schools of thought, I am simply using the terminology in the same way as the person being cited in order to retain the meaning that the author intended.

in terms of their connection to production, or more accurately, the lack of such connection (Hartmann, 1981, p. 4). Eisenstein explains that the sexual division was, for Marx and Engels, part of the class division of labour, rather than created by biological reproduction, and the first class conflicts and first divisions of labour were those between men and women within marriage and child-rearing (Eisenstein, 1979, pp. 10–12). Marxists did not believe there was any difference between the domestic slavery of the wife and the wage-slavery of the husband: both are derived from capitalism (Eisenstein, 1979, p. 15).

This can be explained further through the three approaches of Marxists to theorising women's oppression that Hartmann (1981, p. 5) identifies. First, they argue that women should enter the paid labour force, ending the sexual division of labour. This will not free women immediately but will enable them to join the revolution against private property, after which they will cease to be oppressed. Second, they argue that women's work in the home serves and reproduces capitalism and it is women's exclusion from paid work that causes their oppression. Third, women are exploited by capital through housework, which produces 'surplus value' by allowing capitalists to pay workers less than the value of what they produce (Hartmann, 1981, p. 10) and as such women can be theorized as part of the working class (see further Engels, 1972, pp. 199–200). This illustrates, then, that socialist theory firmly locates women's oppression within the relations of production (as opposed to reproduction) in a capitalist framework.

Socialist feminists have argued that socialism is 'deeply flawed' in that it does not adequately address the 'woman question' (Vogel, 1983, p. 2) or the specificity of women's situation (Kuhn and Wolpe, 1978, pp. 1–10), particularly in relation to the operation of reproduction under capitalism. Furthermore, socialist feminists also criticize radical feminists who, as I have discussed above, maintain that reproductive and sexual (rather than economic) power is central to patriarchy. For radical feminists, the struggle under patriarchy was that between women and men, rather than between the classes, and the determining societal relations were those of reproduction, rather than production (see Eisenstein, 1979, p. 17). As such, socialist feminists, drawing partly on the socialist analysis described above, criticized radical feminists for not taking into account the social context of patriarchy by considering only its biological basis in reproduction (McDonough and Harrison, 1978; Eisenstein, 1979; Vogel, 1983). It is argued that focusing solely on 'sex class', constructed as biologically based, 'artificially separates the sexual and economic spheres' (Eisenstein, 1979, p. 18). Radical feminist notions of patriarchy are also criticized by socialist feminists as ahistorical (Hartmann, 1981, p. 14) in that they do not provide an analysis of the development of patriarchy through time, nor in relation to other (economic and political) forms of domination (McDonough and Harrison, 1978, p. 13). Therefore, for socialist feminists:

> While Marxist analysis provides essential insight into the laws of historical development, and those of capital in particular, the categories of Marxism are sex-blind. Only a specifically feminist analysis reveals the systemic character of relations between men and women. Yet feminist analysis by itself is inadequate because it has been blind to history and insufficiently materialist. (Hartmann, 1981, p. 2)

Therefore, socialism in combination with the insights of (radical) feminism could be used to develop a useful socialist feminist theoretical framework to contribute to an understanding of patriarchy as deriving from both 'class relations of production and the sexual hierarchical relations of society' (Eisenstein, 1979, p. 1; see also Vogel, 1983, p. 2). However, when attempts were made to integrate feminist struggles into Marxist theory, feminism was 'subsumed' into 'the "larger" struggle against capital' (Hartmann, 1981, p. 2). As Heidi Hartmann has famously referred back to the doctrine of coverture to argue:

> The 'marriage' of Marxism and feminism has been like the marriage of husband and wife depicted in English common law: Marxism and feminism are one, and that one is Marxism. (1981, p. 2)

Instead of either simply replacing one 'primary determination' of women's oppression (economy/capitalism) with another (patriarchy), or allowing feminism to be subsumed into socialism, socialist feminists have attempted 'a more complete analysis' (Hartmann, 1981, p. 3) by *synthesising* Marxist and feminist theory. Rather than simply adding one to the other, they are using the conflict between them to redefine both (Eisenstein, 1979, p. 1; see also, more recently, Bryson, 2004, also stressing the need for Marxism itself to be transformed).[5] By doing this, socialist feminists recognize that reproduction and the family not only have 'their own, historically determined, products, material techniques, modes of organization, and power relationships' (Petchesky, 1979, p. 377) – that is, what radical feminists would refer to as patriarchy operating through differences in biological reproduction – but also 'are themselves integrally related to the social relations of production and the state' (Petchesky, 1979, p. 377). As such, Petchesky and other socialist feminists would argue that analysis of patriarchy and the political economy

---

5 This approach is criticized for its exclusion of race. For example, Joseph (1981, p. 93) argues that Marxism is not only sex-blind but is also race-blind and that racism must be addressed as an integral part of Marxist and feminist theory. See also Combahee River Collective (1979).

cannot be separated; women must be theorized as both mothers and workers, in terms of production and reproduction (Eisenstein, 1979, p. 1) and the interconnections between them (Bryson, 2004).

This attempt at synthesis was developed in two ways. First is the 'dual systems' perspective (Young, 1981, p. 44), which, as McDonough and Harrison use it, means that patriarchy derives from *both* the 'control of women's fertility and sexuality in monogamous marriage' *and* the 'economic subordination of women through the sexual division of labour and property' (1978, p. 40). This approach is, however, criticized by Iris Young, who argues that this still makes the mistake of assuming that capitalism and patriarchy are 'two distinct systems of social relations which have distinct structures, movement and histories' (1981, p. 44). Instead, Young argues that Marxism and feminism must be *combined* to understand *capitalist patriarchy* as a single system, in which 'the oppression of women is a *core* attribute' (1981, p. 44, original emphasis). Eisenstein too prefers this approach, also using the term capitalist patriarchy and arguing that capitalism and patriarchy are mutually dependent (1979, p. 22), with patriarchy providing political control through the sexual ordering of society and capitalism using this to create profit (1979, p. 28). For Eisenstein (1979, p. 27), the sexual hierarchical division of labour that is fundamental to both cuts through any attempt to separate them (1979, p. 27). This analysis of the role of the division of labour is also central to Young's (1981) formulation of capitalist patriarchy, as well as to socialist feminist analyses of marriage and the family. Socialist feminists argue that marriage supports the operation of capitalist patriarchy. For example, Carole Pateman argues that 'the employment contract presupposes the marriage contract' (1988, p. 131) in that it assumes that the (male) worker has a woman (housewife) to provide caretaking and housework. As such, there is an assumption in capitalism that marriage will contribute to the 'surplus value' of labour.

The remainder of this section will further demonstrate this link between marriage and capitalism before I move on in the next section to explore whether such arguments can be related to contemporary marriage.

As indicated above through reference to the work of Young (1981) and Eisenstein (1979), the exploitation of women through the sexual division of labour is key to, and supports, their oppression under capitalism (see also Kuhn and Wolpe, 1978, p. 7; Hartmann, 1979, p. 206). This sexual division of labour refers to both the domestic division and that in paid employment, argued to be cyclical and mutually supportive:

> [Sex segregation in jobs] maintains the superiority of men over women because it enforces lower wages for women in the labor market. Low wages keep women dependent on men because

they encourage women to marry. Married women must perform domestic chores for their husbands. Men benefit, then, from both higher wages and the domestic division of labor. This domestic division of labor, in turn, acts to weaken women's position in the labor market. (Hartmann, 1979, p. 208)

The ways in which the division of labour supports capitalist patriarchy can be categorized under four interlinking and overlapping headings: production within the home; reproduction; consumption; and women's paid work.

First, it is argued that women's domestic labour is 'production' in that cooking, laundry and childcare are economic activities, albeit ones that are consumed immediately within the family and before they reach the market-place.[6] As such, women have a slightly different relationship to production than men have (Benston in Vogel, 1983, p. 17) in that women do not 'own' their labour power in the same way that men do: they cannot sell it, or can sell only part of it (Delphy and Leonard, 1992, p. 159). Furthermore, through domestic work, a woman's 'whole work capacity is appropriated...by a particular individual from whom it is difficult or impossible to separate' (Delphy and Leonard, 1992, p. 159). While housework is seen by women as 'real work' (Barrett and McIntosh, 1982, p. 60), it is also different in that it takes place within the isolation of the private family and the tasks themselves contribute to the sexual hierarchy within the family. For example, the assumption is that 'to keep house is a natural adjunct of femininity...rooted in motherhood' (1982, p. 61).

In other words, women's domestic labour is explained by capitalist patriarchy as an extension of the biological facts of child-bearing: there is 'an inevitability so obvious that it does not need to be spelled out' that, having given birth, women will also take primary responsibility for childcare and housework (1982, p. 61). When men do engage in unpaid work in the home it is gendered and of the type that conveys them with more power: for example, by taking responsibility for the car, it becomes *his* car (1982, p. 62) and while women's housework is considered to be necessary (and is constant and often degrading), 'men's work' such as DIY has a more voluntary character (1982, p. 63).

Other socialists and socialist feminists, however, argued that rather than being a distinct form of production, domestic labour is production in the usual Marxist sense in that it creates 'surplus value': for example, by women providing free domestic services for male workers, employers can pay men

---

6 The existence of domestic workers also confirms the economic nature of these activities. For example, Hazel Carby notes the domestic labour done by black women servicing white families (1992, p. 115), asking how that affects (white) feminist understandings of (re)production. There are also many contemporary examples of poor women providing domestic services to middle-class women (for a personal account of such work, see Ehrenreich, 2002, pp. 51–119).

less (Gardiner, 1979, p. 188). This surplus value can be extracted in different ways so the cost of childcare, for example, was historically accommodated through the family wage paid to men (see Gavigan, 1996, pp. 257–8), whereas it could be argued that (in an era of dual incomes) it is now accommodated through 'work-life balance' measures (these are discussed further below). In this way, domestic labour is not *only* for direct consumption in the home, but also provides 'the capacity of a worker to work' (Vogel, 1983, p. 20). This is what led Mariarosa Dalla Costa to argue that 'the woman is the slave of a wage slave, and her slavery ensures the slavery of her man' (quoted in Vogel, 1983, p. 20). Vogel (1983, p. 24) criticizes both sides of this 'domestic labour debate' for leaving the role of child-bearing in capitalism undefined. Production alone, then, cannot fully explain the relationship of the family to capitalism. It does, however, illustrate one of the ways in which capitalist society as a whole benefits from the marriage model's nuclear family; a point to which I will return below.

The second heading is reproduction. This term is contentious but I will adopt Gill and Bakker's definition:

> What feminist theory calls social reproduction has three dimensions: (a) Biological reproduction of the species; (b) Reproduction of the labor force, and (c) Reproduction of provisioning and caring needs. Social reproduction involves fundamental social processes and institutions through which communities are reproduced and develop over time, and upon which all production and exchange ultimately rests. (Gill and Bakker, 2006, p. 41)

The family is the site of child-bearing and rearing. Not only does this provide the next generation of workers, but it is also where the ideologies of capitalist patriarchy are transferred to them. For example, Juliet Mitchell notes the ideological role of the family in cultivating a belief in individualism, freedom and equality (in Eisenstein, 1979, p. 27) and also in reproducing the gendered asymmetry of the parents in the developing notions of masculinity and femininity in boy and girl children (in McIntosh, 1982, p. 112). Chodorow (1979, pp. 92–6) argues that women also reproduce the labour force in acting as mothers for their husbands, providing nurturing and care when he returns home from the alienating, cruel, masculine world of capitalist employment, and so reproducing him physically and emotionally and thus ensuring 'worker stability'. This, Chodorow argues, 'removes the need for employers themselves to attend to such stability or to create contentedness' (1979, pp. 96–7), thus providing an example of the way in which women's domestic labour serves capitalism as well as individual men.

The final dimension cuts across and is evident in all of the four headings that I have identified. It refers to the ways in which capitalist patriarchy is stabilized through women's domestic labour (in that it reinforces the gendered hierarchy of society, for example, by impeding women's ability to engage in paid labour; see Hartmann quote above), through the housewife's role as caring for and 'steadying' male workers (above; Chodorow, 1979, p. 96), and as consumer for the family (Eisenstein, 1979, p. 29; discussed further below).

The third and fourth headings are 'relatively minor' aspects of the relationship between the family and capitalist patriarchy (McIntosh, 1982, p. 11) but both demonstrate ways in which the family serves capitalism. Third, in capitalist society, consumption largely takes place through the family and is performed by women in their role of meeting the food, shelter and other needs of the family (Weinbaum and Bridges, 1979, p. 191). This, Mary McIntosh notes, contributes to raising demand for consumer goods and thus 'helping to combat the tendency to over-production' (1982, p. 111). Finally, as the quote from Heidi Hartmann (above) notes, the preceding three headings combine to reduce the value of women's paid labour power as women are treated as a 'reserve army of labour' (McIntosh, 1982, p. 111), have a 'double shift' (McIntosh, 1982, p. 113) in the form of housework once they finish their paid work day, and are segregated into poorly paid occupations by the existence of a 'dual labour market' (Beechey, 1978).

Based on many of these points, Barrett and McIntosh refer to the family as 'anti-social'. The family is the way in which the social classes reproduce themselves through both bearing and rearing children (passing on the father's social class as well as educational advantage) (1982, p. 45) and through inheritance of wealth (1982, p. 46). Barrett and McIntosh's work is valuable in highlighting how the conservative discourses of individualism and self-sufficiency actually meant privatizing social responsibility within the family because 'the unit of self-support is not the individual but the family' (1982, pp. 47–8). This means that women and children are extensions of and dependent upon the man, reinforcing both male authority and privilege as well as the conservative, capitalist 'economic fantasy' where everyone works to support themselves and those who do not or cannot work outside the home are 'subsumed under those who can' (1982, p. 49), masking both 'interdependence and the necessity of a social conception of needs and a social plan for meeting them' (1982, p. 49; privatization is discussed further below). As such, they argue that rather than the family providing protection and warmth against a pre-existing harsh climate outside of it, the fact that society is predicated upon the assumption that people live in (marital) families that are taking care of dependencies has left the world outside the family 'bereft' (1982, p. 80), concluding that:

> As a bastion against a bleak society it [the family] has made that society bleak. It is indeed a major agency for caring, but

in monopolizing care it has made it harder to undertake other forms of care. It is indeed a unit of sharing, but in demanding sharing within it has made other relations tend to become more mercenary. It is indeed a place of intimacy, but in privileging the intimacy of close kin it has made the outside world cold and friendless, and made it harder to sustain relations of security and trust except with kin. Caring, sharing and loving would be more wide-spread if the family did not claim them for its own. (Barrett and McIntosh, 1982, p. 80)

The ways in which these themes, particularly those of privatization and dependency, are developed by contemporary feminists (writing in the second-wave tradition) are explored below, following an examination of the evolution of family life and marriage since the second-wave. I have demonstrated in this section that socialist feminists built on the theorising of radical feminists and socialists to develop a theory of the role of the family in supporting *capitalist patriarchy*. According to this, there are two beneficiaries of women's domestic labour (Eisenstein, 1979, p. 31). First, capitalism itself benefits from women's work because it stabilizes and cements capitalist patriarchy through the family as it 'reproduces the conditions of production' (Vogel, 1983, p. 28) by producing the next generation of compliant workers and stabilizes the economy through consumption. Some, such as Dalla Costa, would also argue that women contribute to production as housewives by adding to the 'surplus value' produced by their husband. Second, individual men benefit from the domestic work done for them by women: 'men, regardless of class, benefit (although differentially) from the system of privileges they acquire within patriarchal society' (Eisenstein, 1979, p. 31).

For some second-wave feminists, challenges to the division of labour would endanger not only the existence of a free labour pool, but also the sexual hierarchy of society itself (Eisenstein, 1979, p. 31). This focus on the sexual division of labour (both domestic and in the paid labour force) as the root of women's oppression under capitalist patriarchy (see also Hartmann, 1979, p. 208) belies the importance given by these socialist feminist theorists to the institutional, or societal, level as well as to what happens within individual families. With a slightly less explicitly oppressive division of labour in contemporary society (in that at least lip-service, though little more, is paid to women's equality in employment; see, for example, Lister, 2005, p. 451), these analyses may appear to lose significance but, as I will argue in the next two sections, while the division of labour has changed in that the breadwinner/housewife model has declined with more women in the paid labour force (see below), there is evidence that claims of an equal domestic division of labour are a myth, making second-wave theories about women's 'double shift' (McIntosh, 1982, p. 113) of continuing relevance in contemporary society. Furthermore, the increasing individualism and neoliberalism of the third-wave society makes the work that the family does in support of capitalism become more, not less, evident.

Marriage and the (post)modern family

It might be argued that practices within individual marriages have changed significantly since the second-wave (though for a 'cautionary feminist fable' of such suggestions, see Gavigan, 2006). The breadwinner/housewife construct of marriage, itself anything but historically constant (see, for example, Engels (1972) on pre-industrial family forms), is being supplanted by the dual income family as the statistical norm. But does the apparent decline of the family form that was the primary focus of second-wave critiques mean that the latter becomes less relevant? I will begin by interrogating the premise of this claim: that family forms have changed. Although the statistics demonstrate a vast increase in women in the workforce (including those with children), I will use evidence from empirical sociological research and national statistics to demonstrate that the division of labour within the family has nevertheless remained relatively unchanged. Drawing on Betty Friedan's (1963) concept of 'occupation: housewife', I will argue that this becomes 'occupation: superwoman'[7] as third-wave women are expected to both work outside the home on the same terms as men and also take primary responsibility for housework and childcare.

Following this, I will discuss changes in family forms. To what extent can the institution of marriage itself continue to be held responsible for women's oppression at a time when marriage rates are declining and non-marital cohabitation is increasing? I will explore this question by reference to the continuing power of marriage ideology, as evidenced by the strength of the marriage model as a way of organizing non-marital cohabitation. Finally in this section, I will interrogate and problematize the claims from Nan Hunter and others, discussed in Chapter 4, that same-sex marriage might disrupt the gendered assumptions of marriage.

So far in this chapter I have referred to the sex categories of 'men' and 'women' as being advantaged and disadvantaged in different ways through the institutions of marriage and the family. I demonstrated above that the distinction between sex and gender was beginning to be adopted in feminist analysis during the second-wave in that feminists were arguing that it was not biological differences in themselves that oppressed women but rather

---

7 This refers to Shirley Conran's book *Superwoman*, which aims to 'help you [the working mother] do the work you don't like as fast as possible, leaving time for the work you enjoy' (1975, p. 17).

the ways in which gendered feminine roles were denigrated and inevitably assigned to women under patriarchy. However, the evidence from the second-wave was that the gendered feminine roles within the family were in fact being carried out by women. As such, while the sex/gender distinction was being employed as a useful theoretical tool to challenge patriarchal ideology (see Fletcher, 2002, p. 140), generally, second-wave feminist theory makes the reasonable assumption that the position of sexed women within the family related to the feminine gendered role and that of men to the masculine gendered role.

Some of the arguments that I will present next suggest that the household division of labour is (at least becoming) less 'women's work' and more a matter for negotiation. Men may adopt a role that is gendered feminine (for example, caretaking and housework within the family), whether sharing responsibility for some tasks or taking sole responsibility. While I argue that the statistics demonstrate that the feminine gendered role in fact remains *predominantly* the responsibility of women within the family, I acknowledge that to the extent that men do adopt the feminine role they may also be systemically disadvantaged. Where I refer to men benefiting from women's household labour, I am following Martha Fineman's (1995) reasoning when she argued that her terminology of the 'mother/child' dyad included men who had primary or equal responsibility for childcare as 'mothers'.

A few good men?

A 2004 *Feminism and Psychology* special issue on marriage provides examples of some of the ways in which marriage is argued to have changed since the second wave. Many (though not all) of the feminist writers in this collection support marriage on the basis that contemporary couples live or 'do' marriage/relationships differently, defending the institution through the narrative of their own 'feminist marriage' and/or arguing that the oppressive and exploitative aspects of marriage for women can be overcome through 'discursive practice' at the individual level (Elizabeth, 2004, p. 427). They suggest that the partners can and should negotiate egalitarian relationships within the marriage. For example, Marchbank and Marchbank (2004, p. 468) argue, 'We can, to a large extent, make choices that avoid some of the practices of patriarchy' and Elizabeth (2004, p. 429) argues that:

> Increasingly I am convinced that a single recipe for creating an egalitarian heterosexual relationship does not exist. Rather, women who *want* to craft egalitarian partnerships with men need to *strategically deploy* a variety of discourses and engage in a raft of different practices to manage the situational contexts that constitute their lives. (emphasis added)

This inevitably poses the question of the extent to which third-wave women are able to negotiate the household division of labour. Giddens' theory of the 'pure relationship' would suggest that if a gendered division of labour was unacceptable to individual women, they would leave the relationship:

> [A pure relationship is] a social relation ... entered into for its own sake, for what can be derived by each person from a sustained association with another; and which is continued only in so far as it is thought by both parties to deliver enough satisfactions for each individual to stay within it. (Giddens, 1993, p. 58)

If women are able to simply walk away from relationships once the relationships stop providing enough satisfaction, then presumably any economic exploitation happens with the consent of the woman or is at least offset by other benefits of the relationship such as love. For example, Mansfield and Collard (1988) found in their study of recently married people that women were generally prepared to accept 'the inequitable distribution of work and resources in marriage' as long as they were loved and valued (in Jackson, 1997, p. 338). However, this does not take into account the societal forces of economics, socialization and the normative assumptions of 'traditional' marriage that prevent women from exercising this agency to the extent that Giddens assumes they are able to. Although women are not simply puppets who respond unquestioningly to patriarchal forces, the normative values of marriage (powerfully sustained through popular culture: see Geller, 2001) should not be underestimated. In addition, Smart and Neale criticize Giddens' model:

> There is nothing here about class-based inequalities and how they might stop this shift. Nor is there any recognition that racism might in fact exert a push towards traditional marriage rather than away from it for some communities ... [Furthermore] having children often makes it much harder for individuals (usually mothers) to leave relationships and to be financially independent. (1999, p. 12)

In addition to these criticisms, to point to some instances of equal roles in childcare, for example, and argue on that basis that women are capable of negotiating equality in their own relationships demonstrates only the existence of some strong women and some benevolent men. The continued existence of *societal* structures of inequality such as those discussed in this chapter is clear (see also Boyd, 1994b; Fineman, 2004) and will not be challenged by such individualism. Instead, women not lucky enough to have a 'progressive' husband would become more isolated and attribute their stress, exhaustion and anger to their own failings rather than to exploitation. As

Wise and Stanley note, 'the argument that marriage is a private matter can be sustained only by ignoring its contractual basis and how this regulates inter-connections with the community, the family and with parenting children' (2004, p. 332).

I would, therefore, suggest that claims of possibilities for a more equal division of labour if women act on their agency belie continuing societal structures of inequality and gendered power dynamics within the home. Women are working full time outside the home in increasing numbers in addition to taking primary responsibility for a large proportion of the actual housework: the empirical research on household divisions of labour suggests that although housework done by men has increased over this period, 'most of the regular domestic work is still "women's work"' (Armstrong, 1997, p. 50). This is a Canadian study but its findings are also reflected in more recent statistics from the United Kingdom, which show that in the early twenty-first century, although men did four times as much housework than they did in 1942, this still amounted to only around half that done by women (Office for National Statistics, 2006a).

Women also continue to take primary responsibility for the emotional labour of the household (which the arguments of *Feminism and Psychology* contributors implicitly accepted was women's responsibility by reasoning that they should negotiate with men for a fairer division of labour). Emotional labour is, according to Duncombe and Marsden, more onerous for women than physical labour in that it ranges from responsibility for buying birthday cards on behalf of the families to 'recognizing and meeting the emotional needs of household members' to maintaining 'emotional communication' and 'emotional intimacy' with their husbands. When husbands resisted the last of these, women experienced emotional loneliness within the relationship as a *personal* failure (1993, p. 103). This type of emotional labour falls predominantly to wives, who 'felt they were the ones who reassured and were understanding and tender to their husbands, but their husbands failed to reciprocate' (1993, p. 93).

This gulf in the respective levels of housework done by men and women is not greatly affected by women's employment outside the home. Susan Moller Okin examines the difference in the number of hours spent on housework between 'predominantly houseworking wives' and 'predominantly wage-working wives' and their husbands in the United States. She concludes that where both spouses work full-time there are 'gross inequities in the amount and type of work done by each [spouse]' (1989, p. 154). Okin argues that wives in full-time employment do more than twice the amount of housework as their similarly situated husbands (28 hours per week for women compared to 9 for men). Recent statistics in the UK suggest some improvement, though a significant gap remains: the 2005 *Time Use Survey* found that the average amount of time per day spent on housework by women who work full time outside the home was 125 minutes compared with 86 minutes for men who work full time outside the home (Office for National Statistics, 2006b, p. 53). Therefore, the statistics would suggest that, while there have been significant changes in the patterns of women working *outside* the home, this has not been matched by the same level of change within the home.

There remain, then, clear benefits to individual men in contemporary society of women's work in the home, just as feminists argued during the second-wave. As Jackson notes, when women take care of the children and make sure their husbands have clean clothes, this allows men more time for paid work and leisure at the expense of that of their wives (1997, pp. 330–1); increased earning power as a result of this gives men more claim to control the household income and more power generally within the marriage (see, for example, Vogler and Pahl, 1994, p. 130; Dryden, 1999, p. 146). The Equalities Review provided further statistical evidence of the impact of this on women's careers, which is particularly pronounced when they are mothers:

> Our new research reveals clearly that there is one factor that above all leads to women's inequality in the labour market – becoming mothers…although the penalty faced by partnered mothers of young children relative to partnered men fell by around a third since 1975, it still stood at 40 per cent in 2002…In contrast, men's employment rates are not affected by fatherhood. (2007, pp. 66–7)

Therefore, individual men continue to benefit from women's work in the home in three ways: first from the household 'services' his wife performs on his behalf; second, from the resulting free time that enables him to both work and have leisure time (Jackson, 1997, p. 334); and finally, these two advantages work to cement or increase his power within the family because decision-making power within inegalitarian marriages was found to be predominantly determined by a sexist calculation of who contributed the most resources of the type valued outside the family, particularly income and work status (Okin, 1989, p. 158). This benefit to the husband is therefore gained by way of a corresponding detriment to his wife in terms of her power (or ability to exercise the agency that Giddens attributes to her), her leisure time and her career.

As I have noted above, one of the ways in which society has changed since the second wave is the increasing numbers of women in the paid workforce. This has led to a corresponding shift in ideology from the 1960s, when Betty Friedan identified the strength of the 'occupation: housewife' ideology in the United States at a time when the professions were increasingly opening up to women; that is, the depiction in popular culture of the 'happy housewife heroine' who, after having worked outside the home, realized that she really wanted to be a housewife (1963, p. 39):

> I went through issue after issue of the major women's magazines...without finding a single heroine who had a career, a commitment to any work, art, profession, or mission in the world, other than 'Occupation: housewife'. Only one in a hundred heroines had a job; even the young unmarried heroines no longer worked except at snaring a husband.

Now, in an almost complete cycle, while women are working outside the home in increasing numbers, surveys suggest that the '1980s superwoman' combining full-time career and motherhood is recognized by women to be an impossible aspiration (O'Kelly, 2004; Frith, 2005). Instead, there are several media reports that women are romanticising the idea of housewifery and full-time motherhood: a survey by *New Woman* magazine found that, under no illusions as to the difficulties of combining work and family life, a quarter of women planned to stop working outside the home when they had children to return to the 1950s 'traditional' role of carer to their husband's breadwinner (Benn, 2005).

This 'choice' is not, of course, available to single mothers, or women whose partner does not earn enough to support the family; single mothers in particular remain reviled by the political and religious right for a variety of 'social ills' and are viewed with suspicion or even contempt, depending on whether they have access to income other than state benefits (see, for example, Kirkby, 2003; see also Carabine, 2001; Chunn and Gavigan, 2004).

However, despite these media reports, the twenty-first-century 'heroine' is not (yet) the mother who gives up a career outside the home to raise children, instead the heroine is the woman who performs most of the household tasks of the 1960s housewife, but who also has her own career, often working full time.[8] This is a distortion of the goals of second-wave feminists who fought to free women from the constraints of the home. The contemporary economic exploitation of married women is both through the continued appropriation of their household labour (and the resulting disadvantage in terms of the impact this has on their 'career assets': Okin, 1989), and is combined with the increasing family reliance on the second income, creating a double burden for wives. 'Occupation: housewife' becomes 'occupation: superwoman' with the 'ideal' modern woman working at least part time, but for many full time, and also having primary responsibility for the household and children

---

8 Of course, a reasonably well-paid career allows some people to purchase the services of other women in the poorly paid 'feminine' industries, such as childcare and cleaning. See, for example, Carby (1992) and Ehrenreich (2002) for accounts of exploitation of poor, ethnic minority and immigrant women working in these industries.

(see, for example, Armstrong, 1997; Kay, 1997), whether performing the tasks herself or contracting them out, either through negotiation with her partner or in the private sector. There have been societal and political changes to 'accommodate' this double role (or triple role if they have elderly parents as well), which while (perhaps) ameliorating this situation also inevitably serve to entrench it as the norm. For example, the government introduced 'flexible working', which gives parents with a child under the age of six a statutory right to ask their employer for flexible working hours, such as part-time working, flexi-time, compressed hours (i.e. working their hours over fewer days), or job-sharing (Work and Families Act 2006; Department for Trade and Industry, 2006, p. 10). Conaghan and Grabham argue that:

> From the outset it is apparent that the government's approach to work and families is already based on an explicitly heteronormative model, which juxtaposes 'maternity' against 'paternity' and favours a traditional gendered division of labour. The [Work and Families Act 2006] does little to challenge such a model...there remains an assumption that one parent will continue to work, normally full-time, whilst the other remains at home to look after the child. (2007, p. 339)

Thus, despite overwhelming evidence to the contrary and some small policy changes to allow, for example, parental leave in limited circumstances, there remain the same underlying assumptions of the capitalist state as identified by second-wave socialist feminists: that there is a caretaker/housekeeper working in a supporting role within the home for free. It is hardly surprising then that the gender gap remains in all aspects of economic welfare (Fawcett Society, 2005b): despite increases in women's employment outside the home, there remains a pay gap between women and men in full-time work, with women earning on average only 83 pence for every £1 of men's full-time income; women who work part time earn 32 per cent less per hour than a female full-time worker and 41 per cent less per hour than a male full-time worker (Equalities Review, 2007, p. 66).

Martha Fineman also identified these assumptions in the United States context, arguing that:

> On a structural as well as an ideological level, we need reforms that counter the pervasive assumption that the American worker is an unencumbered individual, free to participate in an inflexible nine-to-five schedule, without concern for ill children, school vacations, or other caretaking glitches, because some woman is taking care of all of that at home, for free. (2001, p. 36; see also Boyd, 1997, p. 13)

This issue is clearly not, then, a solely economic one: the dominance of males in the sphere of paid employment gives them power in the family, yet the gendered, hierarchical organization of the paid labour market relies itself on the gendered division of labour within the home (Boyd, 1996, pp. 165–6).

Recent qualitative work has demonstrated that there are also more straight-forwardly patriarchal supports for inequality within contemporary marriage, perhaps supporting the approach of socialist feminists described above. Caroline Dryden found that, although contemporary couples are likely to describe their marriage as a relationship of equals, including in relation to the division of labour (1999, p. 16), this perception would be undermined by their described practices and there was a gender-equality 'issue' for all of her interviewees (1999, p. 146).

That the women were 'actively engaged in challenging the legitimacy of perceived gender power imbalances with their husbands' (1999, p. 146) could be interpreted to support the assertions of the *Feminism and Psychology* con-tributors (above). However, Dryden concludes that, where women were mak-ing these challenges, they were doing so very cautiously and seemingly with little real success; rather than being an equal division of labour, there was an *unequal but 'justified'* division, in that it appeared natural and sensible based on the working patterns of each spouse.

The reasons for women's caution in addressing these inequalities were not simply economic, although women's financial dependence (compounded by interruptions in or an end to full-time employment on the birth of children) remained a factor. In addition, there were 'lurking *emotional* terrors' of being alone or unloved (1999, p. 147). These fears were based on (gendered) psy-chological factors, 'insecurity, lack of confidence and guilt were common' (1999, p. 147). Dryden's research found that these negative emotions were 'intimately linked' to the husband's behaviour in fostering them and play-ing on them by undermining the wife, or blaming perceived inequalities on her own characteristics (such as her disposition or even her biology), or by 'engaging in physical and emotional distancing and separation practices with their wives' (1999, p. 147). These practices were, Dryden argues, an attempt to maintain gender hierarchies, keeping a wife under control, by exploiting and exacerbating her 'already vulnerable social position' (1999, pp. 147–8).

It is fair to conclude, then, that despite some changes the situation of women in both individual marriages and in society (as a result of the mar-riage assumption made by employers and the state, see above) has not changed to the extent that second-wave theories are redundant (see also Boyd 1996, p. 175). Further, Irwin argues that there is 'an emergent consen-sus' among sociologists that 'continuity rather than change is the defining feature of women's position relative to that of men, in both employment and the family' (1999, p. 28). The question remains, however, as to how far the institution of marriage itself remains a key contributing factor in gendered divisions of labour and, more generally, women's exploitation and oppression within the family when the statistical significance of marriage is less than it was during the second wave. This is discussed next, followed by my analysis of the potential impact of same-sex marriage on women's oppression within the family.

Cohabitation and the marriage model

There is little doubt that in statistical terms marriage in the UK is no longer the foundational institution that it was once claimed to be. Although 7 in 10 families are still 'headed' by a married couple, there is an increasing diversity of contemporary family structures, both heterosexual and same-sex (Office for National Statistics, 2005). Perhaps the most striking change from the second wave is the increase in cohabiting non-marital families,[9] though Silva and Smart also identify a more general shift away from family being defined by formal, legal ties:

> A major change in the concept of family is that it has come to signify the subjective meaning of intimate connections rather than formal, objective blood or marriage ties. This subject appreciation binds together people who live in separate households for part of the time, or all of the time, as well as people who have legal links, or people who simply choose to belong together as family. (Silva and Smart, 1999, p. 7)

Recent studies and statistics illustrate that people's stated attitudes and patterns of behaviour have generally been moving away from the idea of marriage that remains embedded in the law and people increasingly see no moral (see, for example, Jamieson et al., 2002) and, mistakenly, no legal (see for example, Barlow et al., 2005, pp. 27–31) difference between marriage and cohabitation.

However, I suggest that this statistical decline in the numbers of people getting married is not a statement about a declining significance of marriage in terms of an *ideal* (see also O'Donovan, 1993). The ways in which people are defining and living their intimate (or couple) relationships remain to a large extent *modelled* on marriage: people are not generally cohabiting as an alternative lifestyle to marriage (although some do feel that there is symbolism in not 'owning' each other through remaining unmarried: Barlow

---

9 The Office for National Statistics *Focus on Families* study (2005) shows that much of this change has been since the mid-1990s: from 1996–2004 the number of cohabitant families increased by 50% from 1.4 million to 2.2 million and there was a slight decrease in the number of married couples between 1996–2004, from 12.6 million to 12.1 million.

and James, 2004, p. 157). Instead, people cohabit as either a precursor to marriage (a 'trial marriage'), or because they are prohibited by the cost of a large traditional wedding (which is conflated with marriage), or because they do not believe there is any moral or legal difference between the marriage and cohabitation (Barlow and James, 2004, pp. 157–8, 161).

I would argue that this lack of (perceived) distinction extends to roles within the relationship including the division of labour, which was never a formal, legal requirement of marriage (although Smart (1984) demonstrated that it was enforced on divorce through punitive measures against 'bad' wives and mothers; see Gavigan (1988) for further discussion of the role of ideology in judicial decisions). This lack of distinction in popular consciousness between marriage and non-marital cohabitation does not mean that the legal framework has become less important in shaping the social relationships within the institutions of marriage and family. Instead, as Shelley Gavigan argues, the law shapes, defines and reinforces the ideology of the family (1988, p. 294). She defines familial ideology as:

> the range of dominant ideas and social practices, discourses and prejudices, common sense and social science, in which relations of gender and generation are held out and generally accepted to be best organized around and through a household comprised of two adults of the opposite sex who (usually) have expressed a primary personal, sexual, and economic commitment to each other and to care for and raise any children they may have. (1995, p. 103)

This ideology, which is clearly much broader than merely encompassing the construction of the legal institution of marriage, is based on the *model* of relationship that is associated with marriage: the private family household (consisting of one man and one women), within which the division of labour is at least presumptively gendered. It also idealizes a particular type of relationship, one that is based on not only its legal structure, but also its history and tradition (including religious ideology), and even its status in popular culture (see, for example, Geller, 2001) as well as the multifarious and interconnecting ways in which each reinforces the 'mythical status' (O'Donovan, 1993, p. 44) of marriage.

This model is thus so strong that it permeates popular consciousness as the natural and inevitable way to live. This is explained by Alison Diduck in terms of Gillis' (1997) distinction between families we live *with* and families we live *by* (2003, p. 20). Although families we actually live with might be different from the traditional nuclear (married) family, families we live by (the picture of the 'ideal' family) remain a version of the model that was critiqued by second-wave feminists. Similarly, Deborah Chambers argues that though there are a variety of living arrangements and though, for some people, the nuclear family has only ever been a transitional phase in their lives,

> the modern nuclear family *does* exist and is flourishing as an ideal: as a symbol, discourse and powerful myth within the collective imagination. This cultural myth is a regulatory force that impacts on our lives at a very personal level. It structures emotions, modes of official knowledge, bodies, identities and definitions of public and private cultural space. (2001, p. 1, original emphasis)

This continuing power of the nuclear family as an ideal is also supported by Joan Chandler who found that although some women were living in various forms of quasi-marriage or non-marriage that were distinct alternatives to marriage, these were simultaneously reflections of 'the nature of marriage and its connections to wider social structure' (1991, p. 167). Furthermore, the legal primacy attached to marriage, as evidenced by its special status in law and legal privileges (such as spouses not being compelled to testify against one another), reinforces the marriage model as the ultimate 'special relationship' (Polikoff, 2003, pp. 201–2).

One way in which the second-wave theories could be adapted to more accurately reflect contemporary society is thus to use the language of the *marriage model* as opposed to (and in addition to) marriage itself as the unit of analysis to bring into focus both the ideological, social, mythological and cultural supports to the legal institution of marriage, and also the extended reach of the marriage model in influencing the ways in which non-marital relationships are lived. It cannot be assumed, as the focus on marriage implies, that non-marital heterosexual cohabitation is less supportive of capitalist patriarchy than marriage itself. To make this assumption would be to overlook the power of the familial ideology that both supports and is supported by the legal framework (see Gavigan, 1988). The remaining question about the changing contemporary family relates to the potential impact of same-sex marriage on women's oppression within the family.

Same-sex marriage: a model of egalitarianism?

Radical feminists, as I have demonstrated above, would contend that it is *heterosexuality* as much as (and more generally than) marriage that oppresses women. Taking this contention one step further (though in a different direction), some feminists, as I discussed in Chapter 4, argue that the existence of *same-sex* marriages would be more egalitarian and destabilize gendered roles within marriage, including heterosexual marriage (Hunter, 1995, pp. 110–12). This is the final aspect of third-wave relationships that I will discuss, before moving on in the next section to analyse the ways in which contemporary feminists are developing second-wave theories of privatization and dependency in relation to contemporary families. This highlights a problem with marriage and the marriage model that is irredeemable no matter how much agency individual women are now able to exercise within their marriages.

The critiques relating to the divisions of labour that have been discussed so far, while important and demonstrably still a major problem with the institution of marriage, relate to the numerically and socially dominant marriage or family form that is white and heterosexual. The disappearance of difference in feminist theorising (more generally than in relation to marriage) has, furthermore, been noted and critiqued by Black feminists and lesbian feminists, among others (see, for example, Rich, 1981; Carby, 1992), and it could be argued that the criticisms outlined so far do not easily translate to same-sex relationships, which have been found to be at least striving for egalitarianism, if not actually achieving it all the time (Dunne, 1997; Weeks et al., 2001; discussed in Chapter 4). However, the discourses of egalitarianism within same-sex relationships have been problematized by Christopher Carrington; and Nancy Polikoff argues that even if same-sex marriages were more egalitarian, this is unlikely to result in greater egalitarianism more generally (1993).

Christopher Carrington (1999) conducted an in-depth qualitative study of 52 lesbian and gay families in San Francisco during the 1990s. Though his research was concerned with a relatively small sample from one (American) city and thus may not be generalizable to the UK context, his findings are interesting. First, both in-depth interviews (with the partners separately) and ethnographic observation revealed that there was 'a chasm' between what the interviewees reported and what he observed in terms of the household division of labour. He found that, like heterosexual couples, same-sex couples tended to assert equality and appeal to myths that hide unequal divisions of labour (1999, p. 14). In fact, he suggests that these tendencies may be stronger for same-sex couples for several reasons, in which gender politics played a prominent role. For example, Carrington claims that some gay men embrace traditional masculinities so that where one partner does most of the housework, this is denied. He also claims that for some lesbians, lesbian identity is seen as a way of resisting gendered inequality and so this ideological commitment to egalitarianism means that any inequality that does exist is denied. Finally, he claims that partners camouflage unequal divisions of labour 'to prevent threats to the gender identities of their partners' (1999, p. 15) so that in a male same-sex relationship one partner is not portrayed as a 'housewife' and in a female same-sex relationship one partner is not portrayed as unfeminine. There was also awareness amongst participants that they were representing same-sex families to the wider world (1999, p. 16).

Second, Carrington absolutely refutes suggestions that same-sex relationships are egalitarian, noting the nearly universal claims of an equal division of household labour while the empirical evidence does not support this (1999, p. 217). He argues that assertions, such as Hunter's, are 'based on the ideology of egalitarianism, not on its actual existence, and on the invisibility, devaluation and diminishment of domesticity' (1999, pp. 217–18). The division of household labour, he found, primarily reflected the influence of paid work (1999, p. 219). There was more likely to be an egalitarian division of labour where both partners worked in female-dominated professional occupations, such as teaching or public sector administration (1999, p. 185).[10] Likewise, wealthier households were able to achieve equity through reliance on the service economy:

> Some lesbigay families achieve partial equity in their relationships through reliance on the labors of mostly working-poor people...These workers are for the most part Latino-, Asian-, and African-American women, and young gay men and lesbians. (1999, p. 185)

However, in the vast majority of households (three-quarters), like Dryden (above), Carrington found an unequal but justified division of labour. The justification was based on the paid work of each partner, with the partner with the lower-paying or less prestigious job picking up 'a disproportionate share' of household labour (1999, p. 188). Carrington concludes that:

> placing the burden of caregiving upon the family unit leads to an unfair distribution of work and resources within families. It is highly problematic to rely upon the unpaid labors of women and some men (including many of the gay men in families studied here) to provide caregiving. It fosters inequality within relationships and requires too much sacrifice on the part of caregivers; it also fosters privatism and an extreme preoccupation with one or two individuals that eclipses the concerns of the wider community. In our public policy and political organizing we should emphasize the public responsibility to create and sustain social institutions that provide care...over expectations of care from legally defined family members. (1999, p. 225)

Nancy Polikoff also argues against Nan Hunter's theory. She highlights research compiled by William Eskridge about same-sex marriages in history and in other cultures, which demonstrated that same-sex marriages often supported gender hierarchy in that traditional gender roles were acted out

---

10 Carrington suggests this is because these occupations offer family-friendly working policies, which provide a more conducive environment for both partners to do some family work (1999, p. 186).

through one partner adopting the roles of the other gender (1993, p. 1538). More significantly, she argues that this research would be more likely to lead pro-marriage advocates to argue that there would be no difference between heterosexual and same-sex marriages (1993, pp. 1540–1), an argument that has subsequently been proven correct. Polikoff demonstrates, by reference to examples from abortion and 'gays in the military' campaigns that, while same-sex marriage *could* be transformative, the pro-marriage discourse is likely to be de-radicalized in order to 'win'. For example, in the case of abortion campaigns, she demonstrates how the argument evolved from one of women's sexual freedom and liberation from male dominance to one of privacy and choice; abortion becoming constructed as a 'difficult, even morally ambiguous, personal choice…as a matter of last resort' (1993, p. 1543). Polikoff argued that same-sex marriage would:

> Require a rhetorical strategy that emphasises similarities between our relationships and heterosexual marriages, values long-term monogamous coupling above all other relationships, and denies the potential of lesbian and gay marriage to transform the gendered nature of marriage for all people. (1993, p. 1549)

In the light of this prediction being borne out (see Chapters 3 and 4) it is difficult to imagine how Hunter would maintain her argument today, particularly as she agrees with Polikoff and others, such as Cheshire Calhoun (2000, p. 130), that the arguments made for same-sex marriage will, in fact, impact on its radical potential and possibly much more so than the legal reform itself:

> The impact of law often lies as much in the body of discourse created in the process of its adoption as in the final legal rule itself. What a new legal rule is popularly understood to signify may determine more of its potential for social change than the particulars of the change in law. (Hunter, 1995, p. 121)

Although same-sex marriage might have some impact, its potential to 'dismantle the legal structure of gender in every marriage' (Hunter, 1995, p. 114) diminishes with the adoption of sameness arguments in support of it. Susan Boyd also demonstrated the difficulties with trying to disrupt problematic legal concepts whilst working within the legal structure in relation to a lesbian spousal support case in Canada, arguing that:

> the ways that the legal arguments had to be formulated [in order to succeed] meant that the potentially disruptive lesbian subject was absorbed back into familiar roles and, to a large extent, her disruptive potential was displaced. In many ways the dominant

> relations of production and ruling were reproduced by our equal-
> ity arguments: the role of the family in absorbing social costs
> of dependency and social reproduction was explicitly rein-
> forced...(1999, p. 381)

The discussion in this section demonstrates that, though there are arguably some ways in which marriage has changed, these changes took place
on the individual, rather than structural level of marriage. Furthermore,
the changes in family form demonstrate not that marriage has weakened
or evolved as an institution but instead that the way in which its normative
power operates has been adapted or even *extended* in that there is little difference between marriage and non-marital (heterosexual) cohabitation. The
argument that same-sex marriages would challenge the gender hierarchies of
marriage has been questioned in light of empirical evidence to the contrary
and the discourses that are being adopted in favour of same-sex marriage.
Such 'challenges' to marriage, while they perhaps should not be dismissed
entirely, are unlikely to have any significant effect on the institution because
they do not challenge one of the central ways in which it reinforces capitalist patriarchy: the privatization of domestic labour within the family. This is
discussed next.

Marriage and the privatization of care

As I have demonstrated in the previous section, marriage on an individual
level has not changed as much as might be assumed on the basis of women's
increasing participation in paid employment, particularly in relation to the
division of labour. However, the issue is not only an individual but also a
structural one: as Susan Boyd notes, even if all men would 'assume a greater
share of social reproductive labour, the costs of social reproduction are merely
redistributed as between women and men, while still privatized within "the
family"' (1999, p. 377). As such, despite any (small) progress that may have
been made with regard to the sexual division of labour *within* the family, the
key issue is actually that the burdens of social reproduction, and its costs,
are privatized within the family as a whole. The second-wave socialist feminist analyses, including those of contemporary feminists such as Susan Boyd,
Brenda Cossman, Martha Fineman, and Shelley Gavigan who have subsequently developed these analyses, are particularly valuable in their *collective*
emphasis: the focus on the societal functions of marriage and its interconnections with other institutions of society, particularly the state.

Although the distinction between the public and private spheres is the
subject of debate, particularly because the boundaries of public/private vary
according to factors such as race, class, or sexual identity (for discussion of

these debates see Boyd, 1997, pp. 12–15), it remains a useful one (see Cossman and Fudge, 2002). In terms of the privatization of dependency, the language of public/private *norms* (Fletcher, 2002, p. 146) is especially useful in examining the ideology that leads the state to impose caretaking responsibilities on the family unit. For example, Boyd argues that an expectation that childcare will be done in the home for free by mothers 'is reciprocally connected to both the underpaid nature of child care labour (often performed by women of colour) and to the lack of publicly funded day care that would enable women to work outside the home' (1997, p. 14, references omitted). So, as noted above, capital and the state (the public sphere) rely on (historically women's) unpaid work in the private sphere (Boyd, 1997, p. 13; Fineman, 2001, p. 36), specifically, that 'particular responsibilities will be taken care of in the private sphere of family, which in turn rests on women's unpaid or poorly paid labour' (Boyd, 1997, p. 17). Efforts to alleviate the impact of this on families (such as extending parental leave and other employment rights) have merely entrenched the notion that they are private and primarily women's responsibilities (see above; Fawcett Society, 2005a; 2005b).

Privatization can refer to a number of different processes. The one that is generally referred to in this context is 'the transfer of public goods and services to the private sector' (Cossman, 2005, p. 422), more specifically, the family. This is broadly associated with fiscal conservatism (often used interchangeably with neoliberalism: Cossman, 2005, p. 436), aiming to shift responsibility for social reproduction away from the collective (public/state) to the individual (private/family). This process of privatization can be clearly seen within family law and the 'reductions and inadequacies' in state support effectively puts pressure on family members to provide support, either by taking full financial responsibility or topping up the shortfall in state funding, such as in the case of elderly people's care (Fox Harding, 1996, p. 107). There do, also, remain areas in which there is a legal obligation of support, such as in the case of divorce and 'absent parents', thus, as Fox Harding argues, 'extending the scope of private dependency and restricting dependency on state benefits' (1996, pp. 107–8).

At the same time as privatization means the state is rolling back provisions for social reproduction, such as welfare benefits and state-funded childcare (see Fudge and Cossman, 2002, p. 15), the private sphere of the family is 'expected to assume greater responsibility for things that were once viewed as "public"…[this] has highly gendered implications and is intrinsically connected to the familial ideology' (Boyd, 1997, p. 19; see also Kline, 1997, p. 349, arguing that privatization is motivated by ideology as well as financial concerns). This shifting of responsibility from the public to the private sphere means that 'family law is being called upon to address the economic needs of women and children at precisely the moment when the welfare state is being dismantled and public financial assistance is becoming scarce' (Cossman, 2002b, p. 169). The state is arguably engaged in a process of extending the definition of family where it is financially advantageous for it to do so, such as imposing on unmarried heterosexual (and now unregistered same-sex) relationships the same assumptions of mutual financial support as married couples. The state must recognize a broader range of family forms because 'the need continues for stable, and intelligible, family forms capable of absorbing and discharging a considerable proportion of the care burden' (Conaghan and Grabham, 2007, p. 332). As such, the state needs to encourage lesbians and gay men to take on these care burdens:

> the loosening of family forms and the opening up of new possibilities for gay and lesbian 'families' must be understood not just (or even) as a product of the success of liberal egalitarian strategies but also (or rather) as a response to the decline of the housewife family model in the context of post-industrial transformation and widescale welfare retrenchment. (Conaghan and Grabham, 2007, p. 333)

This is clearly demonstrated by the discourses used by the Canadian Supreme Court in *M v H* [1999] 2 SCR 3 (discussed in Chapter 3).

The ideal of self-sufficiency is central to privatization (Boyd, 1994b, pp. 42–3; Cossman and Fudge, 2002, p. 16; Fineman, 2004, p. 34). The 'self' here is not only the individual but also the family unit; the capitalist state reinforces 'private familial economic responsibilities' for dependent people (Boyd, 1994b, p. 61). Although there is something to be said for women being compensated for their domestic labour by the men who have directly benefited from it, such as in spousal support claims (see, for example, *White v White* [2001] AC 596, at 605–6), Boyd argues that, in the absence of broader public policy recognizing the value of domestic work, cases in which women are compensated through claims on men's property simply shift women's dependence onto individual men. As such, they let society 'off the hook' for women's dependency by not tackling its root cause (privatized social reproduction) or 'dealing with the way in which women's roles, responsibilities and economic dependence are entrenched' (1994b, p. 67). Furthermore, Boyd also argues that this strategy of privatization relies on a woman having provided domestic labour to a man with the means to financially support her, neglecting the fact that many women will not be in this position (1994b, p. 67). More significantly, however, it fails to acknowledge the 'benefit that society as a whole receives from women's (usually unpaid) domestic labour, particularly in the context of raising children' (Boyd, 1994b, p. 67). Privatization, therefore, allows society to benefit from women's social reproduction work while failing to take responsibility for the economic consequences to individual women, instead attempting where possible to make individual men responsible (see also Gavigan, 1993): in the UK the Child Support Agency website proudly displays the headline: 'Helping parents take financial responsibility for their children' (www.csa.gov.uk, 1 March 2007; for a critique of this discourse, see Sheldon, 2003, pp. 191–3).

This attempt to transfer responsibility for women's derivative dependency to individual men both reinforces a more powerful position for men, compounding women's economic vulnerability, and also stigmatizes those women who do not have access to either their own or a man's resources for financial support. Furthermore, as Fineman argues, privatizing dependency within individual family units in this way obscures the fact that everybody is dependent on others at some point in their lives, whether as a child or as an elderly person, or during a period of unemployment, for example. She refers to this as 'inevitable dependency' (2004, pp. 34–5) and argues that it, in turn, results in the 'derivative dependency' of others. This is particularly the case for the inevitable dependencies of children, which in turn render their caretakers (usually mothers) derivatively dependent on 'material and monetary resources…[as well as] institutional support and accommodation' (2004, p. 36). As Fineman argues, there is an illusion of independence which would be undermined through recognition of inevitable dependency and which leads to a stigmatization of those who are seen as undeservingly dependent such as the 'welfare mother' (2004, p. 32). This illusion is arguably maintained because the (marital) family usually takes care of derivative dependency, which therefore only becomes evident when the family breaks down (through divorce) or when the dependency occurs outside of it (such as single mothers). It is this obfuscation that allows social conservatives to argue that the solution to such dependencies is marriage (see Cossman, 2005, pp. 436–7).

Privatization therefore refers to both the privatization of social reproduction (inevitable dependency) within the family and the privatization of (women's) poverty (or exhaustion through the double shift if she is also working outside the home) as a result of this caretaking role (derivative dependency). The privatization of social reproduction within the family not only continues to affect individual women who are derivatively dependent within the family but also puts the *family as a whole* (including lesbian and gay families) in a situation relative to the state and to capital that is analogous to that of the second-wave housewife: it takes responsibility for reproductive work, often to its collective detriment (and, as demonstrated above, predominantly to that of women within the family), thereby, as Fineman argues, concealing the inevitable nature of dependency (2004, p. 35). Just as in the case of the second-wave housewife, these functions are unrecognized, uncompensated and undervalued by the capitalist society that benefits from them. Though the organization of both domestic and paid labour has changed somewhat since the second wave, primarily in that many more women are now working outside the home (although, as I argued above, this has not necessarily resulted in changes in the domestic division of labour), responsibility for social reproduction under the neoliberal state has arguably shifted *towards* rather than away from the private family (Gill and Bakker, 2006, p. 48). The legal recognition of same-sex relationships supports this privatization. The form that the family takes has become less significant to the neoliberal state than the functions it performs on behalf of capitalism (Gavigan, 1999). Whether or not Hunter and others are correct that same-sex marriage has the potential to destabilize gender in marriage, there is no doubt that it fits seamlessly into a neoliberal privatizing agenda without disrupting *this* ideology of family. As Cossman notes:

> It is absolutely no coincidence that the first major legal victory in the recognition of same-sex relationships [in Canada] involved spousal support, or alimony…The ruling is consistent with the agenda of fiscal responsibility – of expanding the private support obligations of individual family members, and thereby reducing the demands on the state. It is no coincidence that the very first same sex relationship victory is one that fits within the agenda of fiscal conservatism, the privatization of support obligations, and the demise of the welfare state. (2000, p. 56)

Drawing this analogy between the services to capitalism (and individual men) provided by women during the second wave through the family and the services that the third-wave family *as a whole* (though usually women within that family) continues to provide to an increasingly neoliberal capitalist state demonstrates why engagement with second-wave theory continues to be necessary.

Conclusion

I have argued in this chapter that the second-wave critiques of marriage from radical and socialist feminist perspectives are still relevant to third-wave families. First, because, although there have been some changes in the ways 'family' is lived, the gendered division of labour continues to be a significant concern and the traditional nuclear family retains its powerful ideology and mythology, particularly within the marriage model. Second, even if there had been significant changes in women's position within families, second-wave socialist feminists were also concerned with the role of the family as a whole in relation to privatization of care. The neoliberal state of the third wave makes this concern more, not less, relevant today. It is in highlighting the relationship between the privatization of social reproduction, the benefit to the state and capital of the work that the family as a whole does, and the still gendered division of labour within those families that the continuing relevance and importance of the second-wave critique of marriage in relation to same-sex marriage becomes particularly evident.

The claims by same-sex marriage advocates, particularly Nan Hunter, that same-sex marriages could destabilize the gendered definition of all marriages were also refuted. Christopher Carrington and Nancy Polikoff's work indicates that same-sex marriage may not necessarily have the impact that Hunter suggests. Furthermore, this argument would not overcome the privatization critique. However, there were also other plausible arguments for same-sex marriage on the grounds of the necessity of recognition and the possibilities for transgression. These arguments are discussed in the next chapter.

6
Of Outlaws and In-Laws: The 'Ambivalent Gift' of Legal Legitimation

> There is no question that gays and lesbians are threatened by the violence of public erasure, but the decision to counter that violence must be careful not to reinstall another in its place. Which version of lesbian or gay ought to be rendered visible, and which internal exclusions will that rendering visible institute? (Butler, 1993, p. 311)

Introduction

In Chapter 4, I highlighted the two sets of arguments that I consider to be the strongest in terms of potentially overcoming the feminist critiques of marriage in the context of same-sex marriage. In Chapter 5, I responded to the first set of arguments, which suggest that it might transform the institution. In this chapter, I focus on the second set of arguments for same-sex marriage, which highlight the need for positive recognition of same-sex relationships and/or suggest that same-sex marriage may have a transgressive impact on the institution of marriage. I use the terms transformation and transgression in distinct, though linked, ways. Transformation refers to (perhaps fundamental) changes *within* the marriage model, such as the egalitarianism that Hunter and others suggest will result from same-sex marriage. In contrast, transgression of the marriage model would involve *challenging* the model in a way that goes beyond or destabilizes the existing parameters of marriage, or queers marriage.[1]

As I outlined in Chapter 4, recognition arguments suggest that same-sex marriage is necessary because, due to lesbians and gay men having been

---

1 Here, I am using Nikki Sullivan's characterization of 'to queer': 'to make strange, to frustrate, to counteract, to delegitimize, to camp up' (2003, p. vi).

constructed as outsiders to the family, it is essential that the law recognizes same-sex relationships as familial. Furthermore, it is argued that public recognition of same-sex relationships by the state is necessary to challenge the more general invisibility of lesbian and gay sexualities in the public sphere. In other words, recognition of same-sex relationships in the form of marriage is necessary as a positive acknowledgment of lesbian and gay sexualities and desires, as being every bit as significant and familial as heterosexual ones.

Transgression arguments refer to the suggestion that same-sex marriage may be radical in subverting, or transgressing, marriage as a heteronormative institution. Marriage is, to some extent, an example of Butler's theory of performativity (1990, p. 173) in that it is constructed through repetitions of its rituals and ideologies, yet there is no original. I argued in Chapter 1 that, while we can identify a marriage model or framework, it does not have a fixed essence. Rather marriage is (legally) something of an empty shell in that it is based on a *perceived* shared understanding of what marriage is but there appears to be no legal origin of this, at least according to Poulter's (1976; 1979) and Probert's (2007) analyses of *Hyde v Hyde and Woodmansee* [1866] L Rev 1 P&D 130 (set out in Chapter 1). The common law definition of marriage began with the perceived shared ideology that Lord Penzance articulated in his judgment. In Butler's terms, this may be reformulated as a theory of marriage being continually created and recreated through repeated performances of its rituals and utterances of its ideologies; a performance that has no original essence. If same-sex couples perform marriage differently, perhaps this creates an opening to transgress or subvert the heteronormative boundaries of the institution as they are currently interpreted. However, in this chapter, I problematize this claim, arguing that transgressive possibilities are limited by engagement with law reform in this area.

I begin this chapter by critically examining what it means to seek *legal* recognition as a means to a subversive or otherwise progressive end. To do this, I draw upon the work of Carol Smart (1989) in *Feminism and the Power of Law*, identifying the potential problems of using the law in this way, and Vanessa Munro's (2001) critique of Smart. My analysis of the arguments for same-sex marriage demonstrates that, in spite of the useful distinction that Munro draws between the juridical and the legal, arguments that conform to the marriage model are likely to be taken up and reproduced through *both*. I conclude, in agreement with Smart, that while there may be some strategic use in engaging with law, this must be approached cautiously. It is by no means clear that legal recognition of same-sex relationships would result in the type of recognition that would challenge or problematize the institution of marriage as it is currently formulated.

In order to think about the value of recognition it is necessary to ask *who* is being, or is likely to be, recognized. As such, I then turn to the issues raised by the opening quote: which versions of lesbian, gay, or queer are being rendered visible through same-sex marriage and which remain excluded? I begin with the 'outlaws', looking first at the way in which same-sex marriage may contribute to shifting the boundaries between good/bad sex(ualities). I argue that this good/bad distinction is moving away from a direct relationship to straight/gay sexualities towards a focus on responsible/irresponsible sexual practices, which crosses hetero/homo sex boundaries. The discourses of same-sex marriage advocates (and the UK government in the context of the Civil Partnership Act 2004) support and, perhaps, rely on this shift. However, it means that same-sex relationships (or encounters) that fall into the 'irresponsible' side of the binary remain stigmatized and unrecognized or, in Fraser's terms, perhaps *mis*recognized (1997a). I then turn to two examples of non-normative relationships (non-monogamy/polyamory and chosen families) that would remain excluded from the positive recognition that some same-sex relationships may gain through marriage. My argument is not that these types of relationships should (or could) be included within the marriage model but rather that it is important to acknowledge where and how *inclusion* within this model for some will mean continued *exclusion* from any form of recognition for others.

I then examine the argument that same-sex marriage is assimilationist in the context of the UK's Civil Partnership Act 2004. This provision is an interesting case study because, as I discussed in Chapter 2, it is marriage-like and very closely follows the marriage model whilst leaving open a clear opportunity for legal transgression. While it is possible that marriage could be transgressed, such transgression would always be limited by the boundaries provided by the legal structure of the marriage model. The Civil Partnership Act 2004, however, by omitting sex from the provision, leaves unspoken, and therefore potentially outside of its legal structure, one of the central aspects of the marriage model. Therefore, this provides an opportunity not only to transgress the social norms but also potentially part of the legal structure of the marriage model. However, the absence of sex in the Act can equally be read as an erasure of lesbian and gay sexuality, despite the legal recognition of relationships.

I then go on to discuss this further in the wider context of marriage, returning to some of the themes of my preceding discussion of outlaws/in-laws. I argue that the legal recognition of same-sex relationships in a form that further marginalizes non-normative lesbian and gay sexualities is another manifestation of compulsory heterosexuality.

Finally, I return to the concept of recognition in light of these discussions. I ask what a progressive or radical politics of recognition would require in the context of same-sex relationships. Recognition, as Nancy Fraser argues, is not inherently conservative or radical. Instead, it may be affirmative, in that it upholds existing structures and allows an outsider group access to them; or it may be transformative, in that it challenges existing structures through the recognition of outsiders (1997a, p. 23). Applying the Butler/Fraser debate on recognition/redistribution to same-sex marriage, I conclude by arguing that in order for recognition to be transformative, it must be accompanied by a politics of redistribution that is also transformative, rather than affirmative. Despite the absence of a fixed essence of marriage potentially paving the way for transgressive possibilities, the marriage model is socially and politically entrenched to the extent that a transformative and redistributive form of recognition is unlikely in the context of marriage.

Becoming in-laws: legal recognition as liberation?

> [W]e should not make the mistake that law can provide the solution to the oppression that it celebrates and sustains. (Smart, 1989, p. 49)

The resort to law and the assumption that law reform, particularly access to legal marriage, is necessary to overcome the oppression of lesbians and gay men has been almost universal in the West. However, the opening quote suggests that some level of caution should be employed when attempting to use law reform as a tool for social change. Carol Smart questions whether the way in which law exercises its definitional power can be effectively challenged by further law reform. Instead, she suggests that such legal 'tinkering' (Smart, 1997) simply reinforces law's power, 'legitimat[ing] law even while individual legal statutes or legal practices are critiqued' (Smart, 1989, p. 161). This is a particularly important question in the context of same-sex relationships because much of the debate about same-sex marriage and other forms of relationship recognition for same-sex couples centres on the possibilities for normalization and assimilation of same-sex couples through the legal framework of marriage, as against the transformative or transgressive possibilities of expanding the definition of marriage.

In this section, I begin this chapter's engagement in the debate about the deployment of the law's definitional and regulatory power in seeking a progressive goal of liberation for lesbians and gay men. I am not suggesting here that there is one monolithic entity – 'the law' – which strategically engages in certain prohibitions and recognitions in order to achieve a coherent set of pre-determined goals (see Smart, 1989; Boyd, 1994b). Instead, incoherence and disorder are inherent characteristics of the legal system (in the context of family law, see Dewar 1998; 2000) and the postmodern insights of queer theory are critical of 'gay rights' strategies because they fail to 'interrogate the assumption that power is monolithically held by state institutions' (Morgan, 1995, p. 3).

Smart's concern is with law and legal discourse as a power to 'define and disqualify' (1989, p. 164). She argues that what Foucault terms 'juridical power' (which she uses interchangeably with legal power), 'law as a system of knowledge rather than simply as a system of rules' (1989, p. 162), disqualifies other forms of knowledge, particularly feminism. This is not to claim that law does not engage with other 'disciplinary mechanisms'; in the context of marriage law, we need look no further than Lord Justice Ormrod's judgment in *Corbett v Corbett* [1971] P 83 for evidence of the law's readiness to borrow from medical discourse (although the House of Lords has more recently recognized the limits of the courts' ability to engage fully with such discourses and their policy implications through the use of the declaration of incompatibility in *Bellinger v Bellinger* [2003] UKHL 1). Instead, Smart is identifying law's 'claim to truth', which she compares to Foucault's identification of the scientist's claim to truth as an exercise of power 'because, in claiming scientificity, other knowledges [faith, experience, biography] are accorded less status, less value' (1989, p. 9). In the same way, she argues, law claims to be able to find 'the truth' through legal method and processes (such as the criminal trial) thereby claiming power through the disqualification of 'other knowledges like psychology, sociology or common sense' (1989, p. 10).

This disqualification is not always through *silencing* other discourses but may be through appropriating, 'translating' them 'into something the law can digest and process' (1989, p. 11). This translation is evident in the ways that arguments for same-sex marriage were constructed by lawyers and activists (see Chapter 3). It is also evident in the cases that are not explicitly about seeking same-sex marriage, but in recognizing same-sex relationships as familial and spousal for specific purposes, such as in the majority judgments in *Fitzpatrick v Sterling Housing Association* [2001] 1 AC 27 and *Ghaidan v Godin-Mendoza* [2004] 2 AC 557. In order to receive legal recognition (and despite the cases not being about seeking same-sex marriage), the couples in these cases needed to present themselves in the (legally) recognizable terminology of marriage, such as that of 'a stable and monogamous' relationship (per Lord Nicholls in *Mendoza* at 564). The law would not be able to process, and would not recognize, a same-sex relationship which was not analogized to a heterosexual relationship (nor, presumably would it recognize a 'non-traditional' heterosexual relationship that was not analogous to marriage), as evident from the reasoning of Lord Nicholls:

> Security of tenure for the survivor of [a cohabiting heterosexual] couple in the house where they live is, doubtless, an important and legitimate social aim. Such a couple share their lives and make their home together.... A homosexual couple, as much as a heterosexual couple, share each other's life and make their home

together. *They have an equivalent relationship*. There is no rational or fair ground for distinguishing the one couple from the other in this context. (at 568, emphasis added)

This means that alternative discourses about ways of being intimate, or having relationships, or being single, have no place in the legal arena and are effectively silenced in legal and policy debates, as is evident in the absence of radical critiques during the Civil Partnership Act 2004 debates in the UK. When the public discourse is a legal one of equality and recognition, those lesbians and gay men who are politically opposed to same-sex marriage are in the difficult position of either having to engage with these issues on this liberal terrain or else potentially finding themselves as uncomfortable bedfellows with right-wing homophobes in constructing an argument *against* (liberal) equality and non-discrimination (Boyd, 1994a; Butler, 2002, p. 25). The engagement with law inevitably makes it necessary to demand and defend 'gay rights' and 'equality' against homophobic opposition, excluding the possibility of articulating arguments for more radical alternatives (Herman, 1994a). Arguing that same-sex couples should have 'equal rights and responsibilities' precludes the question, not only of whether legal 'rights and responsibilities' are in themselves a good, but also of whether law *can* provide 'the solution' to inequality.

In conceding this point, Smart would argue, we empower law: 'the idea that law is the means to resolve social problems gains strength and the idea that the lawyers and the quasi-lawyers are the technocrats of an unfolding Utopia becomes taken for granted' (1989, p. 161). This is problematic because of what Smart terms 'juridogenesis', the idea that law can create harm in the process of trying to 'cure' it. In the context of rights claims, an example that is readily analogized to same-sex marriage, itself often framed as a 'right', the claimant must fit:

the category of persons to whom the rights have been conceded.... [As such] [m]ore rights come at the cost of the potential for greater surveillance and greater conformity and the claim for new rights brings about the possibility of new forms of regulation. (Smart, 1989, p. 162)

Smart is therefore arguing that juridical power could be more effectively challenged through non-legal means (and this has, in fact, been the strategy of the queer campaigning group Gay Shame). Judith Butler argues along similar lines: 'we ask for an intervention by the state in one domain (marriage) only to suffer excessive regulation in another (kinship)' (2002, p. 17). Perhaps more insidiously, the forms of regulation that accompany rights claims include self-regulation. As David Halperin argues, regulation of behaviour does not only operate through prohibitions but actually is more effective and complete when it operates through processes of normalizing, responsibilizing and disciplining (1995, p. 18). Legal recognition may not, then, bring the wider social recognition that was suggested in Chapter 4 and will inevitably be accompanied by regulation. It is for these reasons that Butler characterizes legal recognition as an 'ambivalent gift' (2002, p. 17).

Vanessa Munro (2001) disagrees with Smart's reading of Foucault based on an alternative interpretation of his work which claims that he intended a distinction to be made between the juridical and the legal. According to the interpretation that Munro favours, the term juridical refers to 'a specific theory of power as sovereignty', a concept of power relations that is 'command-based' but not necessarily legal, nor is law necessarily always juridical (2001, pp. 555–6). As such, Foucaultian theory does not require the 'expulsion of law' from social analysis, as Munro argues is Smart's assumption, but instead that 'the veil of the juridical be lifted' so that the operation of legal power can be seen more clearly (Munro, 2001, p. 557). Based on this distinction between juridical and legal power, Munro contends that 'expulsion of legal reform will not obliterate juridical power in the way that Smart assumes' (2001, p. 562). Instead, she claims that there is a 'need for both legal and non-legal means of reform as appropriate to the circumstances and to the original impetus of unveiling the artificiality of juridical power, both legal and otherwise' (2001, p. 563), describing the rejection of legal reform as an 'effective paralysis' for feminist theory (2001, p. 565).

Munro argues that it is possible to deconstruct and transform law from within: 'the most appropriate means of challenge and resistance are themselves subversive and infiltrating' (2001, p. 566). This possibility of subversion of legal institutions through law reform is explored further below in the context of same-sex marriage, but Munro does not explain why and how it is law that would be 'infiltrated' by feminist/queer theory, rather than feminist/queer theory being complicit in its *own* infiltration by law as Halperin's interpretation of Foucault suggests (above). Munro's description of law as 'a constructing and constituting discourse and structure' (2001, p. 566) illustrates why Smart believes we should be cautious in our resort to law. Furthermore, it is the *uncritical* resort to and arguably reification of (liberal) legal reform that has effectively paralysed radical critique (as argued above), closing down possibilities for radical change. We cannot abandon law as a site of struggle; even the most radical argument that marriage should be abolished as a legal institution (see, for example, Fineman, 1995; 2004) would require a certain (if temporary) engagement with law reform in that a statute to abolish marriage would be required. Following this, some other form of (even minimal) legal intervention in intimate relationships would almost inevitably be required, for example, the use of undue influence in trusts law

(Auchmuty, 2003) or the use of private contracts to determine division of assets (Fineman, 1995).

Instead of engaging with law reform on its own terms by accepting the legal framework already in place and merely seeking access to it, radical lesbians and gay men (and heterosexuals) could seek reform of the legal framework itself in a way that challenges law's normative and definitional power.[2] This may fall into the trap that Smart identifies of assuming that new law or more law would be an improvement on the old law (1989, p. 160). Smart's argument, however, is not to ignore law or abandon legal struggle. On the contrary, she is trying to develop a 'clearer vision of law' (1989, p. 163):

> Law cannot be ignored precisely because of its power to define, but feminism's strategy should be focused on this power rather than on constructing legal policies which only legitimate the legal forum and the form of law. (1989, p. 165)

Instead, Smart is arguing that we need to be aware of and weigh the risks involved in using law in each case, and 'resist the temptation that law offers, namely the promise of a solution' (1989, p. 165). Munro ascribes a level of cynicism about law reform to Smart that seems a little strong, with Munro attributing to Smart an 'assumption that legal reform has *no* fruitful role to play in the contemporary project of challenging both juridical and disciplinary power' (Munro, 2001, p. 566, emphasis added). However, Smart recognizes that there is sometimes a need to engage strategically with law reform once the risks of doing so have been identified and weighed. This is not to say that the outcome of an engagement with law reform is certain or predictable, nor are the short-term and long-term results necessarily the same (Herman, 1994a). However, a critical awareness of how and why one is engaging with law reform and a resistance to simply accepting the existing parameters of law and legal discourse will go a long way towards avoiding the reification of law's power at the expense of more radical discourses, as is Smart's concern, and opening up a space for a more progressive discourse about the purpose and function of relationship recognition.

While Munro understandably seeks to occupy 'a middle ground between the expulsion of legal reform and the insertion of legal imperialism' (2001, p. 566), the history of marriage law reform, which has had, at best, mixed results (see Smart 1984; Diduck, 2003), means that any attempt to 'incorporate legal reforms within [our] overall strategies for subversive resistance' (Munro, 2001, p. 565) in relation to marriage must indeed be very cautious. At the same time, we must also recognize that ostensibly extra-legal social

---

2 It is not my intention in this book to seek to recommend new legal frameworks that may fit this bill, however, I do briefly examine some possibilities in the concluding chapter.

change plays a part in 'subverting' law. For example, in the context of marriage, law reform is attempting to *respond* to the changing ways in which
people live their relationships through the Law Commission's consultation
on possible legal recognition of cohabitants, albeit restricted to ones which
are legally analogous to marriage and confined to property division on relationship breakdown (see further Barker, 2006; Wong, 2006). Similarly, while
we should be cautious about reinforcing the power of law through seeking
law reform as a strategy for social change, we must also recognize Munro's
assertion that:

> the law is not a discrete area of social activity but, rather, has
> implications well beyond the remit of what are normally con-
> sidered 'legal' concerns…Law exerts an influence in a variety of
> contexts, such as the family and the private sphere, despite the
> alleged profession of juridical discourse to the contrary. (2001,
> p. 566)

Munro and Smart agree that legal discourse should not be rejected alto-
gether but instead deployed carefully and strategically. In the context of
same-sex marriage, one of the arguments that will be made in this chapter
is that law reform may well result in assimilation, particularly because of
the arguments that have been deployed in order to gain access to marriage.
However, engagement with law may, as Munro suggests, provide opportunities for subversion. For example, Carl Stychin (1995, p. 156) argues that
law can sometimes, even if unintentionally, provide a mechanism for social
change:

> opportunities for resistance within the legal realm may be opened
> up through the spaces in the reasoning left by the law and it is
> through these gaps that the weakness in the system might be sub-
> verted or even queered. (1995, p. 140)

One of the spaces left by law in the context of same-sex relationship recognition in the UK is the absence of sex in the Civil Partnership Act 2004.
Through the sexual silences of the Act, such opportunities for subversion,
resistance or 'queering' of the law may be opened up.

In the remainder of this chapter, I explore the ways in which recognizing same-sex relationships may be assimilationist, and the ways in which it
might provide opportunities for more radical transgression or subversion.
However, I begin from Smart's position of caution with respect to claims,
such as Munro's, about the ability of a strategy of engagement with legal
reform to effectively subvert or transform law, especially in the light of previous attempts to do so in the context of marriage. Any engagement with
law reform that does not challenge the existing parameters and discourse of

law is likely to reinforce law's power and legitimacy at the expense of real progressive change. Therefore, the legal reforms with the most subversive or transgressive potential in this context will be those that challenge the existing marriage model.

Outlaws

> Society wants its intimate relationships, particularly but not only if there are children involved, to be stable, responsible and secure. It is the transient, irresponsible and insecure relationships which cause us so much concern. (Baroness Hale, *Ghaidan v Godin-Mendoza* at 608)

The House of Lords' judgments in *Fitzpatrick* and *Mendoza* along with the other recent legislative reforms discussed in the introduction to this book indicate that there is an increasing tolerance or acceptance of lesbians and gay men in law. The quotation from Baroness Hale's judgment in *Mendoza* suggests that, for liberals at least, the good/bad distinction between heterosexuality/homosexuality is being overtaken by concern with encouraging 'responsible' (sexual) behaviour. This is consistent with a broader emphasis on responsibility and social inclusion that characterized the New Labour government's policy, particularly in relation to family and sexuality (see, for example, Reece, 2003; Stychin, 2003). While not wishing to deny the importance of many of the gains that have been made in the last ten years, the agenda of inclusion necessarily has a corollary of exclusion; the 'responsible' is in opposition to the 'irresponsible'. This changing political landscape is particularly apparent in relation to the legal recognition of same-sex relationships. For example, in the second reading of the Civil Partnership Bill 2004 Lord Higgins said:

> I support the Bill, in one way for the most simple of reasons: one must surely be more in favour of stable homosexual relationships than those that are not...In some ways, that is a very important aspect of the Bill. (Lord Higgins, HL Hansard, 22 April 2004, c. 427).

It is clear from such discourse that, as Stychin argues, 'the [Civil Partnership] Act is designed to encourage "responsible" relationship behaviour by lesbians and gay men' (2006a, p. 83). Lord Higgins sounds rather grudging in his favour towards 'stable' same-sex relationships but these discourses of supporting stable relationships that are evident in many of the arguments and judgments in favour of same-sex marriage across jurisdictions do suggest that the definitional boundaries of 'good sex' and 'bad sex' are shifting. Gayle Rubin articulated the significance of these boundaries in 1984 and their evolution since then is evident.

In 'Thinking Sex', Rubin describes a sexual value system:

> According to this system, sexuality that is 'good', 'normal', and 'natural' should ideally be heterosexual, marital, monogamous, reproductive, and non-commercial. It should be coupled, relational, within the same generation, and occur at home. It should not involve pornography, fetish objects, sex toys of any sort, or roles other than male and female. Any sex that violates these rules is 'bad', 'abnormal', or 'unnatural'. Bad sex may be homosexual, unmarried, promiscuous, non-procreative, or commercial. It may be masturbatory or take place at orgies, may be casual, may cross generational lines, and may take place in 'public', or at least in the bushes or the baths. It may involve the use of pornography, fetish objects, sex toys or unusual roles. (1984, pp. 13–14)

Although most other forms of lesbian and gay sexualities (as well as, among others, sadomasochism, fetishism and sex work) were firmly on the 'bad' side of the line, interestingly, long-term stable same-sex couples were already a 'major area of contest' (Rubin, 1984, p. 14) and 'moving in the direction of respectability' (1984, p. 15). Despite this, however, it is clear from Rubin's discussion that her definitions of good sex and bad sex in 1984 did map on to a heterosexual/homosexual binary. Heterosexuality (as long as it did not violate other sexual norms) could be 'sublime or disgusting, free or forced, healing or destructive', while homosexuality (and all other 'bad' sex acts) was considered 'devoid of all emotional nuance' (Rubin, 1984, pp. 14–15). The discourses (from not only same-sex marriage advocates but also legislators and judges) are shifting away from this binary. Instead, the 'good' becomes the stable, monogamous, private[3] perhaps even (inter)dependent relationship between two adults, whereas the bad is the unstable, the fleeting sexual encounter, the non-monogamous or polyamorous, the public (see also Warner, 1999; Seidman, 2002, pp. 150–61). Following gay rights activism in several contexts, including lowering of the age of consent and repeal of s. 28 as well as relationship recognition, it is now recognized by the legal systems in the UK and several other jurisdictions, discussed in Chapters 2 and 3, that lesbian and gay sexualities also have 'emotional nuance' in that they may also be 'good' or 'bad'. Thus, the boundaries between the good and the bad begin to cut across lesbian/gay and heterosexual identities and communities,

---

3 Here, this refers to private as opposed to public sex in line with Rubin's use of the term but, in the context of the 'good' (sexual relationship) as opposed to the 'bad' (sexual encounter), it could also refer to the privatized responsibility for dependencies that were discussed in the previous chapter.

'recognising, in economically and racially coded ways, the mature and immature, the ruly and unruly, responsible and irresponsible in both' (Davina
Cooper, 2004, p. 103). The legal recognition of same-sex relationships is arguably both necessary to and a result of this process.

However, using a queer framework to examine same-sex marriage illustrates the ways in which this has meant the continued exclusion of many
lesbian and gay (and hetero)sexualities from the boundaries of respectability.
Steven Seidman argues that as 'the normal gay' has become represented as
a respectable citizen, 'the "bad" sexual citizen' is defined by his or her 'violation of a romantic, monogamous intimate norm'. The fears that the 'normal gay' evokes of 'unleashing an unbridled eroticism that will bring chaos
and decline' mean that sexual controls for *all citizens* are tightened (2002,
pp. 156–7). The quote at the beginning of this section from Baroness Hale's
judgment in *Mendoza* provides an example of this: Baroness Hale notes that
since *Dudgeon v United Kingdom* (1981) 4 EHRR 149 it is no longer legitimate
under Article 8 of the European Convention on Human Rights to 'discourage' same-sex relationships. However, instead it is the 'transient, irresponsible and insecure' relationships (implicitly of all sexualities) that must be
discouraged.

The newfound respectability for same-sex relationships through marriage
may go some way towards demonstrating that lesbianism is a choice available to all women, or may challenge the binary between the respectable
hetero and the unrespectable homo. However, this does not mean that the
boundaries have broken down, merely that they have shifted and, as Steven
Seidman argues, 'as the "normal gay" is integrated as a good citizen, other
sexual outsiders may stand in for the homosexual as representing the "bad"
or dangerous sexual citizen' (Seidman, 2002, p. 17; see also Warner, 1999,
p. 25). Critiquing this shift in boundaries does not entail simply adopting
a libertarian view that any regulatory boundaries are problematic. Instead,
I simply suggest that if sexual activities are to be stigmatized and/or marginalized it should be on grounds relating to those specific sexual practices
rather than by default through reification of 'responsible' or stable relationships. I return to the issue of good/bad sex later in the context of a discussion
of public sex but for the remainder of this section I examine two relationship forms that will be outside of the 'recognition' that same-sex marriage is
supposed to convey.

Non-monogamy and polyamory

> Once upon a time Deardra loved Carol. Deardra also loved Margo,
> Toni and Kathy, but was just coming out of a primary relationship
> with Jan and so didn't want to get into anything heavy with any-
> one. Carol loved Deardra and also Margo and sometimes Renalda,

but she didn't give a hang about Toni and she hated Kathy's guts.
Actually, Carol loved Deardra best, but Deardra wasn't into loving
anyone best and claimed she was equally noncommitted to them
all. (Waters in Altman, 1982, p. 289)

Though this quote, a tongue-in-cheek reference to lesbian non-possessive
multiple relationships, ends with an expression of non-commitment, those
practising non-monogamy and polyamory emphasize the commitment of
their relationships (Klesse, 2006b).[4] There are different forms of polyamory
but in general: 'Polyamory describes a form of relationship where it is possible, valid and worthwhile to maintain (usually long-term) intimate and sexual relationships with multiple partners simultaneously.' (Haritaworn et al.,
2006, p. 515) Non-monogamy is a more general term that can encompass not
only polyamorous relationships but also a couple where one or both partners
have sexual encounters outside of the relationship. The term non-monogamy has been criticized because it is a negative definition in opposition to a
monogamous norm (Ritchie and Barker, 2006, p. 590) so I restrict my use of
it to describing couple relationships that sometimes deviate from monogamy,
while using polyamorous (poly) to describe multiple committed relationships
in various forms.

In his study of gay male non-monogamy, Jeffrey Ringer identified five
types of non-monogamy. First, the partners agree to tell each other about
sexual encounters with others, which may then 'evolve into an erotic epi-
sode for the couple' (2001, p. 145). Second, the partners may be free to have
sexual encounters with others but only when they are in different cities.
Third, Ringer found some couples who agreed to be monogamous for the first
few years while the relationship became 'solid' and then eventually be non-
monogamous. Fourth, some couples believed it inevitable that their partner
would have sex with other people but did not want to know about it. The
final category that Ringer identifies I would characterize as a form of polyamory: on the basis that no two people can completely fulfil each others'
needs, a couple agree that one or both parties can have another sexual partner who then becomes a friend of both and 'fully integrated into the relationship as someone who is important in helping one partner meet his sexual
needs' (2001, p. 145). This could be based on a primary/secondary partner
model where the primary partners' needs are prioritized over other relationships or, alternatively, there could be a polyamorous 'unit' of several primary

---

4 Further to my earlier discussion of the responsible/irresponsible sexual binary, it is interesting that Christian Klesse problematizes the way in which these discourses often contrast 'committed' (or good) poly relationships to 'other' forms of non-monogamy, such as
swinging. There is, for some, an attempt to distinguish 'responsible non-monogamy' from
those who 'seek sex for the sake of sexual pleasure, have "unreasonable" numbers of sexual
partners, or do not look for long-term intimate relationships' (2006b, p. 577).

relationships. For example, Elizabeth Emens describes a four-partner family ('quad') consisting of three men and a woman (2004, p. 312).

Though non-monogamy is (stereo)typically associated with gay male rather than lesbian relationships, there is empirical evidence of female non-monogamy in bisexual and lesbian relationships (Weeks et al., 2001, p. 105; Klesse, 2005). There is also a feminist critique of (heterosexual) monogamy as resting on a man's ownership of a woman so that the lines of property inheritance can be maintained and that 'men also benefit from women's over-investment in one man both emotionally and physically' (Robinson, 1997, p. 145). As Rosemary Auchmuty argues, (heterosexual) monogamy serves patriarchy, 'by ensuring that each woman is kept under the personal control of a man' (2004, p. 122). Furthermore:

> As a form of social organisation, the couple is convenient and relatively easy to manage, but limited and risky, too, as too great a dependence on one person involves putting all one's eggs (emotional, financial, sexual) in one basket. (Auchmuty, 2004, p. 122)

There are also arguments that monogamy in heterosexual relationships serves to isolate women from each other (Rosa, 1994; Robinson, 1997) and that non-monogamy may be a way to 'reconstruct the gendered power relationships of heterosexuality' (Robinson, 1997, p. 152). I do not intend to posit non-monogamy and polyamory as a utopian feminist alternative to monogamy. Non-monogamous practices may be more or less compatible with feminist politics and there are good reasons why feminists should pay close attention to the gendered power relations within non-monogamy, particularly in heterosexual and bisexual contexts. For example, Elisabeth Sheff describes the fetishisation of the (female) 'hot bi babe' amongst some poly men. However, she concludes that while what she terms 'poly-hegemonic masculinities' do in some ways reinforce traditional power structures (such as scheduling and 'emotion work' falling mainly to female partners), there was also a 'markedly increased gender flexibility' available to poly men (2006, p. 638) and attempts to create equitable power structures within relationships, though with varying degrees of success. As such, she concludes that poly relationships have 'innovative potential' to 'resist the demands of hegemonic masculinity' (2006, p. 639).

The purpose of this section is to note the types of relationship that would continue to be excluded from marriage rather than make a feminist argument for or against such relationship forms. However, I would take seriously a feminist argument that monogamy supports capitalism and patriarchy despite the associations that some feminists have made between non-monogamy and a libertarian politics that is about men's exploitation of women rather than women's sexual freedom (see, for example, Jeffreys, 1990).

There is nothing to stop a non-monogamous couple from marrying (though in some circumstances this marriage may be voidable: for example, the Matrimonial Causes Act 1973 s. 12(f) provides that a marriage is voidable if 'at the time of the marriage the respondent was pregnant by some person other than the petitioner') but the current legal structure of marriage is monogamous so, for example, if two people of a three-person poly relationship marry or register this would create an unequal legal relationship in relation to the third party. Further, non-monogamy (in a heterosexual marriage context) is grounds for divorce so it would mean that the marriage was always legally unstable in the sense that a party would potentially have grounds for divorce based on the others' adultery (assuming the sexual acts meet the test for adultery and they can successfully claim that the adultery made it intolerable to live with the defendant). In theory then, a non-monogamous couple or two members of a poly relationship could marry. However, marriage formalizes, fixes at a particular moment, and makes legally explicit a 'primary/secondary partner distinction' within a poly relationship (Klesse, 2006a, p. 168). Where the polyamorous relationship is a bisexual one, it is noteworthy that in most cases, the other-sex partner was the primary partner (Klesse, 2006a); where the different-sex partner is also a spouse, 'legal marriage results in a structural heterosexualisation of the primary/secondary partner distinction' (Klesse, 2006a, p. 170). The unequal legal relationship of married/not-married partners is reflected in an interpersonal dynamic within the relationship, particularly when this also feeds into heteronormative privileging and prioritizing of other-sex relationships over same-sex ones (Klesse, 2006a). As such, Klesse concludes that as long as relationship recognition is based on coupledom (whether heterosexual through marriage or same-sex through civil partnership), it will continue to be problematic for poly and non-monogamous relationships.

This legal enforcement of a monogamous ideal through marriage has been connected to compulsory heterosexuality. For example, Becky Rosa (1994, p. 107) argues that non-monogamy, or in her terms 'anti-monogamy', 'provides a positive and profound challenge to the institution of compulsory heterosexuality'. Furthermore, also drawing analogies to Adrienne Rich's theory of compulsory heterosexuality, Elizabeth Emens refers to 'compulsory monogamy' as being about privileging a primary, sexual relationship, the 'institutionalization of coupledom and the presumed "ownership" of another individual' (2004, p. 152). I examine the issue of compulsory heterosexuality in more detail below and argue that the further marginalization of public sex (which I define broadly in a way that includes non-monogamy) through same-sex marriage constitutes a form of compulsory heterosexuality. However, it is noteworthy in this context that Weeks et al. found that, for lesbians as well as gay men, monogamy was negotiated within the relationship

and primary importance was placed on emotional rather than sexual fid
ity (2001, p. 122). Monogamy was thus an issue to be discussed rather than
assumed (2001, p. 150) and for some people non-monogamy (along with
independence rather than mutual dependency) was a conscious rejection
of what were seen as heterosexual values (2001, p. 125). Same-sex marriage
therefore would not provide recognition for non-monogamous (same-sex)
relationships, which reject 'heterosexual values' of monogamy. This is one
type of non-normative relationship form that would remain 'outlaws'; unrecognized despite same-sex marriage and possibly further marginalized by the
shifting boundaries of respectability.

In contrast to the privileging of coupledom in monogamous relationships,
Barker and Ritchie found that some polyamorous people rejected the pri-
oritization of sexual relationships over non-sexual friendships and that the
distinctions between friends and lovers may become blurred in poly relationships (2006, p. 592). The privileging of sexual relationships is explored next
in the context of chosen family networks.

Families we choose

The phrase 'families we choose' is from Kath Weston's (1991) study of lesbian
and gay kinship networks. Despite adopting the discourse of families, she
argues that chosen families are not merely replicas of heteronormative ones
(1991, p. 107), though they are partly a response to homophobic rejection
and isolation from birth families (1991, p. 116; see also Naples, 2001). Instead,
many lesbians and gay men in chosen families referred to the absence of
models (1991, p. 116) and Weston treats chosen families as 'historical *trans-
formations* rather than derivatives of other sorts of kinship relations' (1991,
p. 106, original emphasis; see also Weeks et al., 2001, p. 11).

The use of the term 'family' could be said to risk the creativity of chosen families (Weeks et al., 2001, p. 16), impede a more radical project of
'decentring' family (Roseneil and Budgeon, 2004, p. 135), and 'direct attention away from the extra-familial, radically counter-heteronormative nature
of many of these relationships' (2004, p. 137). However, as Weeks et al. argue,
its use could also be constructed as an appropriation, part of a broader 'struggle over meaning' (2001, p. 17) in which lesbians and gay men are asserting
the significance and legitimacy of their ties to each other. The ways in which
non-heterosexuals are expanding the notion of family potentially challenge
traditional family values (Weeks et al., 2001, p. 16). This debate appears to
parallel the debate over the meaning of marriage. However, I would argue
that both the legal framework and social meanings of marriage differ from
the broader discourses and framework of family. I do not intend to make an
argument for or against broader legal recognition of families here but, instead,
to merely note some of the ways in which 'families we choose' have played

significant roles in lesbian and gay communities. It is, then, ironic that same-sex marriage could centre the couple unit at the same time as sociological research is finding an increased centring of friendship and de-emphasis of sexual relationships across a 'range of lifestyles and sexualities' (Roseneil and Budgeon, 2004, p. 146; see also Levin, 2004, discussing the prevalence of 'living apart together' as an emerging relationship form; and Heath, 2004, p. 163, on house-sharing amongst young adults as 'the institutionalisation of friendship within a domestic setting').

Further, Roseneil and Budgeon argue that this change is much more radical than simply blurring the boundaries between family and friend categories. Instead, there was also a blurring of the boundaries and meaning of physical space: 'Space normatively constructed as "private" and heterosexual is reconfigured as collective' (2004, p. 150). Friendship networks as families of choice are, then, about more than simply including friends within an expanded category of family and decentring sexual relationships.

Weston found that chosen families tended to have 'extremely fluid boundaries' (1991, p. 108) and were organized around the individual rather than a couple unit so that even the most 'merged' (Weston, 1991, pp. 150–2) couple could theoretically have distinguishable families. There are also multiple ways in which chosen families could be constructed: 'Fluid boundaries and varied membership meant no neatly replicable units, no defined cycles of expansion and contraction, no patterns of dispersal. ... [Chosen families are] the product of unfettered creativity.' (Weston, 1991, p. 109) Yet, there were some identifiable commonalities among the chosen families in Weston's research. For example, both lesbians and gay men consistently included lovers within their chosen family and some included ex-lovers, sometimes a lover's biological or adoptive kin, or people who shared ties to children or a common household. The defining feature of chosen families was love: 'they quite consciously incorporated symbolic demonstrations of love, shared history, material or emotional assistance, and other signs of enduring solidarity' (1991, p. 109). As such, chosen families were described in similar terms to non-chosen families, as people who could be relied on emotionally and materially (p. 113).

Criteria for distinguishing chosen families from 'just friends' included: a shared past, with the time that the relationship had existed providing a measure of closeness (1991, p. 114); 'a co-operative history' (p. 115), in that they provide practical and emotional support networks for things such as giving advice and affection, helping to move house and babysitting; and relationships that had 'weathered conflict' (p. 115). In general, most participants understood chosen families 'to be customized, individual creations that need not deny conflict or difference' (p. 136). This differs from the normative, or nuclear family through the emphasis on choice, which, as noted above, allows for both a creativity that is arguably lacking in the construction of legal families and for 'new patterns of relationship' to be invented (Weeks et al., 2001, p. 11).

Weeks et al. (2001) found what they termed 'families of choice' and 'life experiments' among non-heterosexuals in the UK, which they argue parallel similar changes for heterosexuals. They note a wider sense that individuals are not restricted to families created by biology or law (such as adoption and marriage) and they describe families of choice as:

> Flexible, informal and varied, but strong and supportive networks of friends and lovers, often including members of families of origin. They provide the framework for mutual care, responsibility and commitment for many non-heterosexual people – and indeed for many heterosexuals as well. (Weeks et al., 2001, p. 4)

Thus, 'families of choice' not only involves choosing family members but also choosing how to *be* family. There was an ethic of egalitarianism (though not always achieved in practice) and negotiation within chosen families, particularly between partners (Weeks et al., 2001, pp. 109–24; see also Dunne, 1997, pp. 181–97). Furthermore, chosen rather than biological families were consistently identified as sources of caretaking support, particularly as a response to AIDS (Weston, 1991, p. 113; Weeks et al., 2001, pp. 101–2; Stacey, 2004). There are, however, some limitations of chosen families in terms of cross-generational support, for example, Valerie Lehr (1999, pp. 4, 6–7) notes the neglect of gay and lesbian elders and youths (cf. Stacey, 2004).

The law has no mechanism for recognizing chosen families; created kinship networks, while they may play a significant role in the wedding ceremony (see Chapter 4) and afterwards as chosen family members, could not be legally recognized as such. As Ettelbrick argues, the injustice in marriage is not the exclusion of same-sex couples, but that 'all of the legal and social benefits and privileges constructed for families are available only to those families joined by marriage or biology' (1996, p. 122). Seeking same-sex marriage merely reinforces 'the primacy of marriage in family definitions' (ibid.) and also the primacy of 'the family' over other forms of kinship and intimacy, such as friendship. While there are arguments that the definition of family should be 'recast and reformulated in a way which embraces the authenticity and validity of a wide range of families' (Bailey-Harris, 1999, p. 565), it is unlikely that the definition of marriage could be stretched very far, despite the 'slippery slope' arguments made by anti-gay conservatives in opposition to same-sex marriage (Arkes, 1996; Bennett, 1996).

In this section, I have outlined some practices and relationship forms that will not be recognized by same-sex marriage. I am not arguing that these relationship forms should (or could) be included within the marriage framework. Instead, I intend only to note alternative ways in which same-sex (and, increasingly hetero and non-sexual) significant relationships are constructed. It is also important to acknowledge *which* relationships are referred to in the argument that same-sex marriage will result in positive and necessary state recognition. I am not denying the recognition value of same-sex marriage to some but rather suggesting, as others have previously done in the US context (Ettelbrick, 1996), that it is the most marginal same-sex relationships (or, in other words, those furthest from the dominant ideological norm) that will remain excluded. I focused first on the shifting binary of good/bad sex, before examining two types of non-normative relationship in more detail: non-monogamy; and families of choice. These themes are connected in interesting ways, for example, Stacey found that the recreational sex of gay male cruising not only disrupted ideas of conventional family and private sexuality but also 'generates bonds of kinship and domesticity' (2004, p. 183). This is not to suggest that cruising leads to couple relationships (although there were some examples of this), but rather that 'not infrequently they commence enduring friendships that evolve into kin-like ties, whether or not sexual interest continues' (2004, p. 190). Furthermore, as Stevi Jackson and Sue Scott argue:

> If sexual relationships were de-prioritized as the basis for our most meaningful social ties and if they were not exclusive, then who one related to sexually might come to be of less pervasive social significance. Heterosexuality would then lose its privileged, institutionalized status and non-sexual friendships would no longer be regarded as intrinsically less significant than sexual ones (2004, p. 155).

It is the absence of same-sex marriage that is credited with providing space for these alternative forms of relationships and living arrangements to develop (Altman, 1982). Nevertheless they are not limited to same-sex relationships and I am not arguing that they will cease to exist with the introduction of same-sex marriage. Instead, I am simply noting that same-sex marriage takes the legal recognition of same-sex relationships in a direction that moves away from the less normative relationship forms. Overlooking significant aspects of same-sex relationships constitutes both *mis*recognition (see Fraser, below) and a lost opportunity to revisit the basis on which relationships are supported and recognized by the state.

In-laws

In Chapter 4, I discussed the possibility that same-sex marriage might be transgressive in the sense that it may offer opportunities to challenge, or even queer, the marriage model. However, while transgression is a key strategy in queer theory, in this section I discuss those queer theorists who argue that same-sex marriage would not be transgressive but rather assimilationist in the sense that same-sex marriage is a way of seeking 'normality' and acceptance rather than destabilizing or challenging the institution.

The term assimilation is often used with the similar language of domestication or normalization. For example, Michael Warner uses the term 'normalization' based on his analysis of the politics behind Andrew Sullivan's book *Virtually Normal*, which argues that most gay men and lesbians want to be normal, an aspiration that is close to being achieved with the two remaining issues for gay civil rights in the US being marriage and military service (Sullivan, 1995; Warner, 1999, pp. 53 and 60). For Warner, normalization means creating a desexualized respectability for lesbians and gay men: 'a gay movement you could take home to Mom' (1999, p. 42). Though she uses 'assimilation' in her more recent work, Ruthann Robson prefers the term 'domestication' due to its 'gendered connotations' (2002, p. 711). For Robson:

> Domestication also captures the process inherent in colonization and imperialism of the substitution of one way of thinking for another. Domestication occurs when the views of the dominant culture are so internalized that they seem like common sense. Domestication occurs when the barbed wire enclosures are believed to exist for protection rather than restriction (1992, p. 18).

There are nuanced differences between the theories and languages of assimilation, normalization and domestication that are outside the scope of this discussion but what they have in common is that they each highlight the denial of differences between lesbians, gays and normative heterosexuals and the aim for lesbians and gays to be accepted as 'normal' within society. The term assimilation has a history embedded in the legal culture, particularly in the United States (see Robson, 2002). As such, like Robson, I will continue to use assimilation rather than one of these alternatives.

The goal for assimilationists is to gain 'minority rights' and recognition as 'good citizens' for gays and lesbians rather than seeking to challenge existing sexual norms (Seidman, 2002, p. 175). A vital component of assimilation is to display 'appropriate' behaviour in order to 'conform to the role that has been placed on our marginalized identity in the hope of achieving social inclusion' (Stychin, 2005a, p. 101; see also Patton, 1993). Robson goes further, arguing that same-sex couples must not only be *like* (normative) families but they must also express the belief that they *are* familial relationships (Robson, 1998, p. 166). To successfully argue for same-sex marriage, lesbian and gay organizations must be able to present couples who look like and are *normal* married couples 'but for' the fact that they are the same sex.[5] This links in with Robson's notion of the 'but for' perfect lesbian, by which she refers to 'lesbians who "but for" their sexuality are otherwise perfect; they are the "whitest and brightest" among us' (2002, p. 731), and Warner's description of 'good gays' who are: 'the kind who would not challenge the norms of straight culture, who would not flaunt sexuality, and who would not insist on living differently from ordinary folk' (1999, p. 113; see also Weeks et al., 2001, p. 109). In contrast, the 'bad' are the single, the promiscuous and the queer, who are posited as irresponsible or immature.

Therefore, an assimilationist approach or strategy means that the 'good gays' with long-term, stable, monogamous, couple relationships and (often) with children are presented as representatives of 'the gay community' while the 'bad queers' are discouraged from destabilizing this image. Craig argues that the strategic presentation of a singular, 'good' gay identity is complicit in the oppression of those 'sexual lifestyles and gender variations' (2004, p. 414) that are threatening to heteronormativity:

> Those sexual minorities who can or do conform to the more palatable notion of the [good] 'homosexual' and who as a result enjoy new found rights and power, have a vested interest in silencing those sexual minorities whose lifestyles and gender identities do not support the gay identity developed and marketed to heterosexual society. (2004, p. 414)

This is not a recent phenomenon, nor is it linked solely to the marriage issue (though it is arguably heightened in this context). For example, Carol Queen gives an account of an exchange between an assimilationist lesbian and a female drag queen[6] at a 1993 March on Washington event in the United States, along of the lines of: 'I'm here to march for my civil rights! When they see *you*, it'll ruin everything!' (2004, p. 83)

Neither assimilation nor anti-assimilation, however, is inherently conservative or progressive (Robson, 2002). Robson cites assimilationist policies as responsible for implementing 'English language only' policies on public documents in an attempt to foster 'unity' through one common language and anti-assimilationist policies which provided 'justification' for keeping sex segregation in some occupations (2002, pp. 723–4). As such, 'both assimilation

---

5 See, for example, the couples and families depicted in the advertising campaigns supporting same-sex marriage from the Human Rights Campaign (www.hrc.org/Content/NavigationMenu/Press_Room/HRC_PSAs_and_Ads.htm) and MassEquality (www.massequality.org/ads/) in the United States.

6 A female drag queen is, according to Queen, a woman with a 'larger-than-life femme personae' (2004, p. 82). Queen describes the drag queen in this narrative: 'She wore a 1950s foundation garment with the cups cut out, so that her own very splendid breasts could serve as the garment's focal point, and she had personally sewn a couple of zillion strings of pearl Mardi Gras beads onto it.' (2004, p. 82)

and anti-assimilation can be exercised in a repressive manner by the dominant culture' (2002, p. 730); in the context of marriage the repressive form of anti-assimilation could be the enforced segregation of the separate but equal provisions such as civil partnership. Stychin also argues that the politics of assimilationism and anti-assimilationism is 'a highly indeterminate politics, in which neither social assimilation nor separatism (and neither normalization nor transgression) alone can be politically viable or desirable' (2003, pp. 10–11).

With this discussion in mind, I turn now to the UK's Civil Partnership Act, which provides an interesting case study to examine civil partnership's transgressive and assimilationist possibilities in relationship recognition, or whether, in Fraser's terms, it could actually be an affirmative or a transformative remedy (1997a; 1997b; 2003a; 2003b). As I outlined in Chapter 1, sex is central to the legal structure of marriage in that a marriage must be consummated (subject to specific exceptions) and that either adultery or the absence of a sexual relationship may provide grounds for divorce. The absence of any references to sex in the Civil Partnership Act 2004 is unlikely to be an intentional move away from sex as a central part of the marriage model. The government made it very clear that civil partnerships were intended to mirror marriage as closely as possible and Baroness Scotland explained the absence of adultery in the Act through reference to the complexity of its legal definition. She refers to the specific definition of the sexual component of adultery (penetration of the vagina by the penis) and the difficulties that this test poses in relation to heterosexual couples (Baroness Scotland, HL Hansard, 10 May 2004, c. GC19). These difficulties would be compounded in the context of same-sex relationships to the extent that a whole new definition would be required. Moreover, the government demonstrated its intention for 'adultery' to be cause for dissolution of a civil partnership through Baroness Scotland's suggestion that it would fall within the category of behaviour such 'that the applicant cannot reasonably be expected to live with the respondent' under s. 44(5)(a) (Baroness Scotland, HL Hansard, 10 May 2004, c. GC19; this was also suggested in the practitioner's guides to the Act: Gray and Brazil, 2005; Harper et al., 2005). This is one of the four facts that could provide evidence of the irretrievable breakdown of the relationship in order to dissolve a civil partnership.

However, the absence of adultery as a specific ground for dissolution is significant because it means that it is possible to make an argument that non-monogamy does not necessarily constitute unreasonable behaviour in the context of a same-sex relationship. As noted above, Weeks et al. (2001) and Dunne (1997) found that in the absence of a heteronormative 'script' for same-sex relationships, lesbians and gay men negotiate the 'rules' of intimate relationships. Furthermore, the absence of a consummation requirement means that non-sexual relationships can potentially be legally recognized within the marriage model, assuming that they are prepared to accept the legal consequences (financial and otherwise) of marriage.

An argument may be made that both of these are possible within marriage: there are some circumstances in which a marriage that is not consummated is not voidable; and adultery only provides grounds for divorce if the petitioner also finds it intolerable to live with the defendant (see Chapter 1). However, the rules relating to consummation and adultery in marriage contain an assumption that marriage will be a sexually monogamous relationship. It is arguable that this assumption does not exist within the Civil Partnership Act 2004. Therefore, despite the contrary intention of the legislators, the sexual silences of the Act may provide opportunities to queer civil partnerships for two reasons: first, in that there appears to be no legal presumption of monogamy; and second, it potentially extends relationship recognition to non-sexual relationships.

However, despite these possibilities (and the critiques of consummation in Chapter 5), the absence of sex can also be read as a denial of lesbian and gay sexuality and it does have homophobic or, at the very least, heterosexist connotations in that the 'real' sex act enshrined in the law remains a heterosexual, penetrative one. In this context, then, perhaps the omission of consummation and adultery from the Act is a negative gap: a place where lesbian and gay sexuality is left unspoken. Members of Parliament avoided having to discuss, identify, legally define and thus recognize non-penetrative sexual acts (Barker, 2006). For example, Heather Brook argues that the absence of non-normative forms of sex in the law means that heterosexual penetrative sex remains *the* definition of sex:

> While sex in general can be understood as a range of actions and behaviours, consummation refers to one specific type of sex which was legally invested with meaning such that it, rather than other sexual acts, came to stand as 'sex' as such, or as *all* sex. (2001, p. 140, original emphasis)

In this sense, the invisibility of lesbian and gay sex in the public (legal) sphere is an aspect of 'compulsory heterosexuality'. It could be argued that if legal invisibility of lesbian and gay sexualities is a form of compulsory heterosexuality then same-sex marriage is a remedy. However, the Civil Partnership Act 2004 demonstrates that relationship recognition does not necessarily remedy *sexual* invisibility and, as I argue next, the same may be said about marriage.

The marginalization of 'public sex' as compulsory heterosexuality

> If the price for being within the law is symbolic obliteration, I for one would rather remain an outlaw. (Morgan, 1995, p. 6)

Public sex is sometimes referred to as part of the 'malestream gay male agenda' (Jeffreys, 2003, p. 6) that I discussed in the introductory chapter. However, I would argue that the marginalization of public sex through same-sex marriage is also a problem for feminists for two reasons. First, public sex is not necessarily outside of feminism. For example, Davina Cooper has demonstrated that a (revised) feminist conception of care exists in the Toronto Women's Bathhouse: 'women's bathhouses, as new feminist spaces, exemplify ethical conceptions of care, particularly in the way they promote compassion, self-empowerment, and reciprocity' (2007, p. 257). This illustrates not only that 'public sex' activities (stereo)typically associated with gay men are also of interest to lesbians but also that they may take place within a feminist understanding of care. Though specific instances or practices may be criticized for supporting, for example, domination/submission frameworks or what is characterized by Jeffreys as a 'male' approach to sex and public space (2003), this criticism should not be universally extended to all situations (equally, this does not mean that feminists must never critique specific practices or instances: see, for example, Herman's (1996) critique of sadomasochism). Furthermore, for Michael Warner (1999), public sex refers to any non-normative sexual acts that are not within the 'zone of privacy' given to heterosexual married couples by (in the US context)[7] *Griswold v Connecticut* 381 US 479, rather than simply sex in a public place.[8] Second, more broadly, it may also refer to sex being public in the sense of being in the public sphere (publicly acknowledged), as opposed to being a 'private matter' that is not 'flaunted'. For example, Sarah Lamble argues that, though lesbians and transgender people are winning legal rights, their bodies and sexualities 'are *actively rendered invisible* via legal knowledge practices, norms and rationalities' (2009, p. 112; emphasis added). She refers to this as 'limited knowing/thinking' of queer and trans sexualities (2009, p. 118). I will argue in this section that both of these forms of public sex are marginalized in the same-sex marriage debates albeit in different ways and that this marginalization, through desexualising same-sex relationships, constitutes a form of compulsory heterosexuality, even as marriage may be transgressed or even queered in other ways.

Compulsory heterosexuality is a term that Adrienne Rich uses to describe the way in which 'women's choice of women as passionate comrades, life partners, co-workers, lovers, tribe, has been crushed, invalidated, forced into hiding and disguise' (Rich, 1981, p. 4). The question is whether same-sex

---

7 In the UK context, see Katherine O'Donovan: 'The couple is a unit, a black box, into which the law does not purport to peer. What goes on inside the box is not perceived as the law's concern.' (1985, p. 12)

8 Following the US Supreme Court's ruling in *Lawrence v Texas* 539 US 558, Warner's concept of public sex may need to be re-evaluated, but for the purposes of this chapter I am using the term in line with his original meaning, that is, to refer to non-normative sexual acts.

marriage would challenge compulsory heterosexuality by bringing same-sex relationships out of the closet and into the registry office (as discussed in Chapter 4), or whether same-sex marriages would be 'in disguise' in the sense that they would be embracing and fitting within a heteronormative institution, and thus represent what Morris Kaplan (1997, p. 210) terms the 'cultural triumph of compulsory heterosexuality'. This question implies two possible interpretations of 'compulsory heterosexuality'. In the narrower sense, it refers to lesbian and gay relationships being, in Rich's terms, crushed, invalidated and forced into hiding. That is, it is a failure to acknowledge the existence and legitimacy of same-sex relationships and lesbians and gay men. The final word, disguise, also indicates a wider meaning in addition to the closet, relating to the enforcement of the dominant norms of heterosexual society, such as coupledom, monogamy and private rather than public sexuality. To the extent that they adopt (or are assumed to adopt) these norms, same-sex relationships could be said to be disguised as 'straight'.

As I argued above, the dichotomy of the responsible and the irresponsible (and also the normal and the abnormal, the respectable and the scandalous, and the private and the public, among others) replacing that of gay and straight should not necessarily be celebrated. However, it is not my intention to make an argument for the decriminalization of sexual activity in public places. Instead, I want to highlight the role that same-sex marriage claims play in seeking a respectable 'good gay' image, part of which includes the gentrification, including desexualisation, of urban (gay) space.

Gentrification refers to 'a campaign designed to privatize, sanitize, and control public spaces' in order to make those paying high rents 'feel at home' (Shepard, 2004, pp. 106, 110). As Dean Spade demonstrates in the US context, the single-issue politics of marriage has consumed lesbian and gay organizations struggling 'for the rights of a few race-and-money-privileged people' to be able to inherit each other's wealth (2004, p. 36). At the same time, 'queer and trans youth of color who have found each other and formed community in the public spaces of [now wealthy neighbourhoods] for years' (2004, p. 32) are being chased out by vigilantism and police harassment at the instigation of a coalition of high-income gays and straights (see also Shepard, 2004). Michael Warner also gives examples of the gay community (*sic*) 'let[ting] things go' rather than fighting zoning laws and police harassment, which severely restrict 'adult establishments' (including not only sex clubs and sex shops, but also gay nightclubs and bars), and increased policing in cruising areas, including the use of entrapment (1999, pp. 149–59). This suggests that some gays and lesbians are interested in moving sexual taboos just far enough to accommodate same-sex desire without considering the wider issue of sexual repression (Califia, 1999, p. 39) or social justice measures such as improved public housing or (in the US) universal health coverage (Spade, 2004). Warner does not believe that 'this erosion of queer publics' (1999, p. 161) is driven by homophobia, but by 'real estate interests', the privatisation and ownership of public space that was previously used by queers. However, I would argue that it constitutes a wilful unknowing of, a 'deliberate refusal to know or consider' (Lamble, 2009, p. 124), sexualities, bodies, practices and uses of 'public' space that are non-normative. This is not limited to heterosexual oppression of queers: Pat Califia notes that the objections made by middle-class gay homeowners halted plans to build a shelter for homeless queer youth in the Castro (2004, p. 71; see also Bell and Binnie, 2000, pp. 144–5, for discussion of the class dimensions of this in the UK context). This gentrification of public (queer) space and erosion of public sex culture is 'too often cheered on by [some] lesbian and gay advocates' (Warner, 1999, p. 163) as well as lifestyle magazines and celebrities:

> Gay journalists are repudiating the legacy of safer sex, depicting lesbians as sexless homebodies whom gay men should imitate and gay male sexual culture as a zone of irresponsibility, narcissism, and death. Gay marriage is understood by many to offer a post-political privacy now described as the only thing we ever wanted. (Warner, 1999, p. 163)

Though it may be stereotypically 'malestream', this sexual culture is not only a gay male one (see Cooper, 2007; Lamble, 2009) and the wider class politics as well as the manifestation of compulsory heterosexuality through the enforced invisibility of same-sex desire and 'strategic desexualising' of lesbians and gay men (Stychin, 2003, p. 36) should be of concern to feminists.

The second, related, point is that same-sex marriage does not, as illustrated in the context of civil partnerships, necessarily mean that lesbian and gay *sexuality* is recognized within the provision. Mary Bernstein found that the likely success of domestic partner or same-sex marriage provisions could be explained in the extent to which the challenge they pose to heteronormativity can be circumvented (2001, p. 437). She argues that, although these provisions assume an intimate relationship between same-sex partners, this relationship is usually presented in financial terms (for example, some domestic partnership provisions require the partners to demonstrate that they are financially dependent on each other) rather than the sexual consummation or emotional aspects of the relationship. Furthermore, claims for domestic partnership (and to some extent marriage), by focusing to a large extent on health insurance coverage in the US (and pensions/taxation in the UK), 'can be easily framed in terms of equal pay for equal work' (Bernstein, 2001, p. 437) rather than an endorsement or validation of same-sex relationships. Because legal change is 'dependent on the ability to frame the challenge in a way that leaves heteronormativity untroubled', it is unlikely to in itself 'create acceptance or transform dominant cultural values' (Bernstein, 2001, pp. 439–40).

Therefore, engagement with the state requires non-normative behaviour to remain hidden and, as such, the transgressive potential of same-sex marriage is subverted: 'the bargains [same-sex marriage advocates] must make with lawmakers ensure that dominant norms underlying the opprobrium associated with homosexuality remain unchanged' (Bernstein, 2001, p. 422). That is, compulsory heterosexuality and heteronormativity remain unchallenged. It is necessary, as Mark Graham argues, that in order to 'demolish heteronormative regimes' we must 'dethron[e] heterosexuality from its pedestal as the only true and natural form of human sexuality' (2004, p. 29). It is not possible to do this without talking about sex, and without,

> heightening the social and cultural visibility of sexuality, exploring the options, interrogating the pleasures, anxieties and inequalities sexuality gives rise to, and examining how inequalities associated with age, race, gender, and other characteristics are implicated in sex. (Graham, 2004, pp. 29–30)

However, this is a risky strategy because, as Graham notes, it 'opens sexuality up to further intervention without any guarantee that this will take a desirable form' (2004, p. 29). Without taking this risk, though, lesbian and gay sexuality remains invisible; there is, as Adrienne Rich argues, a continued 'denial of reality and visibility to women's *passion* for women' (1981, p. 29, emphasis added) and hetero sex remains the unquestioned norm. Similarly, Boyd and Young conclude that 'a focus on sex' in same-sex partnership recognition may not be necessary, 'except to the extent that it is needed to ensure the visibility of lesbian and gay lives, and that they are not erased in the very process of receiving recognition' (2003, p. 787).

I am not arguing that same-sex relationship recognition should include specific reference to same-sex sexuality but merely noting the limitations of same-sex marriage as a way of recognizing lesbians and gay men as *sexual* citizens, particularly where the form that lesbian and gay sexuality takes is non-normative. It is likely that any form of argument would be construed in a de-sexualized way by the courts and legislature because of the wilful ignorance/unknowing that has been evident (see Lamble, 2009). Although it is, as mentioned above, impossible to predict with any certainty what the impact of law reform would be, particularly in the long term (Herman, 1994a, p. 145). Furthermore, as Bernstein recognizes, positive legal recognition for same-sex couples may disrupt heteronormativity not only in law through the legal system recognizing, forming and dissolving familial relationships between same-sex couples, but also in society through indirectly providing a safer environment for more lesbians and gay men to come out (2001, pp. 439–40).

My argument is that what Lamble (2009, p. 124) terms the 'deliberate refusal to know' lesbian and gay sex is a manifestation of compulsory heterosexuality that is *likely* to continue despite any supposedly positive recognition effects of same-sex marriage. I make this argument in order to problematize the assumptions that recognition would be the result of same-sex marriage and that recognition would be the same for all queers.

Towards a radical conception of recognition: a return to redistribution

Recognition is, according to Nancy Fraser, a question of social status and thus misrecognition should be situated within a larger social framework that 'cannot be understood in isolation from economic arrangements' (Fraser, 2003a). This is not to imply that Fraser views recognition as the key to remedying social injustice. In fact, she disagrees with Axel Honneth on this point when he argues that a claim for redistribution is a sub-variety of recognition claim (Fraser and Honneth, 2003). Instead, she maintains that a politics of recognition must exist *alongside* one of redistribution; one without the other (more specifically, recognition without redistribution) is an incomplete strategy. In this final section, I explore the meanings of recognition and the connection between recognition and redistribution in the context of same-sex marriage debates. This allows for a clearer picture to develop of the link between the feminist critiques of marriage explored in Chapter 5 and the limitations of marriage as a tool for recognition, as highlighted by the preceding discussion in this chapter.

In her earlier work on the issue, Fraser distinguishes recognition claims from redistributive claims. Although she argues that both are linked and mutually reinforcing, she contends that they must be distinguished analytically and that they have different kinds of remedy (1997a, p. 15). Fraser's concept of recognition is perhaps more clearly defined through *non*-recognition or *mis*recognition: 'being rendered invisible by means of the authoritative representational, communicative, and interpretative practices of one's culture' (Fraser, 1997a, p. 14). Fraser argues that this is a form of cultural injustice as distinct from socio-economic injustice. The remedy for cultural injustice, Fraser argues, is:

> some sort of cultural or symbolic change. This could involve upwardly revaluing disrespected identities and the cultural products of maligned groups. It could also involve recognising and positively valorising cultural diversity. More radically still, it could involve the wholesale transformation of societal patterns of representation, interpretation, and communication in ways

that would change *everybody's* sense of self. (Fraser, 1997a, p. 15,
original emphasis)

Fraser is arguing that some types of injustice are distributive (economic),
others are rooted in misrecognition (cultural), while some are both. For Fraser,
the oppression of lesbians and gay men lies in heterosexism ('the authoritative construction of norms that privilege heterosexuality') and homophobia ('the cultural devaluation of homosexuality') and as such is rooted in
'an unjust cultural-valuation structure' rather than the economic structure
(1997a, p. 18).

Butler critiques Fraser's approach to the recognition/redistribution dichotomy, arguing that they cannot be distinguished from each other and that to
try to do so risks positing misrecognition as 'merely cultural' rather than central to the way that resources are distributed through the family and, as such,
has the potential to 'ameliorate the political force of queer struggles' (Butler,
1997, p. 44). She argues that sexualities are produced through the capitalist
mode of production just as genders are:

> It would be a mistake to understand such productions as 'merely
> cultural' if they are essential to the functioning of the sexual
> order of political economy, that is, constituting a threat to its very
> workability. The economic, tied to the reproductive, is necessarily
> linked to the reproduction of heterosexuality. It is not that non-
> heterosexual forms of sexuality are simply left out, but that their
> suppression is essential to the operation of that prior normativity.
> This is not simply a question of some people suffering a lack of
> cultural recognition by others, but rather, *a specific mode of sexual
> production and exchange that works to maintain the stability of gen-
> der, the heterosexuality of desire, and the naturalization of the family.*
> (1997, p. 42, emphasis added)

This is a particularly important point in relation to same-sex marriage
claims, which, while using the discourse of recognition, is also centrally
concerned with access to legal provisions and economic resources that are
distributed through the family.

Fraser responds that her distinction is not intended to 'derogate' recognition to the 'merely cultural' but to 'conceptualize two equally primary,
serious, and real kinds of harm that any morally defensible social order must
eradicate' (1997b, p. 280). Although Fraser argues that 'misrecognition constitutes a fundamental injustice, whether accompanied by maldistribution or
not' (p. 281), the way that Fraser applies the distinction to sexual orientation (a recognition issue) as distinct from gender (a 'bivalent' issue, that is
one requiring both recognition and redistribution) is problematic. Leaving

aside the issue of whether gender and sexuality (including sexual orientation) can be distinguished as analytical and political categories, as Butler argues, the oppression of lesbians and gay men is rooted in the economic structure as much as the cultural-valuation structure. This is particularly evident in the discourses surrounding same-sex marriage claims. In fact, the most successful arguments for same-sex marriage have been on the basis of access to economic structures as much as (if not more than) recognition of same-sex relationships. I therefore disagree with Fraser's categorization of 'the despised sexuality' as being at one of the extremes of her spectrum (see also Butler, 1997, p. 39).

Instead, I argue that the law uses recognition and non-recognition to control access to economic justice. As Butler also notes, the family has long been the site of socialist feminist concern because of the way that it produces and reproduces economic exploitation. Through marriage, law defines family and sets up a system whereby this exploitation is (re)produced and rewarded, for example it provides some tax breaks in recognition of privatized caretaking that takes place within the family (historically defined through marriage, though an increase in cohabitation has meant that the Law Commission has recommended partially extending this to non-married cohabitants: Law Commission, 2007). In response to Butler's criticism on this point, Fraser does argue that misrecognition may be material in the same way as injustices of distribution; she is not claiming that recognition has no material consequences (1997b, p. 282). My concern here though is that, in the context of marriage, the distribution issue is integral to the recognition issue, rather than consequential. The 'despised sexualities' should be categorized as one of Fraser's 'bivalent collectivities'; that is, one that suffers 'injustices that are traceable to both political economy and culture simultaneously' (1997a, p. 19). She argues that bivalent collectivities 'may suffer both socioeconomic maldistribution and cultural misrecognition in forms where neither of these injustices is an indirect effect of the other, but where both are primary and co-original' (ibid.). Recognition (or misrecognition) is the primary way in which inclusion and exclusion from the legal framework is determined and, through offering cultural and economic recognition, the law (and leaving aside the question of how intentional or coherent this was) regulates sexual behaviour through setting the parameters of respectability and normality. In other words, in this context I agree with Butler's (1997, p. 41) argument that it is impossible to separate social or cultural recognition from economic redistribution, and also from regulation, because the construction of the legal family is central to all of these models.

Fraser also discusses the remedies to recognition and distributive injustices. These can be either 'affirmative' or 'transformative'. Affirmative remedies merely seek access to existing structures without challenging the underlying frameworks that structure injustices of recognition and distribution (1997a, p. 23). A transformative remedy is one which is 'aimed at correcting inequitable outcomes precisely by restructuring the underlying generative framework' (1997a, p. 23). For example, a transformative recognition remedy would, in terms of sexual orientation, 'deconstruct the hetero–homo dichotomy' (1997a, p. 24), while a transformative redistributive remedy would seek to transform 'the underlying political–economic structure' (1997a, p. 25).[9] The more mainstream recognition arguments and all of the access to economic benefits (redistributive) arguments that are made for same-sex marriage are affirmative in that they do not (and do not seek to) challenge existing structures and frameworks, but rather seek access to them. In contrast, the more radical recognition arguments that seek to destabilize the current understandings of marriage through transgressing, subverting, or queering the institution via same-sex marriage could map on to Fraser's transformative recognition.

In this chapter, I have sought to problematize these more radical recognition arguments in a number of ways, including through questioning the inclusion/exclusion binary that would see some (same-sex) relationship forms remain 'outsiders'. This discussion also maps on to problems with (gay) identity politics more generally from queer theory perspectives. However, Fraser later refined her theory of recognition, arguing that recognition strategies based on identity politics are problematic because they contribute to the displacement of struggles for economic justice by those of recognition (2003a, p. 24), reify group identities leading to the exclusion of those who do not conform, and replicate wider power hierarchies (2003a, p. 26). Nevertheless, these problems do not mean that recognition claims must be abandoned. Instead, Fraser argues that recognition can be reformulated in a way that incorporates redistributive claims (2003a, p. 27). Fraser's claim is that recognition must be treated as 'a question of *social status*' (Fraser, 2003a, p. 27, original emphasis) rather than group identity. The status model situates recognition within larger society so it acknowledges that society has economic as well as cultural ordering, though 'neither is wholly reducible to the other' (2003a, p. 30). The economic and the cultural remain, for Fraser, analytically distinct; recognition (an issue of status) referring to 'different actors' capacities for social participation' whereas distribution (an issue of economic class) is about the 'systemic effects of economic structures on the relative economic position of social actors, which also affects their capacities for participation'

---

9 Nancy Fraser's use of 'transformative' here is slightly different to the way I have been using it in that Fraser's transformative remedies could also include what I have been referring to as transgression. However, this is not wholly inconsistent with my use of the terms because, as I noted in the introduction to this chapter, though I make a distinction between them, I do maintain that they overlap and are interlinked concepts.

(2003a, p. 30). Therefore, the status model of recognition, which focuses on individuals rather than groups (as opposed to an identity model), 'works against tendencies to displace struggles for redistribution' (2003a, p. 31):

> Unlike the identity model, then, the status model views misrec-ognition in the context of a broader understanding of contempo-rary society. From this perspective, status subordination cannot be understood in isolation from economic arrangements. Nor can the recognition dimension of justice be viewed in abstrac-tion from distribution. On the contrary, only by considering both dimensions together can one determine what is impeding partici-patory parity in any case. (Fraser, 2003a, p. 31)

Fraser uses the issue of same-sex marriage to illustrate her argument: mis-recognition requires changing social institutions to enable or foster partici-pation. For Fraser, this could be achieved *either* through legalizing same-sex marriage or deinstitutionalizing heterosexual marriage. There may be, she suggests, other good reasons for choosing one of these over the other, but, in terms of recognition, either would provide a remedy. Despite her move away from identity politics and its associated problems, then, this revised form of recognition is not necessarily any more radical than an identity politics model, nor is it intended to be. The remedy for the misrecognition of same-sex marriage may be either transformative or affirmative and which is chosen does not necessarily, for Fraser, affect the 'quality' of the recognition.

However, this leaves aside two important issues: the role of redistributive justice in the context of same-sex marriage; and how that relates to Fraser's earlier distinction between affirmative and transformative remedies. As I argued above, sexuality is a 'bivalent collectivity' requiring recognition *and* redistribution remedies. Therefore, the role of redistribution in same-sex mar-riage claims is central to a recognition claim. As noted above, (affirmative) redistribution in terms of access to legal and economic benefits and burdens of marriage is one of the key arguments for same-sex marriage; and, as my argument in Chapter 5 suggested, access to marriage is an inherently affir-mative remedy in terms of economic redistribution. In this chapter, I have sought to problematize the claim that same-sex marriage may bring a trans-formative (as opposed to affirmative) recognition. Empirically, that remains a somewhat open question as it is impossible to predict with any certainty what the effect of same-sex marriage might be. However, assuming that the recognition *may* be transformative, I would question whether transformative recognition combined with affirmative redistribution can be a sufficiently radical or progressive remedy. In the absence of transformative redistribution, recognition cannot be any more than partially transformative and the radical impact of recognition would be limited.

Conclusion

Law is used for 'purposive social engineering' (Smart, 1997, p. 312). In terms of family law and relationship recognition this is achieved through the law prescribing the *form* that intimate relationships must take in order to receive recognition. The law is, however, far from unitary or certain and there is a distinction between the legal ideology of 'the family' and the way that people 'do' family (Diduck, 2003). Dewar (2000) argues that there is 'pervasive uncertainty' about what family law is for and, despite judicial assumptions to the contrary, this uncertainty extends to the essence, if not the model, of marriage (see Chapter 1). It is reasonable, then, to argue that marriage may be transgressed, subverted or even queered by same-sex marriage and this is certainly the fear of its right-wing opponents. However, in this chapter, I have sought to problematize that claim by examining what legal recognition through marriage may mean. I argued that Carol Smart's caution in respect of resorting to legal reform is appropriate in this context and demonstrated some of the ways in which legal recognition will be assimilationist in promoting a 'normal gay' ideal and failing to recognize more radical, non-normative, forms of same-sex relationships and (lesbian and gay) sexualities.

Smart's aim in *Feminism and the Power of Law* was to 'challenge law's over-inflated view of itself' as against other forms of knowledge, particularly feminism, that have been 'continuously disqualified by law' (1989, p. 3). In attributing an assimilatory power to law, I may be accused of reinforcing this over-inflated view or of attributing too much power to law in terms of its operation and influence outside of the legal arena. For example, Stychin argues that a much more effective disciplining or normalizing mechanism of social control than the juridical power of law reform itself is the liberal identity politics that must be articulated in order to successfully engage in law reform (2005a, p. 98). This liberal identity politics, however, arguably arises from the necessity of having to 'translate' claims into a language that law can engage with (as demonstrated by Herman (1994a, p. 118) in the context of Christian Right engagements with law) and of having to present a relationship that the law can identify with.

I am not suggesting that people cannot create alternative ways of living outside of and despite the legal framework that is in place; in fact, sociological research has demonstrated that such possibilities are widely exercised and that notions of intimacy and relationships have evolved much faster than, or differently to, the legal framework (see, for example, Giddens, 1993; Silva and Smart, 1999; Smart and Neale, 1999; Budgeon and Roseneil, 2004; cf. Gross, 2005, p. 306). Nor am I denying that radical possibilities may exist, whether through 'loopholes' in the recognition provision (such as the absence of sex in the Civil Partnership Act 2004), or through simply 'displacing the heteronormativity of legal subjectivity in the familial context' (Cossman, 2002a, p. 246). The issue of same-sex marriage is more complicated than setting up an assimilation versus transgression binary would suggest (Stychin, 2003; Richardson, 2004).

Nevertheless, the debate has been framed in terms of 'we are family' or 'we are not family' (Cossman, 1994, p. 3). It is not possible to simultaneously request recognition for same-sex families within the legal framework and to maintain a positionality against the (hetero)normative. Most significantly in terms of the feminist critiques of marriage, it is not possible to simultaneously seek recognition through marriage and argue that family is not an appropriate mechanism through which to distribute social resources. This link between the (re)distribution of social resources and recognition is the key issue. As discussed in Chapter 5, marriage provides a means of distribution that is fundamentally unjust. Seeking recognition through marriage can only be affirmative recognition in that it necessarily (and at the very least) leaves in place the framework of marriage. I have argued that, despite the obvious temptation to seek the positive state recognition of (some) same-sex relationships that marriage would bring, (affirmative) recognition is unlikely to be anything other than partial recognition of the range of relationships within the lesbian and gay communities. Not only is this partial recognition insufficient to justify overlooking the feminist critiques of marriage, these critiques also demonstrate the importance of addressing redistribution as part of a radical politics of recognition. In the context of same-sex marriage claims, legal recognition is, as Butler argues, an 'ambivalent gift'.

Conclusion

Not the marrying kind

In the UK same-sex marriage case, *Wilkinson v Kitzinger* [2006] EWHC 2022, Sir Mark Potter's judgment that the exclusion of same-sex couples from marriage could be justified by reference to the procreation function of marriage was flawed. Not only was his view that procreation is central to marriage explicitly rejected by the House of Lords in *Baxter v Baxter* [1948] AC 274 six decades earlier, I have also argued that it is evident from contemporary judgments and remarks made in *obiter* that the prevailing judicial conception of marriage in the UK is primarily concerned with interdependency, sexual and emotional intimacy, and companionship. However, rather than ask whether same-sex couples should be able to legally marry, my aim has been to question whether marriage has or could evolve to overcome the problems that feminists have identified with the institution. Those seeking same-sex marriage have generally not interrogated the institution and have largely overlooked the feminist critiques. As such, my goals were to explore marriage and the ways that same-sex relationship recognition fits into this framework and to revisit the feminist critiques to discover whether they could be extended to same-sex marriage.

Though the feminist critiques of marriage that I have discussed were largely made during the second wave of feminism, marriage as a legal and social institution has not changed significantly enough to deny the relevance of these critiques to the contemporary marriage model. Furthermore, many of the 'new' provisions that have been created to recognize same-sex relationships map on to this marriage model. There have been some strong arguments made for same-sex marriage, from the necessity of accessing legal protections and the symbolism of legal recognition to feminist claims that same-sex marriage would transform the institution and suggestions that marriage could be queered. In light of these arguments, I revisited the second-wave feminist critiques, asking whether (and how) they need to be revised to make a stronger and more specific critique of *same-sex* marriage.

Second-wave radical feminists problematized penetrative (hetero) sex; Katherine O'Donovan (1993, p. 47) explicitly links this to marriage by highlighting the role of the consummation requirement in constructing it as *the* legally approved form of sexual expression. Radical feminists also focused on the ways in which women's reproductive biology and the denigration of nurturing were used to oppress women, both particularly apparent in the gendered dynamics of marriage. Socialist feminists synthesized these theories of patriarchy with socialist accounts of capitalism to theorize the impact of capitalist patriarchy on women's oppression. This highlighted the ways in which not only individual men but also capitalism as a whole benefits from women's labour within the family. There was a particular focus on women's unpaid labour within the home as reproducing the conditions necessary for capitalism through enabling or supporting men's paid work and stabilizing the economy through consumption work.

While perceptions of the ideal marriage may have shifted to a more egalitarian and negotiated household division of labour, this is far from a universal reality. Women are still doing most of the household labour but the justification for this is no longer always based on gendered notions of marital roles. Instead, it is alternatively (or also) based on a superficially egalitarian pragmatism: it 'makes sense' for the partner with the lowest income to take on more domestic work. While egalitarianism was a strongly held ideal in same-sex relationships, this 'justified' inequality was also demonstrated in Christopher Carrington's (1999) ethnography of same-sex relationships. It is significant that Carrington found that those lesbians and gay men who worked in female gendered occupations (teachers, nurses, administrators) tended to do most of the domestic labour where their partner worked in male gendered occupations. Where both partners worked in female gendered occupations the division of labour tended to be more equal. This strong influence of occupation suggests that there remains a link between both gender *and* capitalism and household division of labour, particularly in that the male gendered occupations continue to assume the 'unencumbered individual' who is available to work long hours because somebody else is taking care of the domestic responsibilities (Fineman, 2001, p. 36). Moreover, a key issue for socialist feminists is that responsibility for care and dependency is privatized within the family. The increasing influence of neoliberalism and the rolling back of the welfare state makes these critiques more relevant to contemporary marriage, including same-sex marriage.

Nevertheless, there are some ways in which feminist critiques should be revised to address same-sex marriage more specifically. The first is to acknowledge the declining statistical significance of marriage, though not its ideological influence, by referring to the *marriage model* rather than marriage itself. The critiques that I have outlined apply just as much to relationships that are based on the marriage model, such as cohabitation, as they do to marriage. For example, the government will, for the purposes of calculating entitlement for state benefits, treat a cohabiting couple in the same way as a married couple, thus encouraging the privatization of dependency within the household even in the absence of marriage. Referring to the marriage model as the focus of critique also more explicitly encompasses the marriage-like but separate provisions that have been created for same-sex relationships, such as civil partnership. It is necessary to do this because civil partnership has been embraced by some heterosexuals who reject marriage on feminist grounds and seek access to this provision as an alternative (see, for example, Equal Love, 2011).

Second, it is necessary to respond more directly to the ways in which same-sex marriage might transform, transgress, or queer marriage and suggestions that same-sex marriage might be necessary despite the feminist critiques of it. Feminist theory alone can respond to some of these claims, but a more complete rebuttal can be made through reference to queer theoretical perspectives. Though a combination of feminism and queer theory is not unproblematic due to a number of theoretical conflicts between them, queer theorists and feminists share some concerns in relation to marriage. In particular, Carol Smart's Foucaultian feminist theory (1989) and the queer critiques of assimilationist strategies provide a useful addition to second-wave theories of marriage in problematizing the resort to law generally (and marriage in particular) in attempts to overcome homophobia and heterosexism. Furthermore, there are also some significant overlaps between second-wave feminist and queer theories, particularly through the development and extension of Adrienne Rich's concept of compulsory heterosexuality.

Compulsory heterosexuality is a second-wave, radical feminist theory that refers to the devaluing or invisibility of women's love for women (Rich, 1981). It could be argued, then, that same-sex marriage would counter this devaluation or invisibility through legally recognizing lesbian relationships. However, queer theorists argue that same-sex marriage would be assimilationist, or 'the cultural triumph of compulsory heterosexuality' (Kaplan, 1997, p. 210) because marriage could only recognize those same-sex relationships that fit into the heteronormative marriage framework. In other words, same-sex relationships must be 'in disguise' as hetero (or perhaps homo) normative relationships, with the accompanying marginalization of public sex. Furthermore, as I discussed in relation to the UK civil partnership provision, the recognition occurs in a context that desexualizes same-sex relationships, with some even attempting to analogize them to 'spinster sisters'. This suggests a very dubious recognition of lesbian and gay sexualities.

Feminist critiques of marriage remain relevant to both contemporary heterosexual marriage and same-sex marriage and should provide the basis for analysis of the marriage model. However, as I have demonstrated, a stronger critique can be made of same-sex marriage by also drawing upon some of the insights of queer theoretical perspectives. For many queers, the old euphemism 'not the marrying kind' remains apt despite same-sex marriage.

In the introduction, I suggested that part of feminist methodology was to ask the 'question of the excluded', which involves investigating: what is marriage; which relationships are included and excluded; what assumptions are made by the law; and who stands to gain and lose from inclusion within marriage? The final part of this, which was outside the scope of this book, is how could the interests of those who are invisible or peripheral to marriage law be taken into account? I conclude with a brief examination of three law reform proposals that may provide a basis for future research to answer this question in a way that is compatible with the concerns of second-wave feminist and queer critics of marriage.

Recognizing all families? Beyond marriage and beyond conjugality[1]

> Advocating marriage for same-sex couples is a sensible way to champion equal civil rights for gay men and lesbians. Unfortunately, it is not a sensible approach toward achieving just outcomes for the wide range of family structures in which LGBT people, as well as many others, live. Those outcomes depend on eliminating the 'special rights' that only married couples receive and meeting the needs of a range of family forms. (Polikoff, 2008, p. 84)

In her recent book, Nancy Polikoff argues that law should recognize and value all family forms, whether or not they are based on marriage or sexual relationships. Her proposal for doing this involves a multi-tiered system. The first is marriage, re-named civil partnership in order to distance it 'from its past and from the components of marriage that religions define' (2008, p. 132). However, she would fundamentally alter the legal consequences of marriage/civil partnership. Rather than a fixed set of legal consequences accompanying marriage/civil partnership, the particular laws that accompany an individual relationship would depend on the relationship's function rather than legal status. For example, with regard to a legal consequence of marriage that is designed to facilitate child-rearing, 'a marriage without children would be excluded and *any household* raising children would be included' (2008, p.133,

---

1 This subheading references the title of Nancy Polikoff's (2008) book, the Beyond Marriage (2006) movement in the United States, and the Law Commission of Canada's (2001) report.

emphasis added). The principle behind this is that not all marriages share the same characteristics and so should not share the same legal consequences; similarly, any households that do provide the function that the law intends to recognize or facilitate should attract the legal consequences. Polikoff argues that marriage/civil partnership then becomes a genuine choice because it is 'neither necessary nor sufficient to access particular laws' (2008, p. 133).

Additionally, Polikoff proposes that states should create a system of registration for 'designated family relationships'. This would allow someone who does not have a spouse or partner to identify someone as 'designated family' to be treated as a spouse (2008, p. 134). The examples that Polikoff gives of this are the authority to make medical decisions and disposition-of-remains decisions, and intestacy inheritance rights. This system 'would be open to all unmarried/unpartnered people who wanted a chosen family relationship to be legally recognized' (2008, p. 135). This would not have to be someone who shares a home. Finally, in relation to those who do not have a spouse/ partner and have not designated a family relationship, Polikoff proposes that the law should consider someone to be a family member 'based on the circumstances of the relationship', including friends, if they can show that they had a close relationship with the person and were the most likely to know their wishes (2008, p.136).

Polikoff's argument was partly inspired by those of a group of American academics and activists (of which she was one) who formed a project, Beyond Marriage, advocating for what I would refer to as a 'marriage plus' system. This refers to the fact that they seek not only same-sex marriage but also recognition of a broader range of relationships that are currently excluded from the marriage framework. Their list includes: senior citizens who live together as partners, carers, or constructed family members; extended families; queer couples/individuals who are jointly raising children, perhaps across two households; close friends and siblings who live together (Beyond Marriage, 2006).

By centring households and including families of choice (designated families), these proposals attempt to avoid legally privileging the monogamous conjugal unit. However, by leaving marriage in place,[2] both Polikoff's and the Beyond Marriage's proposals risk creating a hierarchy of relationships where marriage remains the 'ideal', even when it is no longer privileged in terms of its legal status. Furthermore, though Polikoff is concerned with the

---

2 Polikoff recommends changing marriage slightly in terms of a) changing its name to civil partnership and b) removing the legal distinction between civil partners (spouses), cohabitants and her new category of designated family members. However, this slightly revised marriage does not otherwise depart from the structure, legal consequences and ideologies of the marriage model in significant ways.

effects of dependency,[3] she does not explicitly examine the implications that her proposals (and those of Beyond Marriage) might have for the further privatization of care (and enforced interdependency through legal assumptions that 'spouses' will financially support each other) within this wider range of household or family units. This is one of the key issues that I have identified in terms of how second-wave feminist critiques of marriage provide an important insight into contemporary same-sex marriage debates. I argued, in agreement with Conaghan and Grabham (2007), that recognizing more diverse families is (perhaps in addition to any recognition benefits the families may experience) actually a way for the state to reinforce expectations of family-based care. Polikoff seeks to move away from marriage but, by overlooking the ways in which her proposal may support privatization of care and enforced interdependency within family units, she incorporates a central aspect of the marriage model within her proposals.

I would argue that any reform proposals in this area should not merely be seeking to expand the marriage model to include more diverse relationships but to actively avoid this blanket privatization of care, which means that an intimate, cohabiting, or self-identified designated family relationship results in an assumption of mutual responsibility for care and dependency across the board. While Polikoff's proposals and those of Beyond Marriage both, perhaps for strategic or political reasons, keep the marriage model as a framework for recognizing relationships (albeit a revised and/or expanded version that is more inclusive and takes account of many critiques of marriage), the Law Commission of Canada took a more radical approach. Its report, *Beyond Conjugality*, moves away from the marriage model, advocating 'a fundamental rethinking of the way in which governments regulate relationships' (2001, p. ix). This approach, I would suggest, has more potential than Polikoff's or the Beyond Marriage approach to result in a form of relationship recognition that moves away from the problems of the marriage model that I identified in previous chapters.

Noting the diversity of adult relationships, including non-conjugal households of both relatives and non-relatives and caretaking relationships, the Law Commission of Canada recommended a 'more principled and comprehensive approach' (2001, p. 7) that would be based on the values of equality and autonomy (2001, p. 13). This involves a focus on the functional characteristics of the relationship rather than its status, especially whether there is emotional and/or financial interdependence. It also involves paying attention to equality *within* relationships, with particular mention made of

---

3 The three key principles for 'valuing all families' are: 'place the needs of children and their caretakers above the claims of able-bodied adult spouses/partners'; 'support the needs of children in all family constellations'; and 'recognize adult interdependency' (Polikoff, 2008, pp. 137–8).

inequality between men and women and the need for the state to ensure the personal security (physical, psychological and economic) of those in relationships (2001, p. 19). The principles of autonomy, privacy and religious freedom mean that the state should 'remain neutral with regard to the form or status of relationships and not accord one form of relationship more benefits or legal support than others' (2001, p. xi) and should 'avoid, wherever possible, the establishment of legal rules that cannot be administered effectively without intrusive examinations into, or forced disclosure of, the intimate details of personal adult relationships' (2001, p. 21). Finally, the principles of coherence and efficiency require that 'laws have clear objectives, and that their legislative design corresponds with the achievement of these objectives' (2001, p. xii).

Some of these principles are potentially problematic: for example, the principle of state neutrality refers to supporting 'any and all relationships that have the capacity to *further relevant social goals*' (2001, p. 18, emphasis added). The relevant social goals in question may not necessarily be feminist goals. However, their approach provides a valuable starting point for a feminist alternative to the marriage model by rejecting any 'one size fits all' framework for relationship recognition, including those based on caretaking rather than sex. Instead, the Law Commission of Canada recommended that four questions be asked of any law that 'employs relational terms':

> First, are the objectives of the law still legitimate? If the objectives of a law are no longer appropriate, the response may be to repeal or fundamentally revise a law rather than to adjust its use of relational terms. Second, if a law is pursuing a legitimate objective, are relationships relevant to the objective at hand? If relationships are not important, then the legislation should be redesigned to allocate the rights and responsibilities on an individual basis. Third, assuming that relationships are relevant, could the law allow individuals to decide which of their close personal relationships should be subject to the law? Fourth, if relationships do matter, and self-definition of relevant relationships is not a feasible policy option, is there a better way for the government to include relationships? (2001, pp. 29–30)

This approach provides the opportunity to move beyond not only marriage but also the marriage model. As such, with Carol Smart's caution regarding law reform in mind (1989), the arguments that I have made in this book would suggest this approach as a starting point for future research.

Bibliography

ACLU (2011) *Verified Complaint: Wiessmann and Resko v State College Area School District* www.aclupa.org/downloads/Wiessmannfinal.pdf

Aikau, H, K Erickson and W Leo Moore (2003) 'Three Women Writing/Riding Feminism's Third Wave' **26**(3) *Qualitative Sociology* 397

Altman, D (1982) 'Sexual Freedom and the End of Romance' in A Sullivan (ed.), *Same-Sex Marriage Pro and Con: A Reader* (New York: Vintage, 1997)

Amnesty International (2011) 'Argentina Legalizes Same-Sex Marriage' www.amnesty.org/en/news-and-updates/argentina-legalizes-same-sex-marriage-2010-07-15

Arkes, H (1996) 'The Role of Nature' in A Sullivan (ed.), *Same-Sex Marriage Pro and Con: A Reader* (New York: Vintage, 1997)

Armstong, P (1997) 'Restructuring Public and Private: Women's Paid and Unpaid Work' in S B Boyd (ed.), *Challenging the Public/Private Divide: Feminism, Law and Public Policy* (Toronto: University of Toronto Press)

Association for Civil Rights in Israel (2006) 'Court orders the state to register overseas same-sex marriages' www.acri.org.il/eng/Story.aspx?id=344

Auchmuty, R (1997) 'Last In, First Out: Lesbian and Gay Legal Studies' **5**(2) *Feminist Legal Studies* 235

Auchmuty, R (2003) 'When Equality is not Equity: Homosexual Inclusion in Undue Influence Law' **11**(2) *Feminist Legal Studies* 163

Auchmuty, R (2004) 'Same-Sex Marriage Revived: Feminist Critique and Legal Strategy' **14**(1) *Feminism and Psychology* 101

Auchmuty, R (2007) 'Out of the Shadows: Feminist silence and liberal law' in V E Munro and C F Stychin (eds), *Sexuality and the Law: Feminist Engagements* (Oxon: Routledge-Cavendish)

Baatrup, S and K Waaldijk (2005) 'Major Legal Consequences of Marriage, Cohabitation and Registered Partnership for Different-Sex and Same-Sex Partners in Denmark' in K Waaldijk (ed.), *More or Less Together: Levels of Legal Consequences of Marriage, Cohabitation and Registered Partnership for Different-Sex and Same-Sex partners. A comparative study of nine European countries* www-same-sex.ined.fr/publica_doc125 .htm#

Bailey-Harris, R (1999) 'Third Stonewall Lecture – Lesbian and Gay Family Values and the Law' **29**(Aug) *Family Law* 560

Bailey-Harris, R (2002) 'Case Reports: Divorce: *Hadjimilitis (Tsavliris) v Tsavliris (Divorce: Irretrievable Breakdown)*' **32** *Family Law* 883

Bainham, A (2002) 'Does Sex Matter?' *Cambridge Law Journal* 44

Baird, R M and S E Rosenbaum (eds) (1997) *Same-Sex Marriage: The Moral and Legal Debate* (New York: Prometheus Books)

Baird, R M and S E Rosenbaum (eds) (2004) *Same-Sex Marriage: The Moral and Legal Debate* (New York: Prometheus Books) (2nd edn)

Bamforth, N (2007) 'Same-Sex Partnerships: Some Comparative Constitutional Lessons' **2007**(1) *European Human Rights Law Review* 47

Barker, N (2004) 'For Better or for Worse? The Civil Partnership Bill [HL] 2004' **26**(3) *Journal of Social Welfare and Family Law* 313

Barker, N (2006) 'Sex and the Civil Partnership Act: The Future of (Non)Conjugality?' **14**(2) *Feminist Legal Studies* 241

Barker, N (2011) 'Ambiguous Symbolisms: Recognising Customary Marriage and Same-Sex Marriage in South Africa' **7**(4) *International Journal of Law in Context* 447

Barlow, A, S Duncan, G James and A Park (2005) *Cohabitation, Marriage and the Law: Social Change and Legal Reform in the 21st Century* (Oxford: Hart)

Barlow, A and G James (2004) 'Regulating Marriage and Cohabitation in 21st Century Britain' **67**(2) *Modern Law Review* 143

Barlow, A and R Probert (1999) 'Reforming the Rights of Cohabitants – Lessons from Across the Channel' 29 *Family Law Journal* 477

Barnes, T (2011) 'Brazil Becomes Largest Nation Yet to Legalize Civil Unions' *Christian Science Monitor,* 6 May 2011 www.csmonitor.com/World/Americas/2011/0506/Brazil-becomes-largest-nation-yet-to-legalize-civil-unions

Barnett, L (2007) 'Mother is First Lesbian Guilty of Bigamy' *TimesOnline* 10 July 2007 www.timesonline.co.uk/tol/news/uk/crime/article2051926.ece

Barrett, M and M McIntosh (1982) *The Anti-Social Family* (London: Verso)

Barter, S and R Hodgwood (2005) 'Ménages à Trois – Relationships and the Taxman' **35** *Family Law* 568

Bartlett, K T (1990) 'Feminist Legal Methods' in K T Bartlett and R Kennedy (eds), *Feminist Legal Theory: Readings in Law and Gender* (Boulder: Westview Press, 1991)

Beauvoir, S de (1949) *The Second Sex* (London: Vintage) (1997 edn)

Bedau, H A (1961) 'On Civil Disobedience' *The Journal of Philosophy* 653

Beechey, V (1978) 'Women and Production: A Critical Analysis of Some Sociological Theories of Women's Work' in A Kuhn and A Wolpe (eds), *Feminism and Materialism: Women and Modes of Production* (London, Boston and Henley: Routledge & Kegan Paul)

Bell, D and J Binnie (2000) *The Sexual Citizen: Queer Politics and Beyond* (Cambridge: Polity Press)

Benn, M (2005) 'When Did You Last See Your Husband?' *The Guardian* 9 April 2005

Bennett, W (1996) 'Leave Marriage Alone' in A Sullivan, *Same-Sex Marriage Pro and Con: A Reader* (New York: Vintage, 1997)

Bernstein, M (2001) 'Gender, Queer Family Policies, and the Limits of Law' in M Bernstein and R Reimann (eds), *Queer Families Queer Politics: Challenging Culture and the State* (New York: Columbia University Press)

Beyond Marriage (2006) *Beyond Same-Sex Marriage: A New Strategic Vision for All our Families and Relationships* www.beyondmarriage.org/full_statement.html

Blumberg, G G (2004) 'Legal Recognition of Same-Sex Conjugal Relationships: The 2003 California Domestic Partner Rights and Responsibilities Act in Comparative Civil Rights and Family Law Perspective' **51** *UCLA Law Review* 1555

Bonthuys, E (2007) 'Race and Gender in the Civil Union Act' **23** *South African Journal on Human Rights* 526

Booth, P and S Jenkinson (2007) 'From Our Own Co-Respondents' **37** *Family Law* 530

Borrillo, D (2001) 'The "Pacte Civil de Solidarité" in France: Midway Between Marriage and Cohabitation' in R Wintemute and M Andenaes (eds), *Legal Recognition of Same-Sex Relationships: A Study of National, European and International Law* (Oxford: Hart)

Borrillo, D (2005) 'Who is Breaking with Tradition? The Legal Recognition of Same-Sex Partnership in France and the Question of Modernity' **17** *Yale Journal of Law and Feminism* 89

Borrillo, D and K Waaldijk (2005) 'Major Legal Consequences of Marriage, Cohabitation and Registered Partnership for Different-Sex and Same-Sex Partners in France' in K Waaldijk (ed.), *More or Less Together: Levels of Legal Consequences of Marriage, Cohabitation and Registered Partnership for Different-sex and Same-sex Partners. A comparative study of nine European countries* www-same-sex.ined.fr/publica_doc 125.htm#

Bourassa, K and J Varnell (2006) 'The Final Vote. Really. Mean it this Time. Getting on with Married Life Thank You Very Much' www.samesexmarriage.ca/legal/fin071206.htm

Boyd, S B (1994a) 'Expanding the "Family" in Family Law: Recent Ontario Proposals on Same-Sex Relationships' 7 *Canadian Journal of Women and Law* 545

Boyd, S B (1994b) '(Re)Placing the State: Family, Law and Oppression' 9 *Canadian Journal of Law and Society* 39

Boyd, S B (1996) 'Best Friends or Spouses? Privatization and the Recognition of Lesbian Relationships in *M v H*' 13 *Canadian Journal of Family Law* 321

Boyd, S B (ed.) (1997) *Challenging the Public/Private Divide: Feminism, Law and Public Policy* (Toronto: University of Toronto Press)

Boyd, S B (1999) 'Family, Law and Sexuality: Feminist Engagements' 8(3) *Social and Legal Studies* 369

Boyd, S B (2004) 'The Perils of Rights Discourse: A Response to Kitzinger and Wilkinson' 4(1) *Analyses of Social Issues and Public Policy* 211

Boyd, S B and C F L Young (2003) ' "From Same-Sex to No Sex"?: Trends Towards Recognition of (Same-Sex) Relationships in Canada' 1(3) *Seattle Journal for Social Justice* 757

Bradney, A (2000) 'Case Comment: Formalities to the Marriage Ceremony' *Law Quarterly Review* 351

Brook, H (2001) 'How to Do Things with Sex' in C Stychin and D Herman (eds), *Law and Sexuality: The Global Arena* (Minnesota: University of Minnesota Press)

Brook, H (2004) 'Just Married: Adversarial Divorce and the Conjugal Body Politic' 14(1) *Feminism and Psychology* 81

Brunner, K (2001) 'Nullity in Unconsummated Marriages' 31 *Family Law* 837

Bryson, V (2004) 'Marxism and Feminism: Can the "Unhappy Marriage" Be Saved?' 9(1) *Journal of Political Ideologies* 13

Buckel, D S (2005) 'Government Fixes a Label of Inferiority on Same-Sex Couples when it Imposes Civil Unions and Denies Access to Marriage' 16 *Stanford Law and Policy Review* 73

Budgeon, S and S Roseneil (2004) 'Editor's Introduction: Beyond the Conventional Family' 52(2) *Current Sociology* 127

Bunch, C (1972) 'Lesbians in Revolt: Male Supremacy Quakes and Quivers' 1 *The Furies: Lesbian/Feminist Monthly* 8–9 http://scriptorium.lib.duke.edu/wlm/furies/

Burnett, W B (1998–1999) 'Hawaii's Reciprocal Beneficiaries Act: An Effective Step in Resolving the Controversy Surrounding Same-Sex Marriage' 37 *Brandeis Law Journal* 82

Buseck, G (2004) 'Civil Marriage for Same-Sex Couples' 38 *New England Law Review* 495

Bush, G W (2004a) 'State of the Union Address' www.whitehouse.gov/news/releases/2004/01/20040120-7.html

Bush, G W (2004b) 'A Call for a Constitutional Amendment Protecting Marriage' in R M Baird and S E Rosenbaum (eds), *Same-Sex Marriage: The Moral and Legal Debate* (New York: Prometheus Books) (2nd edn)

Butler, J (1990) *Gender Trouble: Feminism and the Subversion of Identity* (New York and London: Routledge) (1999 10th anniversary edn)

Butler, J (1993) 'Imitation and Gender Insubordination' in H Abelove, M A Barala and D M Halperin (eds), *The Lesbian and Gay Studies Reader* (New York: Routledge)

Butler, J (1997) 'Merely Cultural' 15(3/4) *Social Text 52/53* 265

Butler, J (2002) 'Is Kinship Always Already Heterosexual?' 13(1) *Differences: A Journal of Feminist Cultural Studies* 14

Calder, G (2009) 'Penguins and Polyamory: Using Law and Film to Explore the Essence of Marriage in Canadian Family Law' 21 *Canadian Journal of Women and Law* 55

Calhoun, C (2000) *Feminism, the Family, and the Politics of the Closet: Lesbian and Gay Displacement* (New York: Oxford University Press)

Califia, P (1999) 'Gay Marriage' in *Speaking Sex to Power: The Politics of Queer Sex* (California: Cleis Press, 2002)

Califia, P (2004) 'Legalized Sodomy is Political Foreplay' in Mattilda, aka M Bernstein Sycamore (ed.), *That's Revolting! Queer Strategies for Resisting Assimilation* (Brooklyn: Soft Skull Press)

Callan, M E (2003) 'The More the Not Marry-Er: In Search of a Policy Behind Eligibility for California Domestic Partnerships' **40** *San Diego Law Review* 427

Carabine, J (2001) 'Constituting Sexuality through Social Policy: The Case of Lone Motherhood 1834 and Today' **10**(3) *Social and Legal Studies* 291

Carby, H V (1992) 'White Women Listen! Black Feminism and the Boundaries of Sisterhood' in Centre for Contemporary Cultural Studies (eds), *The Empire Strikes Back: Race and Racism in 70s Britain* (London: Routledge)

Card, C (1998) 'Radicalesbianfeminist Theory' **13**(1) *Hypatia* 206

Carrington, C (1999) *No Place Like Home: Relationships and Family Life among Lesbians and Gay Men* (Chicago and London: University of Chicago Press)

Casswell, D G (2001) 'Any Two Persons in Canada's Lotusland, British Columbia' in R Wintemute and M Andenaes (eds), *Legal Recognition of Same-Sex Relationships: A Study of National, European and International Law* (Oxford: Hart)

Chambers, David L (2001) 'For the Best of Friends and for Lovers of All Sorts, a Status Other Than Marriage' **76**(5) *Notre Dame Law Review* 1347

Chambers, Deborah (2001) *Representing the Family* (London: Sage)

Chandler, J (1991) *Women without Husbands: Exploration of the Margins of Marriage* (Basingstoke: Macmillan)

Chodorow, N (1979) 'Mothering, Male Dominance, and Capitalism' in Z R Eisenstein (ed.), *Capitalist Patriarchy and the Case for Socialist Feminism* (New York and London: Monthly Review Press)

Chunn, D E and S A M Gavigan (2004) 'Welfare Law, Welfare Fraud, and the Moral Regulation of the "Never Deserving" Poor' **13**(2) *Social and Legal Studies* 219

City of Cleveland Heights (2007) *Criteria and Procedures for Domestic Partner Registry* http://clevelandheights.com/citydept_community_domestic.asp

City of Minneapolis (2007) *Equal Benefits Ordinances* www.ci.minneapolis.mn.us/domestic-partner-registration/docs/chapter142.pdf

Coad, J (2001) 'Privacy – Article 8. Who Needs It?' *Entertainment Law Review* 226

Collier, R (1995) *Masculinity, Law and the Family* (London: Routledge)

Combahee River Collective (1979) 'A Black Feminist Statement' in Z R Eisenstein (ed.), *Capitalist Patriarchy and the Case for Socialist Feminism* (New York and London: Monthly Review Press)

Conaghan, J (2000) 'Reassessing the Feminist Theoretical Project in Law' **27**(3) *Journal of Law and Society* 351

Conaghan, J and E Grabham (2007) 'Sexuality and the Citizen Carer' **58**(3) *Northern Ireland Legal Quarterly* 325

Conran, S (1975) *Superwoman: Everywoman's Book of Household Management* (London: Sidgwick & Jackson)

Constitutional Marriage Amendment Campaign (2006) 'Let's unite in prayer for the defeat of the Civil Unions Bill' www.defendmarriage.co.za/index.htm

Coolidge, D O (2002) 'Widening the Lens: Chapter 6 of the ALI Principles, Hawaii and Vermont' **4** *Journal of Law and Family Studies* 79

Cooper, Davina (2001) 'Like Counting Stars?: Re-Structuring Equality and the Socio-Legal Space of Same-Sex Marriage' in R Wintemute and M Andenaes (eds), *Legal Recognition of Same-Sex Relationships: A Study of National, European and International Law* (Oxford: Hart)

Cooper, Davina (2004) *Challenging Diversity: Rethinking Equality and the Value of Difference* (Cambridge: Cambridge University Press)

Cooper, Davina (2007) ' "Well You Go There to Get Off": Visiting Feminist Care Ethics through a Women's Bathhouse' **8**(3) *Feminist Theory* 243

Cooper, Donna (2004) 'The Proprietary Consequences of Loving and Living Together' **23** *University of Tasmania Law Review* 45

Cossman, B (1994) 'Family Inside/Out' **44** *University of Toronto Law Journal* 1

Cossman, B (2000) 'Canadian Same Sex Relationship Recognition Struggles and the Contradictory Nature of Legal Victories' **48** *Cleveland State Law Review* 49

Cossman, B (2002a) 'Lesbians, Gay Men, and the Canadian Charter of Rights and Freedoms' **40** *Osgoode Hall Law Journal* 223

Cossman, B (2002b) 'Family Feuds: Neo-Liberal and Neo-Conservative Visions of the Reprivatization Project' in B Cossman and J Fudge (eds), *Privatization, Law, and the Challenge to Feminism* (Toronto: University of Toronto Press)

Cossman, B (2005) 'Contesting Conservatisms, Family Feuds and the Privatisation of Dependency' **13** *American University Journal of Gender, Social Policy and Law* 415

Cossman, B, D Danielsen, J Halley and T Higgins (2003) 'Gender, Sexuality and Power: Is Feminist Theory Enough?' **12**(3) *Columbia Journal of Gender and Law* 601

Cossman, B and J Fudge (eds) (2002) *Privatization, Law, and the Challenge to Feminism* (Toronto: University of Toronto Press)

Cossman, B and B Ryder (2001) 'What is Marriage-like Like? The Irrelevance of Conjugality' **18** *Canadian Journal of Family Law* 269

Cotler, I (2006) 'Marriage in Canada: Evolution or Revolution?' **44** *Family Court Review* 60

Cox, B (1994) 'A (Personal) Essay on Same-Sex Marriage' in R M Baird and S E Rosenbaum (eds), *Same-Sex Marriage: The Moral and Legal Debate* (New York: Prometheus Books, 2004) (2nd edn)

Cox, B (2000–2001) 'But Why Not Marriage: An Essay on Vermont's Civil Unions Law, Same-Sex Marriage and Separate But (Un)Equal' **25** *Vermont Law Review* 113

Craig, E (2004) ' "I Do" Kiss and Tell: The Subversive Potential of Non-Normative Sexual Expression from within Cultural Paradigms' **27** *Dalhousie Law Journal* 403

Cretney, S (2003) 'The Family and the Law – Status or Contract?' **15**(4) *Child and Family Law Quarterly* 403

Cretney, S M, J M Masson and R Bailey-Harris (2003) *Principles of Family Law* (London: Sweet & Maxwell) (7th edn)

Cruz, D (2002) 'The New "Marital Property": Civil Marriage and the Right to Exclude?' **30** *Capital University Law Review* 279

Cuomo, C J (1998) 'Thoughts on Lesbian Differences' **13**(1) *Hypatia* 198

De Vos, P (2007a) 'Separate is *Never* Equal: The Same-Sex Marriage Debate in South Africa' **8**(1) *Lesbian and Gay Psychology Review* 45

De Vos, P (2007b) 'The "Inevitability" of Same-Sex Marriage in South Africa's Post-Apartheid State' **23** *South African Journal on Human Rights* 432

Delphy, C and D Leonard (1992) *Familiar Exploitation: A New Analysis of Marriage in Contemporary Western Societies* (Cambridge: Polity Press)

Department for Trade and Industry (2006) *Flexible Working: The Right to Request and the Duty to Consider: A Guide for Employers and Employees* www.dti.gov.uk/files/file21364.pdf

Dewar, J (1998) 'The Normal Chaos of Family Law' **61**(4) *Modern Law Review* 467

Dewar, J (2000) 'Family Law and its Discontents' **14** *International Journal of Law, Policy and the Family* 59

Diduck, A (2003) *Law's Families* (London: Butterworths)

Diduck, A and Kaganas, F (2006) *Family Law, Gender and the State: Text, Cases and Materials* (Oxford and Portland, Oregon: Hart) (2nd edn)

Dobson, J (2003) 'Marriage: The South African Context' *Dr Dobson Newsletters: Focus on the Family, Africa* www.safamily.org.za/newsletter_dob?mode=content&id=2558 2&refto=3644

Dobson, J (2005) 'An Open Letter to South Africans on Same-Sex Marriage' www.cft. org.za/articles/dobson_gay_marriage_sa.htm

Douglas, C A (1990) *Love and Politics: Radical Feminist and Lesbian Theories* (San Francisco: Ism Press)

Dryden, C (1999) *Being Married, Doing Gender: A Critical Analysis of Gender Relationships in Marriage* (London and New York: Routledge)

Duncombe, J and D Marsden (1993) 'Love and Intimacy: The Gender Division of Emotion and "Emotion Work": A Neglected Aspect of Sociological Discussion of Heterosexual Relationships' in G Allan (ed.), *The Sociology of the Family: A Reader* (Oxford: Blackwell, 1999)

Dunne, G A (1997) *Lesbian Lifestyles: Women's Work and the Politics of Sexuality* (Hampshire and London: MacMillan Press)

Eagleton, T (1991) *Ideology: An Introduction* (London and New York: Verso)

Eekelaar, J and M Maclean (2004) 'Marriage and the Moral Bases of Personal Relationships' **31**(4) *Journal of Law and Society* 510

Ehrenreich, B (2002) *Nickel and Dimed: Undercover in Low-wage USA* (London: Granta Books)

Eichler, M (1997) *Family Shifts: Families, Policies, and Gender Equality* (Toronto: Oxford University Press)

Eisenstein, Z R (ed.) (1979) *Capitalist Patriarchy and the Case for Socialist Feminism* (New York and London: Monthly Review Press)

Elizabeth, V (2004) 'To Marry or Not to Marry: That is the Question' **13**(4) *Feminism and Psychology* 426

Emens, E (2004) 'Monogamy's Law: Compulsory Monogamy and Polyamorous Existence' **29** *New York University Review of Law and Social Change* 277

Engels, F (1972) *The Origin of the Family, Private Property, and the State* (New York: Pathfinder) (2003 edn)

Eskridge, W N Jr (1996) *The Case for Same-Sex Marriage: From Sexual Liberty to Civilized Commitment* (New York and London: Free Press)

Eskridge, W N Jr (2001) 'Equality Practice: Liberal Reflections on the Jurisprudence of Civil Unions' **64** *Albany Law Review* 853

Ettelbrick, P (1989) 'Since When is Marriage a Path to Liberation?' in A Sullivan (ed.), *Same-Sex Marriage Pro and Con: A Reader* (New York: Vintage Books, 1997)

Ettelbrick, P (1996) 'Wedlock Alert: A Comment on Lesbian and Gay Family Recognition' **5** *Journal of Law and Policy* 107

Ettelbrick, P (2001) 'Domestic Partnership, Civil Unions or Marriage: One Size Does Not Fit All' **64** *Albany Law Review* 905

Equal Love (2011) *Application in Ferguson et al. v United Kingdom, Lodged with the European Court of Human Rights on 2 February 2011* http://equallove.org.uk/the-legal-case/

Equalities Review (2007) *Fairness and Freedom: The Final Report of the Equalities Review* www.communities.gov.uk/publications/corporate/fairnessfreedom

Fawcett Society (2005a) *A Little Something for the Ladies – Are Politicians Stereotyping Women Voters in 2005?* www.fawcettsociety.org.uk/generalelection2005.htm

Fawcett Society (2005b) 'Are We There Yet? 1975–2005: 30 Years of Closing the Gap Between Women and Men' www.fawcettsociety.org.uk/documents/Fawcett%20 30%20years%20full%20-%20low.pdf

Feldblum, C R (1997) 'The Moral Rhetoric of Legislation' **72** *New York University Law Review* 992

Feldblum, C R (2001) 'The Limitations of Liberal Neutrality Arguments in Favour of Same-Sex Marriage' in R Wintemute and M Andenaes (eds), *Legal Recognition of Same-Sex Relationships: A Study of National, European and International Law* (Oxford: Hart)

Feldblum, C R (2005) 'Gay is Good: The Moral Case for Marriage Equality and More' 17 *Yale Journal of Law and Feminism* 139

Ferguson, A (1998) 'Cheshire Calhoun's Project of Separating Lesbian Theory from Feminist Theory' 13(1) *Hypatia* 214

Fineman, M A (1995) *The Neutered Mother, the Sexual Family and Other Twentieth Century Tragedies* (New York: Routledge)

Fineman, M A (2001) 'Dependencies' in N J Hirschmann and U Liebert (eds), *Women and Welfare: Theory and Practice in the United States and Europe* (London: Rutgers University Press)

Fineman, M A (2004) *The Autonomy Myth: Lies We Tell Ourselves about Dependency and Self-Sufficiency* (New York: The New Press)

Firestone, S (1970) *The Dialectic of Sex: The Case for Feminist Revolution* (New York: Farrar, Straus & Giroux)

Fisher-Hertz, L (2006) 'West Looks Back on Battle that Fizzled: DA's Motives are Questioned' *Poughkeepsie Journal* 26 February 2006 www.gpnys.org/?p=237

Fletcher, R (2002) 'Feminist Legal Theory' in R Banakar and M Travers (eds) *Introduction to Law and Social Theory* (Oxford: Hart)

Fox Harding, L (1996) *Family, State and Social Policy* (Hampshire and London: Macmillan)

Fraser, N (1997a) *Justice Interruptus: Critical Reflections on the 'Postsocialist' Condition* (New York and London: Routledge)

Fraser, N (1997b) 'Heterosexism, Misrecognition and Capitalism: A Response to Judith Butler' 15(3/4) *Social Text 52/53* 279

Fraser, N (2003a) 'Rethinking recognition: overcoming displacement and reification in cultural politics' in B Hobson (ed.), *Recognition Struggles and Social Movements: Contested Identities, Agency and Power* (Cambridge: Cambridge University Press)

Fraser, N (2003b) 'Social Justice in the Age of Identity Politics: Redistribution, Recognition, and Participation' in N Fraser and A Honneth (eds), *Redistribution or Recognition? A Political–Philosophical Exchange* (London and New York: Verso)

Fraser, N and A Honneth (2003) *Redistribution or Recognition? A Political–Philosophical Exchange* (London and New York: Verso)

Friedan, B (1963) *The Feminine Mystique* (London: Penguin) (1992 edn)

Frith, M (2005) 'Desperate to be Housewives: Young Women Yearn for 1950s Role as Stay-At-Home Mums' *The Independent* 10 March 2005

Frye, M (1977) 'Some Reflections on Separatism and Power' in H Abelove, M A Barale and D Halperin (eds), *The Lesbian and Gay Studies Reader* (New York: Routledge, 1993)

Gaffney-Rhys, R (2006) '*Sheffield City Council v E and Another* – capacity to marry and the rights and responsibilities of married couples' 18(1) *Child and Family Law Quarterly* 139

Gardiner, J (1979) 'Women's Domestic Labour' in Z R Eisenstein (ed.), *Capitalist Patriarchy and the Case for Socialist Feminism* (New York and London: Monthly Review Press)

Gavigan, S A M (1988) 'Law, Gender and Ideology' in A F Bayefsky (ed.), *Legal Theory Meets Legal Practice* (Edmonton: Academic Publishing)

Gavigan, S A M (1993) 'Paradise Lost, Paradox Revisited: The Implications of Familial Ideology for Feminist, Lesbian, and Gay Engagement to Law' 31 *Osgoode Hall Law Journal* 589

Gavigan, S A M (1995) 'A Parent(ly) Knot: Can Heather Have Two Mommies?' in D Herman and C Stychin (eds), *Legal Inversions: Lesbians, Gay Men and the Politics of Law* (Philadelphia: Temple University Press)

Gavigan, S A M (1996) 'Familial Ideology and the Limits of Difference' in J Brodie (ed.), *Women and Canadian Public Policy* (Toronto: Harcourt Brace)

Gavigan, S A M (1999) 'Legal Forms, Family Forms, Gendered Norms: What is a Spouse?' **14** *Canadian Journal of Law and Society* 127

Gavigan, S A M (2006) 'Equal Families, Equal Parents, Equal Spouses, Equal Marriage: The Case of the Missing Patriarch' **33** *Supreme Court Law Review (2d)* 317

Gay and Lesbian Advocates and Defenders (GLAD) (2006) *Why Marriage Matters* www.glad.org/rights/OP1-whymarriagematters.PDF

Gay and Lesbian Advocates and Defenders (GLAD) (2007) *New Hampshire Civil Unions*, July 2007 www.glad.org/marriage/New_Hampshire_Civil_Unions.pdf

Gay and Lesbian Advocates and Defenders (GLAD) (2011) *Family Law in Vermont* www.glad.org/rights/vermont/c/family-law-in-vermont/

Gay and Lesbian Rights Lobby (2005) *'Separate and Unequal': State-Based Marriage* www.glrl.org.au/publications/press_releases/2005/ MarriageMR.pdf

Gay and Lesbian Rights Lobby (2007) *All Love is Equal...Isn't It? The Recognition of Same-Sex Relationships under Federal Law: Consultation Report* www.glrl.org.au/pdf/major_reports/AllLoveisEqual_Isn_tIt.pdf

Gay Liberation Front (1971) 'Manifesto' in L Power (ed.), *No Bath but Plenty of Bubbles: An Oral History of the Gay Liberation Front 1970–1973* (London: Cassell, 1995)

Geller, J (2001) *Here Comes the Bride: Women, Weddings and the Marriage Mystique* (New York and London: Four Walls Eight Windows)

Giddens, A (1992) *The Transformation of Intimacy: Sexuality, Love and Eroticism in Modern Societies* (Cambridge: Polity Press)

Gill, S and I Bakker (2006) 'New Constitutionalism and the Social Reproduction of Caring Institutions' **27** *Theoretical Medicine and Bioethics* 35

Gillis, J (1997) *A World of Their Own Making: A History of Myth and Ritual in Family Life* (Oxford: Oxford University Press)

Glennon, L (2006) 'Strategizing for the Future through the Civil Partnership Act' **33**(2) *Journal of Law and Society* 244

Godard, J (2007) 'Pacs Seven Years on: Is It Moving towards Marriage?' **21** *International Journal of Law, Policy and the Family* 310

Goldblatt, B (2006) 'Case Note: Same-Sex Marriage in South Africa – The Constitutional Court's Judgment' **14**(2) *Feminist Legal Studies* 261

Gordon, R (2004) 'The Battle Over Same-Sex Marriage: Uncharted Territory. Bush's Stance Led Newsom to Take Action' *San Francisco Chronicle* 15 February 2004, A1 http://sfgate.com/cgi-bin/article .cgi?file=/chronicle/ archive/2004/02/15/MNGMN51F8Q1.DTL

Government Equalities Office (2011) *Civil Partnerships on Religious Premises: A Consultation* (London: Crown Copyright)

Graff, E J (1996) 'Retying the Knot' in A Sullivan (ed.), *Same-Sex Marriage Pro and Con: A Reader* (New York: Vintage Books, 1997)

Graham, M (2004) 'Gay Marriage: Whither Sex? Some Thoughts from Europe' **1**(3) *Sexuality Research and Social Policy* 24

Gray, N and D Brazil (2005) *Blackstone's Guide to the Civil Partnership Act 2004* (Oxford: Oxford University Press)

Graycar, R and J Millbank (2000) 'The Bride Wore Pink... to the Property (Relationships) Legislation Amendment Act 1999: Relationships Law Reform in New South Wales' **17** *Canadian Journal of Family Law* 227

Gross, A (2006) 'Israeli Supreme Court Orders Registration: Canada's Marriage Equality Available to Israelis' www.samesexmarriage.ca/advocacy/isr231106.htm

Gross, N (2005) 'The Detraditionalization of Intimacy Reconsidered' 23(3) *Sociological Theory* 286

Guild, E (2001) 'Free Movement and Same-Sex Relationships: Existing EC Law and Article 13 EC' in R Wintemute and M Andenaes (eds), *Legal Recognition of Same-Sex Relationships: A Study of National, European and International Law* (Oxford: Hart)

Halle, R (2001) 'Political Organizing and the Limits of Civil Rights: Gay Marriage and Queer Families' in M Bernstein and R Reimann (eds), *Queer Families Queer Politics: Challenging Culture and the State* (New York: Columbia University Press)

Halley, J (2001) 'Recognition, Rights, Regulation and Normalisation: Rhetorics of Justification in the Same-Sex Marriage Debate' in R Wintemute and M Andenaes (eds), *Legal Recognition of Same-Sex Relationships: A Study of National, European and International Law* (Oxford: Hart)

Halley, J (2006) *Split Decisions: How and Why to Take a Break from Feminism* (Princeton and Oxford: Princeton University Press)

Halperin, D (1995) *Saint=Foucault: Towards a Gay Hagiography* (New York and Oxford: Oxford University Press)

Harding, R (2006) 'Dogs are "Registered", People Shouldn't Be: Legal Consciousness and Lesbian and Gay Rights' 15(4) *Social and Legal Studies* 511

Haritaworn, J, C Lin and C Klesse (2006) 'Poly/logue: A Critical Introduction to Polyamory' 9(5) *Sexualities* 515

Harper, M, M Downs, K Landells and G Wilson (2005) *Civil Partnership: The New Law* (Bristol: Family Law)

Hartmann, H (1979) 'Capitalism, Patriarchy, and Job Segregation by Sex' in Z R Eisenstein (ed.), *Capitalist Patriarchy and the Case for Socialist Feminism* (New York and London: Monthly Review Press)

Hartmann, H (1981) 'The Unhappy Marriage of Marxism and Feminism: Towards a More Progressive Union' in L Sargent (ed.), *The Unhappy Marriage of Marxism and Feminism: A Debate on Class and Patriarchy* (London and Sydney: Pluto Press)

Havas, E (1995) 'The Family as Ideology' 29(1) *Social Policy and Administration* 1

Hawaii Department of Health (2006) http://hawaii.gov/health/vital-records/reciprocal

Hawaii State Department of Health (2011) 'About Reciprocal Beneficiary Relationships' www.hawaii.gov/health/vital-records/vital-records/reciprocal/index.html#termination

Hearn, J (1987) *The Gender of Oppression: Men, Masculinity and the Critique of Marxism* (Brighton: Wheatsheaf Books)

Heath, S (2004) 'Peer-Shared Households, Quasi-Communes and Neo-Tribes' 52 *Current Sociology* 161

Helms, J (1997) 'The Defense of Marriage Act: The Hon. Jesse Helms: In Support' in R M Baird and S E Rosenbaum (eds), *Same-Sex Marriage: The Moral and Legal Debate* (New York: Prometheus Books)

Henson, D M (1993) 'A Comparative Analysis of Same-Sex Partnership Protections: Recommendations for American Reform' 7 *International Journal of Law and the Family* 282

Herman, D (1994a) *Rights of Passage: Struggles for Lesbian and Gay Legal Equality* (Toronto: University of Toronto Press)

Herman, D (1994b) 'A Jurisprudence of One's Own? Ruthann Robson's Lesbian Legal Theory' 7(2) *Canadian Journal of Women and the Law* 509

Herman, D (1996) 'Law and Morality Re-Visited: The Politics of Regulating Sado-Masochistic Porn/Practice' 15 *Studies in Law, Politics and Society* 147

Herman, D (1997) *The Antigay Agenda: Orthodox Vision and the Christian Right* (Chicago and London: University of Chicago Press)

Hibbs, M (2001) 'Why Marry? – Perceptions of the Affianced' **31**(Mar) *Family Law* 197

Hickman, L A (1997) 'Making the Family Functional: The Case for Same-Sex Marriage' in R M Baird and S E Rosenbaum (eds), *Same-Sex Marriage: The Moral and Legal Debate* (New York: Prometheus Books)

Hiltunen, R and K Waaldijk (2005) 'Major Legal Consequences of Marriage, Cohabitation and Registered Partnership for Different-Sex and Same-Sex Partners in Finland' in K Waaldijk (ed.), *More or Less Together: Levels of Legal Consequences of Marriage, Cohabitation and Registered Partnership for Different-Sex and Same-Sex Partners. A comparative study of nine European countries* www-same-sex.ined.fr/publica_doc 125.htm#

Hoagland, S L and J Penelope (eds) (1988) *For Lesbians Only: A Separatist Anthology* (London: Onlywomen Press)

Hogg, P W (2006) 'Canada: The Constitution and Same-Sex Marriage' **4** *International Journal of Constitutional Law* 712

Human Rights and Equal Opportunity Commission (2007) *Same-Sex: Same Entitlements, National Inquiry into Discrimination against People in Same-Sex Relationships: Financial and Work-Related Entitlements and Benefits* www.hreoc.gov.au/human_rights/same-sex/report/pdf/SSSE_Report.pdf

Human Rights Campaign (2007a) 'Top Ten Reasons for Marriage Equality' http://hrc.org/Template.cfm?Section=Center&CONTENTID=14392&TEMPLATE=/ContentManagement/ContentDisplay.cfm

Human Rights Campaign (2007b) 'Rights and Protections Denied Same-Sex Partners' http://hrc.org/Template.cfm?Section=Center&CONTENTID=14698&TEMPLATE=/ContentManagement/ContentDisplay.cfm

Human Rights Campaign (2010a) *LGBT Equality and the Fortune 500* www.hrc.org/issues/workplace/fortune500.htm

Human Rights Campaign (2010b) *Statewide Marriage Prohibitions* www.hrc.org/state_laws

Human Rights Campaign (2011a) *Equal Benefits Ordinances* www.hrc.org/issues/workplace/benefits/equal_benefits_ordinances.htm

Human Rights Campaign (2011b) *Marriage Equality and Other Relationship Recognition Laws* www.hrc.org/state_laws

Human Rights Campaign WorkNet (2007) *How to Achieve Domestic Partner Work Benefits in Your Workplace* www.hrc.org/Template.cfm? Section=Why_Employers_Offer&Template=/ContentManagement/ContentDisplay.cfm&ContentID=10910

Hunt, A (1985) 'The Ideology of Law: Advances and Problems in Recent Applications of the Concept of Ideology to the Analysis of Law' **19** *Law and Society Review* 11

Hunter, N (1995) 'Marriage, Law and Gender: A Feminist Inquiry' in N Hunter and L Duggan (eds), *Sex Wars: Sexual Dissent and Political Culture* (New York: Routledge)

International Gay and Lesbian Human Rights Commission (2003) 'Where You Can Marry: Global Summary of Registered Partnership, Domestic Partnership, and Marriage Laws' www.iglhrc.org/site/iglhrc

International Lesbian and Gay Association (2000) *World Legal Survey: Denmark* www.ilga.info/Information/Legal_survey/europe/denmark.htm

International Lesbian and Gay Association (2005) *In Canada, Equal Marriage is the Biggest Fight since Decriminalisation in 1969* www.ilga.org/campaigning/Canada.pdf

International Lesbian and Gay Association (2006) *Same Sex Partnership in South Africa: Joint Working Group Response to Passing of Civil Union Act* www.ilga.org/news_results.asp? LanguageID=1&FileCategory=3&ZoneID=2&FileID=923

Irwin, S (1999) 'Resourcing the Family' in E B Silva and C Smart (eds), *The New Family* (London: Sage)

Jackson, S (1997) 'Women, Marriage and Family Relationships' in V Robinson and D Richardson (eds), *Introducing Women's Studies: Feminist Theory and Practice* (London: Macmillan)

Jackson, S and S Scott (2004) 'The Personal *is* still Political: Heterosexuality, Feminism and Monogamy' **14**(1) *Feminism and Psychology* 151

Jamieson, L, M Anderson, D McCrone, F Bechhofer, R Stewart and Y Li (2002) 'Cohabitation and Commitment: Partnership Plans of Young Men and Women' **50**(3) *Sociological Review* 356

Jeffreys, S (1990) *Anticlimax: A Feminist Perspective on the Sexual Revolution* (London: Women's Press)

Jeffreys, S (1994) 'The Queer Disappearance of Lesbians: Sexuality in the Academy' **17**(5) *Women's Studies International Forum* 459

Jeffreys, S (2003) *Unpacking Queer Politics* (Cambridge: Polity Press)

Johnson, G (2002) 'In Praise of Civil Unions' 30 *Capital University Law Review* 315

Joseph, G (1981) 'The Incompatible Ménage à Trois: Marxism, Feminism, and Racism' in L Sargent (ed.), *The Unhappy Marriage of Marxism and Feminism: A Debate on Class and Patriarchy* (London and Sydney: Pluto Press)

Kandaswamy, P (2007) 'Enforcing Family Values: State Austerity and the Racial Politics of Gay Marriage' conference paper presented at *Gender Unbound*, 9–11 July 2007, Keele University (on file with author)

Kaplan, M (1997) *Sexual Justice: Democratic Citizenship and the Politics of Desire* (New York: Routledge)

Kay, F M (1997) 'Balancing Acts: Career and Family among Lawyers' in S B Boyd (ed.), *Challenging the Public/Private Divide: Feminism, Law and Public Policy* (Toronto: University of Toronto Press)

Kirkby, J (2003) *Choosing to be Different: Women, Work and Family* (London: Centre for Policy Studies)

Kitzinger, C and S Wilkinson (2004) 'The Re-Branding of Marriage: Why We Got Married Instead of Registering a Civil Partnership' **14**(1) *Feminism and Psychology* 127

Klesse, C (2005) 'Bisexual Women, Non-Monogamy and Differentialist Anti-Promiscuity Discourses' 8 *Sexualities* 445

Klesse, C (2006a) 'Non-Monogamy, Heteronormativity and the Marriage Debate in the Bisexual Movement' **7**(2) *Lesbian and Gay Psychology Review* 162

Klesse, C (2006b) 'Polyamory and its "Others": Contesting the Terms of Non-Monogamy' 9 *Sexualities* 565

Kline, M (1997) 'Blue Meanies in Alberta: Tory Tactics and the Privatization of Child Welfare' S B in Boyd (ed.), *Challenging the Public/Private Divide: Feminism, Law and Public Policy* (Toronto: University of Toronto Press)

Knight, R H (1994) 'How Domestic Partnerships and "Gay Marriage" Threaten the Family' in R M Baird and S E Rosenbaum (eds), *Same-Sex Marriage: The Moral and Legal Debate* (New York: Prometheus Books)

Kohn, S (1999) 'The Domestic Partnership Organizing Manual for Employee Benefits', *NGLTF Policy Institute*, 1 June 1999 www.thetaskforce.org/library/dp_pub.htm

Kovacs, D (2009) 'A Federal Law of De Facto Property Rights: The Dream and the Reality' 23 *Australian Journal of Family Law* 104

Kuhn, A and A Wolpe (eds) (1978) *Feminism and Materialism: Women and Modes of Production* (London: Routledge & Kegan Paul)

Lahey, K A (2001) 'Becoming "Persons" in Canadian Law: Genuine Equality or "Separate But Equal"?' in R Wintemute and M Andenaes (eds), *Legal Recognition of Same-Sex Relationships: A Study of National, European and International Law* (Oxford: Hart)

Lahey, K A (2003) 'Law and Sexuality in Canada: Heteronormativity, Rights and Genuine Equality' paper presented at *Gender, Sexuality, Family Conference,* Queen's University 4 April 2003 (on file with author)

Lambda Legal and The Center Hawai'i (2007) *Register as Reciprocal Beneficiaries* http://data.lambdalegal.org/pdf/734.pdf

Lamble, S (2009) 'Unknowable Bodies, Unthinkable Sexualities: Lesbian and Transgender Legal Invisibility in the Toronto Women's Bathhouse Raid' **18**(1) *Social and Legal Studies* 111

Laursen, S (2010) 'Ban on Assisted Conception for Lesbians Lifted' www.lgbt.dk/1376/

Law Commission of Canada (2001) *Beyond Conjugality: Recognising and Supporting Close Personal Adult Relationships* http://tabletology.com/docs/beyond_conjugality.pdf

Law Society (2002) *Cohabitation: The Case for Clear Law: Proposals for Reform* (July) www.lawsociety.org.uk/influencinglaw/policy inresponse/view=article. law?DOCUMENTID=207751

Leeds Revolutionary Feminist Group (1981) *Love Your Enemy? The Debate Between Heterosexual Feminism and Political Lesbianism* (London: Onlywomen Press)

Lehr, V (1999) *Queer Family Values: Debunking the Myth of the Nuclear Family* (Philadelphia: Temple University Press)

Lent, A (2003) 'The Transformation of Gay and Lesbian Politics in Britain' **5**(1) *British Journal of Politics and International Relations* 24

Leonard, A S (2001) 'Legal Recognition of Same-Sex Partners under US State or Local Law' in R Wintemute and M Andenaes (eds), *Legal Recognition of Same-Sex Relationships: A Study of National, European and International Law* (Oxford: Hart)

Lesbian and Gay Legal Rights Service (1993) 'The Bride Wore Pink: Legal Recognition of Our Relationships' 3 *Australasian Gay and Lesbian Law Journal* 67

Lesbian and Gay Legal Rights Service (1994) 'The Bride Wore Pink: Legal Recognition of Our Relationships: A Discussion Paper' (2nd edn) www.glrl.org.au/pdf/major_ reports/bride_wore_pink.pdf

Levi, J (2004) 'Toward a More Perfect Union: The Road to Marriage Equality for Same-Sex Couples' **13** *Widener Law Journal* 831

Levin, I (2004) 'Living Apart Together: A New Family Form' **52**(2) *Current Sociology* 223

Lewin, E (2001) 'Weddings Without Marriage: Making Sense of Lesbian and Gay Commitment Rituals' in M Bernstein and R Reimann (eds), *Queer Families Queer Politics: Challenging Culture and the State* (New York: Columbia University Press)

L'Heureux-Dubé, C (2001) 'Introduction: Same-Sex Partnerships in Canada' in R Wintemute and M Andenaes (eds), *Legal Recognition of Same-Sex Relationships: A Study of National, European and International Law* (Oxford: Hart)

Lind, C (2001) 'Politics, Partnership Rights and the Constitution in South Africa ... (and the Problem of Sexual Identity)' in R Wintemute and M Andenaes (eds), *Legal Recognition of Same-Sex Relationships: A Study of National, European and International Law* (Oxford: Hart)

Lister, R (2005) 'Being Feminist' *Government and Opposition* 442

Loek, D (2001) 'Sisters Growing Old Together Wish for Spousal Tax Benefits' *Toronto Star* 28 June 2001, p. E03

Loosemore, S (2002) *'EGALE v Canada*: The Case for Same-Sex Marriage' **60** *University of Toronto Faculty of Law Review* 43

Lowe, N and G Douglas (2007) *Bromley's Family Law* (Oxford: Oxford University Press) (10th edn)

Lucas, I (1998) *Outrage! An Oral History* (London and New York: Cassell)

Lund-Andersen, I (2001) 'The Danish Registered Partnership Act, 1989: Has the Act Meant a Change in Attitudes?' in R Wintemute and M Andenaes (eds), *Legal*

Recognition of Same-Sex Relationships: A Study of National, European and International Law (Oxford: Hart)

MacDougall, B (2000) 'The Celebration of Same-Sex Marriage' 32 *Ottawa Law Review* 235

MacKinnon, C (1987) *Feminism Unmodified: Discourses on Life and Law* (Massachusetts and London: Harvard University Press)

Mansfield, P and J Collard (1988) *The Beginning of the Rest of Your Life: A Portrait of Newly-Wed Marriage* (London: Macmillan)

Marchbank, P and H Marchbank (2003) 'Life after Marriage' 13(4) *Feminism and Psychology* 464

Martin, C and I Théry (2001) 'The PaCS and Marriage and Cohabitation in France' 15 *International Journal of Law, Policy and the Family* 135

Matsuda, M (2005) 'Love, Change' 17 *Yale Journal of Law and Feminism* 185

Maxwell, N G (2001) 'Opening Civil Marriage to Same-Gender Couples: A Netherlands–United States Comparison' 18 *Arizona Journal of International and Comparative Law* 141

McCandless, J and S Sheldon (2010) ' "No Father Required"? The Welfare Assessment in the Human Fertilisation and Embryology Act 2008' 18(3) *Feminist Legal Studies* 201

McClain, L C (2007) 'Love, Marriage, and the Baby Carriage: Revisiting the Channelling Function of Family Law' 28 *Cardozo Law Review* 2133

McDonough, R and R Harrison (1978) 'Patriarchy and the Relations of Production' in A Kuhn and A Wolpe (eds), *Feminism and Materialism: Women and Modes of Production* (London, Boston and Henley: Routledge & Kegan Paul)

McIntosh, M (1982) 'The Family in Socialist-Feminist Politics' in R Brunt and C Rowan (eds), *Feminism, Culture and Politics* (London: Lawrence & Wishart)

Merin, Y (2002) *Equality for Same-Sex Couples: The Legal Recognition of Gay Partnerships in Europe and the United States* (Chicago: University of Chicago Press)

Mhlambiso, N (2007) 'Gay Organisations Unravel the Civil Unions Act', *Behind the Mask* 16 March 2007 www.mask.org.za/article.php?cat= southafrica&id=1530

Millbank, J (1999) 'The De Facto Relationships Amendment Bill 1998 (NSW): The Rationale for Law Reform' 8 *Australasian Gay and Lesbian Law Journal* 1

Millbank, J (2000a) 'The Property (Relationships) Legislation Amendment Act 1999 (NSW) versus the De Facto Relationships Amendment Bill 1998 (NSW)' 9 *Australasian Gay and Lesbian Law Journal* 1

Millbank, J (2000b) 'Domestic Rifts: Who is Using the Domestic Relationships Act 1994 (ACT)?' 14 *Australian Family Law Journal* 1

Millbank, J and W Morgan (2001) 'Let Them Eat Cake and Ice Cream: Wanting Something "More" from the Relationship Recognition Menu' in R Wintemute and M Andenaes (eds), *Legal Recognition of Same-Sex Relationships: A Study of National, European and International Law* (Oxford: Hart)

Millbank, J and K Sant (2000) 'A Bride in Her Every-Day Clothes: Same Sex Relationship Recognition in NSW' 22 *Sydney Law Review* 181

Millett, K (1969) *Sexual Politics* (London: Rupert Hart-Davis)

Moats, D (2004) *Civil Wars: A Battle for Gay Marriage* (Florida: Harcourt Books)

Mohr, R D (1997) 'The Case for Gay Marriage' in R M Baird and S E Rosenbaum (eds), *Same-Sex Marriage: The Moral and Legal Debate* (New York: Prometheus Books)

Morgan, W (1995) 'Queer Law: Identity, Culture, Diversity, Law' 5 *Australasian Gay and Lesbian Law Journal* 1

Mullally, S and D O'Donovan (2011) 'Religion in Ireland's "Public Squares": Education, the Family and Expanding Equality Claims' 2011(April) *Public Law* 284

Munro, V E (2001) 'Legal Feminism and Foucault – A Critique of the Expulsion of Law' 28(4) *Journal of Law and Society* 546

Murphy, J (2002) 'The Recognition of Same-Sex Families in Britain – The Role of Private International Law' *International Journal of Law, Policy and the Family* 181

Murphy, J (2004) 'Same-Sex Marriage in England: A Role for Human Rights?' **16**(3) *Child and Family Law Quarterly* 245

Naples, N (2001) 'A Member of the Funeral: An Introspective Ethnography' in M Bernstein and R Reimann (eds), *Queer Families Queer Politics: Challenging Culture and the State* (New York: Columbia University Press)

Nash, K (2002) 'A Movement Moves... Is There a Women's Movement in England Today?' **9**(3) *European Journal of Women's Studies* 311

National Gay and Lesbian Task Force (2011) *Relationship Recognition for Same-Sex Couples in the US* www.theTaskForce.org

Nicholson, The Hon. A (2005) 'The Legal Regulation of Marriage' **29** *Melbourne University Law Review* 556

Nicol, N and M Smith (2007) 'Legal Struggles and Political Resistance: Same-Sex Marriage in Canada and the US' paper presented at *Gender Unbound,* Keele University 9–11 July 2007 (copy on file with author)

Nielsen, L (1990) 'Family Rights and the "Registered Partnership" in Denmark' **4** *International Journal of Law and the Family* 297

O'Donovan, K (1985) *Sexual Divisions in Law* (London: Weidenfeld & Nicolson)

O'Donovan, K (1993) *Family Law Matters* (London: Pluto)

Office for National Statistics (2005) *Focus on Families* www.statistics.gov.uk/CCI/nugget.asp?ID=1161

Office for National Statistics (2006a) *Time Use Survey: We Mostly Sleep, Work and Watch TV* www.statistics.gov.uk/CCI/nugget.asp?ID=7&Pos=1&ColRank=2&Rank=352

Office for National Statistics (2006b) *Time Use Survey 2005: How We Spend Our Time* www.statistics.gov.uk/articles/nojournal/time_use_2005.pdf

O'Kelly, L (2004) 'It Beats Working' *The Observer* 6 June 2004

Okin, S M (1989) *Justice, Gender and the Family* (New York: Basic Books)

Partners Task Force (2005) *Registered Partnership: The Scandinavian Approach* www.buddybuddy.com/d-p-scan.html

Partners Task Force (2006) *Marrying Apartheid: The Failure of Domestic Partnership Status* www.buddybuddy.com/mar-apar.html

Pateman, C (1988) *The Sexual Contract* (Cambridge: Polity Press)

Patton, C (1993) 'Tremble, Hetero Swine!' in M Warner, *Fear of a Queer Planet: Queer Politics and Social Theory* (Minnesota: University of Minnesota Press)

Pawlowski, M (2001) 'Property Rights of Homesharers: Recent Legislation in Australia and New Zealand' **10** *Nottingham Law Journal* 20

Petchesky, R (1979) 'Dissolving the Hyphen' in Z R Eisenstein (ed.), *Capitalist Patriarchy and the Case for Socialist Feminism* (New York and London: Monthly Review Press)

Polikoff, N (1993) 'We Will Get What We Ask For: Why Legalizing Gay and Lesbian Marriage Will Not "Dismantle the Legal Structure of Gender in Every Marriage"' **79** *Virginia Law Review* 1535

Polikoff, N (2003) 'Ending Marriage As We Know It' **32** *Hofstra Law Review* 201

Polikoff, N (2008) *Beyond (Straight and Gay) Marriage: Valuing All Families under the Law* (Boston: Beacon Press)

Poulter, S (1976) '*Hyde v Hyde* – A Reappraisal' **25** *International and Comparative Law Quarterly* 475

Poulter, S (1979) 'The Definition of Marriage in English Law' **42** *Modern Law Review* 409

Probert, R (2007) '*Hyde v Hyde*: Defining or Defending Marriage?' **19**(3) *Child and Family Law Quarterly* 322

Purvis, T and A Hunt (1993) 'Discourse, Ideology, Discourse, Ideology, Discourse, Ideology...' **44**(3) *British Journal of Sociology* 473

Queen, C (2004) 'Never a Bridesmaid, Never a Bride' in Mattilda, aka M Bernstein Sycamore (ed.), *That's Revolting! Queer Strategies for Resisting Assimilation* (Brooklyn: Soft Skull Press)

Radbord, J (2003) 'A Wedding Story' **15** *Windsor Review of Social and Legal Issues* 15

Radbord, J (2005) 'Lesbian Love Stories: How We Won Equal Marriage in Canada' **17** *Yale Journal of Law and Feminism* 99

Radicalesbians (1970) 'The Woman Identified Woman' in S L Hoagland and J Penelope (eds), *For Lesbians Only: A Separatist Anthology* (London: Onlywomen Press, 1988)

Rauch, J (1997) 'Marrying Somebody' in A Sullivan (ed.), *Same-Sex Marriage Pro and Con: A Reader* (New York: Vintage, 1997)

Rauch, J (2004a) *Gay Marriage: Why It Is Good for Gays, Good for Straights, and Good for America* (New York: Times Books, Henry Holt & Company)

Rauch, J (2004b) 'Bush's Case for Same-Sex Marriage' in R M Baird and S E Rosenbaum (eds), *Same-Sex Marriage: The Moral and Legal Debate* (New York: Prometheus Books) (2nd edn)

Redstockings (1969) *Manifesto* http://fsweb.berry.edu/academic/hass/csnider/ berry/ hum200/redstockings.htm

Reece, H (2003) *Divorcing Responsibly* (Oxford: Hart)

Rees, T (1993) 'Criminal Law Act 1977, s. 2(2) – Husband and Wife Cannot be Convicted of Conspiring with Each Other Alone' *Criminal Law Review* 890

Rich, A (1981) *Compulsory Heterosexuality and Lesbian Existence* (London: Onlywomen Press)

Richards, C (2002) 'The Legal Recognition of Same-Sex Couples – The French Perspective' **51** *International and Comparative Law Quarterly* 305

Richardson, D (2004) 'Locating Sexualities: From Here to Normality' **7**(4) *Sexualities* 391

Ringer, R J (2001) 'Constituting Nonmonogamies' in M Bernstein and R Reimann (eds), *Queer Families Queer Politics: Challenging Culture and the State* (New York: Columbia University Press)

Ritchie, A and M Barker (2006) ' "There Aren't Words for What We Do or How We Feel So We Have to Make Them Up": Constructing Polyamorous Languages in a Culture of Compulsory Monogamy' **9** *Sexualities* 584

Robinson, V (1997) 'My Baby Just Cares for Me: Feminism, Heterosexuality and Non-Monogamy' **6**(2) *Journal of Gender Studies* 143

Robson, R (1992) *Lesbian (Out)Law: Survival Under the Rule of Law* (New York: Firebrand Books)

Robson, R (1998) *Sappho Goes to Law School* (New York: Columbia University Press)

Robson, R (2002) 'Assimilation, Marriage, and Lesbian Liberation' **75**(4) *Temple Law Review* 709

Rosa, B (1994) 'Anti-Monogamy: A Radical Challenge to Compulsory Heterosexuality' in G Griffin, M Hester, S Rai and S Roseneil (eds), *Stirring It: Challenges for Feminism* (London: Taylor & Francis)

Roseneil, S and S Budgeon (2004) 'Cultures of Intimacy and Care beyond "the Family": Personal Life and Social Change in the Early 21st Century' **52** *Current Sociology* 135

Rubin, G S (1984) 'Thinking Sex: Notes for a Radical Theory of the Politics of Sexuality' in H Abelove, M A Barale and D M Halperin (eds), *The Lesbian and Gay Studies Reader* (New York: Routledge, 1993)

Schatschneider, R (2004–2005) 'On Shifting Sand: The Perils of Grounding the Case for Same-Sex Marriage in the Context of Antimiscegenation' **14** *Temple Political and Civil Rights Law Review* 285

Schneider, C E (1992) 'The Channelling Function in Family Law' **20** *Hofstra Law Review* 495

Schrama, W M (1999) 'Registered Partnership in the Netherlands' **13** *International Journal of Law, Policy and the Family* 315

Segal, L (1987) *Is the Future Female? Troubled Thoughts on Contemporary Feminism* (London: Virago Press)

Seidman, S (1993) 'Identity and Politics in a "Postmodern" Gay Culture: Some Historical and Conceptual Notes' in M Warner (ed.), *Fear of A Queer Planet: Queer Politics and Social Theory* (Minnesota: University of Minnesota Press)

Seidman, S (2002) *Beyond the Closet: The Transformation of Gay and Lesbian Life* (New York and London: Routledge)

Sharpe, A (1997) 'The Transsexual and Marriage: Law's Contradictory Desires' **7**(1) *Australasian Gay and Lesbian Law Journal* 1

Shaw, M (2002) *The Relationships (Civil Registration) Bill and the Civil Partnerships Bill* (Research Paper 02/17 House of Commons Library)

Sheff, E (2006) 'Poly-Hegemonic Masculinities' **9** *Sexualities* 621

Sheldon, S (2003) 'Unwilling Fathers and Abortion: Terminating Men's Child Support Obligations?' **66**(2) *Modern Law Review* 175

Sheldon, S (2005) 'Fragmenting Fatherhood: The Regulation of Reproductive Technologies' **68**(4) *Modern Law Review* 523

Shepard, B (2004) 'Sylvia and Sylvia's Children: A Battle for Queer Public Space' in Mattilda, aka M Bernstein Sycamore (ed.) *That's Revolting! Queer Strategies for Resisting Assimilation* (Brooklyn: Soft Skull Press)

Shipman, B and C Smart (2007) ' "It's Made a Huge Difference": Recognition, Rights and the Personal Significance of Civil Partnership' **12**(1) *Sociological Research Online* www.socresonline.org.uk/12/1/shipman.html

Silva, E B and C Smart (1999) 'The "New" Practices and Politics of Family Life' in E B Silva and C Smart (eds), *The New Family?* (London: Sage)

Sloane, C A (1997) 'A Rose by any Other Name: Marriage and the Danish Registered Partnership Act' **5** *Cardozo Journal of International and Comparative Law* 189

Smart, C (1984) *The Ties That Bind: Law, Marriage and Reproduction of Patriarchal Relations* (London: Routledge & Kegan Paul)

Smart, C (1989) *Feminism and the Power of Law* (London: Routledge)

Smart, C (1997) 'Wishful Thinking and Harmful Tinkering? Sociological Reflections on Family Policy' **26**(3) *Journal of Social Policy* 301

Smart, C and B Neale (eds) (1999) *Family Fragments?* (Cambridge: Polity Press)

Smith, M (2007) 'Framing Same-Sex Marriage in Canada and the United States: *Goodridge, Halpern* and the National Boundaries of Political Discourse' **16**(1) *Social and Legal Studies* 5

Spade, D (2004) 'Fighting to Win' in Mattilda, aka M Bernstein Sycamore (ed.), *That's Revolting! Queer Strategies for Resisting Assimilation* (Brooklyn: Soft Skull Press)

Stacey, J (2004) 'Cruising to Familyland: Gay Hypergamy and Rainbow Kinship' **52**(2) *Current Sociology* 181

Stamps, R-C (1992) 'Domestic Partnership Legislation: Recognizing Non-Traditional Families' **19** *Southern University Law Review* 441

Stefanec, E (2004) 'Mimicking Marriage: As the Evolution of the Legal Recognition of Same-Sex Marriage Progresses, Civil Unions Currently Represent the Best Alternative to Marriage' **30**(1) *University of Dayton Law Review* 119

Steiner, E (2000) 'The Spirit of the New French Registered Partnership Law – Promoting Autonomy and Pluralism or Weakening Marriage?' **12**(1) *Child and Family Law Quarterly* 1

Stoddard, T (1989) 'Why Gay People Should Seek the Right to Marry' in M Blasius and S Phelan (eds), *We Are Everywhere: A Historical Sourcebook of Gay and Lesbian Politics* (New York: Routledge, 1997)

Stoddard, T (1990) 'Yes: Marriage is a Fundamental Right' **76** *ABA Journal* 42

Stonewall (2003) *Stonewall Response to: Civil Partnership – A Framework for the Legal Recognition of Same-Sex Couples* www.stonewall.org.uk/documents/Stonewall_response_August_2003.doc

Stonewall (2004a) *Parliamentary Briefing: Civil Partnership Bill, House of Lords Second Reading* www.stonewall.org.uk/documents/Lords_Second_Reading_Apr_2004.doc

Stonewall (2004b) *Parliamentary Briefing: Civil Partnership Bill, House of Lords Report Stage* www.stonewall.org.uk/documents/Lords_Report_June_04.doc

Stonewall (2004c) *Parliamentary Briefing: Civil Partnership Bill, House of Commons Second Reading* www.stonewall.org.uk/documents/oahq_Commons_Second_Reading_Sep_2004.doc

Stonewall (2007) *Civil Partnership Act – Frequently Asked Questions* www.stonewall.org.uk/information_bank/partnership/civil_partnership_act/152.asp

Stychin, C F (1995) *Law's Desire: Sexuality and the Limits of Justice* (London and New York; Routledge)

Stychin, C F (2001) 'Civil Solidarity or Fragmented Identities? The Politics of Sexuality and Citizenship in France' 10(3) *Social and Legal Studies* 347

Stychin, C F (2003) *Governing Sexuality: The Changing Politics of Citizenship and Law Reform* (Oxford: Hart Publishing)

Stychin, C F (2005a) 'Being Gay' *Government and Opposition* 90

Stychin, C F (2005b) 'Couplings: Civil Partnership in the United Kingdom' 8 *New York City Law Review* 543

Stychin, C F (2006a) 'Not (Quite) a Horse and Carriage: The Civil Partnership Act 2004' 14(1) *Feminist Legal Studies* 79

Stychin, C F (2006b) 'Family Friendly? Rights, Responsibilities and Relationship Recognition' in A Diduck and K O'Donovan (eds), *Feminist Perspectives on Family Law* (Oxon: Routledge-Cavendish)

Sullivan, A (1995) 'Virtually Normal' in R M Baird and S E Rosenbaum (eds), *Same-Sex Marriage: The Moral and Legal Debate* (New York: Prometheus Books, 1997)

Sullivan, A (1996) 'Three's a Crowd' in A Sullivan (ed.), *Same-Sex Marriage Pro and Con: A Reader* (New York: Vintage Books, 1997)

Sullivan, A (ed.) (1997) *Same-Sex Marriage Pro and Con: A Reader* (New York: Vintage Books)

Sullivan, N (2003) *A Critical Introduction to Queer Theory* (Edinburgh: Edinburgh University Press)

Sumner, I (2002) 'Going Dutch? A Comparative Analysis and Assessment of the Gradual Recognition of Homosexuality with Respect to the Netherlands and England' 9(1) *Maastricht Journal* 29

Sumner, I (2004) 'Happy Ever After? The Problems of Terminating Registered Partnerships' in M Digiox and P Festy (eds), *Same-Sex Couples, Same-Sex Partnerships and Homosexual Marriages: A Focus on Cross-National Differentials* (Documents de travail No. 124; Ined, 2004) www-same-sex.ined.fr/WWW/04Doc124IanSumner .pdf

Tatchell, P (2005) 'Civil Partnerships Are Sexual Apartheid' www.petertatchell.net/

Thomson, M (1997) 'Legislating for the Monstrous: Access to Reproductive Services and the Monstrous Feminine' 6 *Social and Legal Studies* 401

Thomson, M (2006) 'Viagra Nation: Sex and the Prescribing of Familial Masculinity' 2 *Law, Culture and the Humanities* 259

Thomson, M (2008) *Endowed: Regulating the Male Sexed Body* (New York and London: Routledge)

Turner, W B (2000) *A Genealogy of Queer Theory* (Philadelphia: Temple University Press)

Underwood, S G (2003) *Gay Men and Anal Eroticism: Tops, Bottoms and Versatiles* (New York: Harrington Park Press)

United States Department of Justice (2011) 'Statement of the Attorney General on Litigation Involving the Defense of Marriage Act' www.justice.gov/opa/pr/2011/February/11-ag-222.html

Vogel, L (1983) *Marxism and the Oppression of Women: Toward a Unitary Theory* (London: Pluto Press)

Vogler, C and J Pahl (1994) 'Money, Power and Inequality in Marriage' in G Allan (ed.), *The Sociology of the Family: A Reader* (Oxford: Blackwell, 1999)

Waaldijk, K (2001) 'Small Change: How the Road to Same-Sex Marriage Got Paved in the Netherlands' in R Wintemute and M Andenaes (eds), *Legal Recognition of Same-Sex Relationships: A Study of National, European and International Law* (Oxford: Hart)

Waaldijk, K (2003) 'Taking Same-Sex Partnerships Seriously – European Experiences as British Perspectives?' (June) *International Family Law Journal* 84

Waaldijk, K (2004) 'Others May Follow: The Introduction of Marriage, Quasi-Marriage, and Semi-Marriage for Same-Sex Couples in European Countries' **38**(3) *New England Law Review* 569

Waaldijk, K (ed.) (2005) *More or Less Together: Levels of Legal Consequences of Marriage, Cohabitation and Registered Partnership for Different-Sex and Same-Sex Partners. A comparative study of nine European countries* www-same-sex.ined.fr/publica_doc125.htm#

Wade, J H (1982) 'Limited Purpose Marriages' **45** *Modern Law Review* 159

Waites, M (2002) 'Inventing a "Lesbian Age of Consent"? The History of the Minimum Age for Sex Between Women in the UK' **11**(3) *Social and Legal Studies* 323

Wald, J (2004) 'New York Town's Mayor Marries Same-Sex Couples' CNN 28 February 2004 www.cnn.com/2004/US/Northeast/02/27/ny.samesex.marriage/

Walker, P (2007) 'Woman admits bigamy in same-sex partnership' *GuardianUnlimited* 9 July 2007 www.guardian.co.uk/gayrights /story/0,,2122172,00.html

Walters, S D (1996) 'From Here to Queer: Radical Feminism, Postmodernism and the Lesbian Menace (Or, Why Can't a Woman be More Like a Fag?)' **21**(4) *Signs: Journal of Women in Culture and Society* 830

Walters, S D (2001) 'Take My Domestic Partner, Please: Gays and Marriage in the Era of the Visible' in M Bernstein and R Reimann (eds), *Queer Families Queer Politics: Challenging Culture and the State* (New York: Columbia University Press)

Warner, M (1999) *The Trouble with Normal: Sex, Politics, and the Ethics of Queer Life* (Cambridge, Massachusetts: Harvard University Press)

Washington Post (1997) 'Hawaii's Domestic Partners Law a Bust; Relatively Few Sign Up for Country's Broadest Benefits Package' 25 December 1997

Weeks, J (1977) *Coming Out: Homosexual Politics in Britain from the Nineteenth Century to the Present* (London and New York: Quartet Books) (1990 edn)

Weeks, J, B Heaphy and C Donovan (2001) *Same-Sex Intimacies: Families of Choice and Other Life Experiments* (London and New York: Routledge)

Weinbaum, B and A Bridges (1979) 'The Other Side of the Paycheck: Monopoly Capital and the Structure of Consumption' in Z R Eisenstein (ed.), *Capitalist Patriarchy and the Case for Socialist Feminism* (New York and London: Monthly Review Press)

Weston, K (1991) *Families We Choose: Lesbians, Gays, Kinship* (New York: Columbia University Press) (1997 revised edn)

Wilkinson, S and C Kitzinger (2006) 'In Support of Equal Marriage: Why Civil Partnership is not Enough' **8**(1) *The Psychology of Women Section Review* 57

Wintemute, R (2004) 'Sexual Orientation and the Charter: The Achievement of Formal Legal Equality (1985–2005) and its Limits' **49** *McGill Law Journal* 1143

Wise, S and L Stanley (2004) 'Beyond Marriage: The Less Said about Love and Life-Long Continuance Together the Better' **14**(2) *Feminism and Psychology* 332

Wolfenden Report (1957) *Report of the Committee on Homosexual Offences and Prostitution* (London: HMSO, Cmnd 247)

Wolfson, E (1996) 'Why We Should Fight for the Freedom to Marry' in A Sullivan (ed.), *Same-Sex Marriage Pro and Con: A Reader* (New York: Vintage, 1997)

Wolfson, E (1998) 'Lesbians and Gay Men Should Fight for the Freedom to Marry' in T Roleff (ed.), *At Issue: Gay Marriage* (San Diego, California: Greenhaven Press)

Wolfson, E (2001) 'The Hawaii Marriage Case Launches the US Freedom-to-Marry Movement for Equality' in R Wintemute and M Andenaes (eds), *Legal Recognition of Same-Sex Relationships: A Study of National, European and International Law* (Oxford: Hart)

Wolfson, E (2005) 'Just Say No to Civil Union' *The Stranger* 20–26 October 2005 www.thestranger.com/seattle/Content?oid=23780

Women and Equality Unit (2003a) *Civil Partnership: A Framework for the Legal Recognition of Same-Sex Couples* www.womenandequalityunit.gov.uk/research/civ_par_con.pdf

Women and Equality Unit (2003b) *Responses to Civil Partnership: A Framework for the Legal Recognition of Same-Sex Couples* www.womenandequalityunit.gov.uk/publications/CP_responses.pdf

Wong, S (2006) 'Cohabitation and the Law Commission's Project' **14**(2) *Feminist Legal Studies* 145

Young, C and S Boyd (2006) 'Losing the Feminist Voice? Debates on the Legal Recognition of Same Sex Partnerships in Canada' **14** *Feminist Legal Studies* 213

Young, I (1981) 'Beyond the Unhappy Marriage: A Critique of the Dual Systems Theory' in L Sargent (ed.), *The Unhappy Marriage of Marxism and Feminism: A Debate on Class and Patriarchy* (London and Sydney: Pluto Press)

Ytterberg, H and K Waaldijk (2005) 'Major Legal Consequences of Marriage, Cohabitation and Registered Partnership for Different-Sex and Same-Sex Partners in Sweden' in K Waaldijk (ed.), *More or Less Together: Levels of Legal Consequences of Marriage, Cohabitation and Registered Partnership for Different-Sex and Same-Sex Partners. A comparative study of nine European countries* www-same-sex.ined.fr/publica_doc125 .htm#

Index

Printed and bound in Great Britain by
CPI Antony Rowe, Chippenham and Eastbourne